FERMENT IN EDUCATION: A LOOK ABROAD

THE NATIONAL SOCIETY FOR THE STUDY OF EDUCATION
Series on Contemporary Educational Issues

FERMENT IN EDUCATION: A LOOK ABROAD

Edited by
John J. Lane

Editor for the Society
Kenneth J. Rehage

19 NSSE 95

Distributed by THE UNIVERSITY OF CHICAGO PRESS • CHICAGO, ILLINOIS

The National Society for the Study of Education

The National Society for the Study of Education was founded in 1901 as successor to the National Herbart Society. The purpose of the Society is to encourage serious study of educational problems and to make the results of such study available through its publications.

These publications include the annual two-volume Yearbook, the first of which was published in 1902. The two volumes of the 94th Yearbook, published in 1995, are entitled *Creating New Educational Communities* and *Changing Populations/Changing Schools*.

In 1972, the Society established a new series of publications under the series title "Contemporary Educational Issues." The present volume, *Ferment in Education: A Look Abroad*, is one of two published in that series in 1995. The other volume is entitled *Improving Science Education*.

All members of the Society receive its two-volume Yearbook. Members who take the Comprehensive Membership also receive the two current volumes in the series on Contemporary Educational Issues.

Membership in the Society is open to any individual who desires to receive its publications. Inquiries regarding membership and current dues may be addressed to the Secretary-Treasurer, NSSE, 5835 Kimbark Avenue, Chicago, IL 60637.

Library of Congress Catalog Number: 95-67503
ISBN: 0-226-468623

Published 1995 by

THE NATIONAL SOCIETY FOR THE STUDY OF EDUCATION
5835 Kimbark Avenue, Chicago, Illinois 60637

First Printing

Printed in the United States of America

Acknowledgments

The National Society for the Study of Education is indebted to Professor John J. Lane who proposed a book on education abroad for the Society's series on Contemporary Educational Issues. Professor Lane is responsible for planning this volume and for securing contributions from authors who are acquainted with developments in education in various parts of the world.

We are also grateful to the authors for preparing thoughtful analyses of the topics they have chosen to address in their respective chapters for this book.

All who have had a part in bringing this volume to completion have made it possible for the reader to gain a broader perspective on some aspects of developments in education worldwide.

Kenneth J. Rehage
Editor for the Society

Table of Contents

Chapter 1

INTRODUCTION AND
OVERVIEW

John J. Lane

The Berlin Wall has fallen. The Soviet Union has dissolved, and the borders of Eastern Europe continue to be remapped. To the delight of most of its citizens, Central Europe has reclaimed its own identity apart from Eastern Europe. The European Union continues to grow, surpassing for the moment the North American Free Trade Agreement (NAFTA) nations both in numbers of people affected as well as in combined gross domestic product. And, since the 1980s, the burgeoning economies of South Korea, Taiwan, Hong Kong, and Singapore have elevated these nations from "less developed" status to the point where today they are known as "Pacific Rim tigers." Further, the dynamic interplay among Hong Kong, Taiwan, and Mainland China appears certain to have a major impact on the Asia Pacific Economic Cooperation (APECO). Increasingly, so-called "middle powers" like Australia, Canada, Mexico, and New Zealand influence world affairs. And who could have predicted the recent political events in South Africa, the peace accords in the Middle East, or the passage of the General Agreement on Taxes and Tariffs (GATT) in the United States? Triumphalism aside, surely a new world order is in the making.

As the world's leaders debate such matters as market economy, balance of power, sovereignty and nationalism, what role do they see for education? How shall schools help to develop society? How shall schools cultivate the intellect as they prepare citizens for the world of work? Though every nation since the times of the ancient Sumerian, Egyptian, and Hebrew civilizations has asked these questions, none has answered them definitively. These are education's perennial questions. Yet throughout the

world there are currently an unprecedented number of educational inno-
vations, reforms, and experiments designed to respond to these important
questions. So while we have as yet to discover the "one best way" to edu-
cate, there is considerable ferment in education.

This book provides several lenses through which to view the current
unrest in the educational systems of a select number of nations at various stages of economic and political development. Several authors focus
attention on the relative value of research, arguing that the quality and
utility of research depends, for good or ill, largely on who sponsors it.
Others contend that when certain research criteria are met, there is
much to be gained by sharing the results of large cross-national studies.
Still others find that while some governments struggle to overcome the
stifling effects of decades of Communism, public education has been
virtually marginalized resulting in the development of alternative schools
by citizens impatient with government inaction. Other authors attempt
to show that substantive improvement in a nation's schools begins with
the improvement of its teacher education programs.

From a sociological perspective, the proper role of schools in society
has been examined from three major theoretical perspectives: functionalist, interactionist, and conflict. Functionalist theory examines how
schools socialize children in keeping with a society's dominant values in
order to maintain a more or less conflict-free society. Interactionists are
concerned about school processes and procedures like school administration and organization, student grouping, and testing. They focus on
the success or failure of schools to contribute to the social mobility of
citizens. In a similar vein, conflict theorists examine how schools assist or
impede citizens in their quest for power, prestige, and wealth. These
theorists, however, analyze such critical school factors as the effects on
education of the struggle between social groups, the benefits of specific
school reforms and the influence of business and industry on curriculum
(Armstrong, Henson, Savage, 1989). Readers will find elements of each
of these perspectives reflected in several of the essays included in this
volume.

Psacharopoulos (1990, p. 370) argues that as countries reach different stages of economic development, they face different educational
challenges. Low- or middle-income countries (annual income below
$2,000 per capita) are concerned about such basic issues as how to
increase access to primary education toward 100 percent and how to

improve instruction so as to increase a nation's literacy rate. As countries develop, the major educational question becomes how to find the means to expand secondary school opportunities in both college preparatory and vocational educational programs.

When nations are ready to modernize their economies, they look to schools to assist their citizens in developing the technical skills necessary to participate in a global economy. At this point, developed nations typically are concerned with how to strike a balance between nonuniversity educational programs and university studies and how to finance the educational system in ways consistent with principles of fairness and equality of opportunity. Several of the contributors to this book provide insights into how some nations at various points on the Psacharopoulos continuum struggle against tremendous odds to advance the educational system of their respective countries.

In his presidential address to the Comparative and International Education Society, Stephen Heyneman (1993) noted the remarkable increase in the quantity and quality in comparative educational literature but bemoaned the ongoing paradigm wars among educational comparativists. He identified four conflicting sides in the wars. The first are the "irredentists" who maintain "that no educational solution is viable unless autonomously invented by local cultural authorities" (p. 383). The irredentists believe that there are no common educational interests and questions that cross between rich and poor nations. Second, there are "single solution specialists" who assert that no matter how complex the educational problem, they have the answer in such remedies as decentralization, vouchers, management information systems, or educational technology.

Third, there are the "conspiratists," scholars who believe that empirical research based on universal standards not only violates natural complexity but is politically unacceptable as well. Finally, there are the "modelers" who argue for an absolute interpretation of social models and who have a propensity to argue that policy comes from regression equations. Heyneman believes no one group has "the" answer. They are all right.

Among the contributors to this volume are key figures in the development of comparative education whose work may be readily identified with one or the other of Heyneman's four paradigm groups. Others are practitioners and policy analysts who, I suspect, do not regard themselves as aligned with any particular school of thought. Finally, there are those who do not regard themselves as part of the comparative education community at all.

For many developing nations, ferment in education begins with the leaven of financial support from various international agencies. Investment in developing nations typically comes in the form of research support that occasions the involvement of research teams and policy analysts arriving in waves from wealthy nations to diagnose and prescribe cures for that nation's educational ills.

In chapter 2, Joel Samoff challenges the traditional propositions underlying funding and research. The chapter provides a context and comprehensive overview of many of the problems experienced not only in the educational systems of developing countries but also those often encountered in developed countries. Samoff is especially concerned about the influence of the World Bank, which has lent over $11 billion dollars for education, training, and research in over 100 countries since 1963.

In chapter 3, Nobuo Shimahara discusses Japan's school reform, paying particular attention to the final years of secondary education when preparation for university entrance examinations is most intense. He describes the prevailing educational ideology of the 1970s and early 1980s as "catch-up" since during that period Japan sought to develop a world-class elementary and secondary educational system. He shows that in many respects that goal has been achieved, and excellent schools are today producing many highly qualified students for regrettably too few eminent universities.

Shimahara notes the striking differences in academic standing, facilities, and funding among four-year universities, especially those private institutions founded after 1954. The next educational challenge facing the Japanese, he asserts, will be the reform of higher education.

Post-Soviet Russians recognize that the condition of their education system is as bad as the infrastructure of their schools. But how to change the system and rebuild the schools continues to elude them. In chapter 4, Richard Farkas shows that the Russian people are searching for a path to the future, and, like other nations, look to education to show the way. Farkas finds that nationalism and intolerance function like a cancer in Russian society ineluctably compelling its leaders "to face backwards." A frequent consultant to Russian government agencies, Farkas notes that the Soviet educational system remains firmly locked in the rigid patterns of the Stalinist era. Rote learning, narrow and prescribed curricula, and authoritarian classrooms continue to characterize Russian schooling. Farkas maintains that it is important to understand how the interaction of politics, policymaking, and leadership affect the educational system. He argues that the Russians have grossly underestimated the financial and social costs of governing a democratic society. Farkas concludes by showing what it will take to develop a master plan for a new Russian society including an appropriate educational system.

During the Communist era in Romania, civic education consisted largely of lessons designed to indoctrinate children in Communist principles. According to Elena Nedelcu, the subtext of most lessons was that a socialist society was, in every respect, superior to a capitalist society. In chapter 5, Nedelcu attests to the need to revitalize civic education in Romania.

In chapter 6, John J. Lane describes how the Czech Republic's educational system is in transition, just as its social, economic, and political systems are. He shows how recent legislation has changed, in minor ways, the structure of education from preschool through college and university levels. The Czechs are especially concerned to have greater numbers of their children attend college preparatory secondary schools. In response to this demand, there is a movement toward independent secondary schools that has within it the seeds of major systemic reform in the Czech educational system.

The effectiveness of a nation's school reforms depends greatly on its teachers. Without a competent and motivated teaching force committed to proposed change, even the best conceived reform plan will fail at the classroom level. Among the factors contributing to the ferment in education in the United States were the proposals to reform teacher education made by the Holmes Group, an association composed largely of deans of education at research universities.

In chapter 7, Tamar Arias and Aaron Seidenberg describe Israel's effort to change an educational system that continues to reflect the influence of Central Europe and the United States. The authors identify four stages in the development of the process of reforming teacher preparation in Israel. To illustrate how colleges of education have responded to the call for reforms, they report on the experience of their own institution, Beit Berl College, the largest teacher education program in Israel.

Jingbin Zhang explains in chapter 8 the new role and heightened expectations for teachers in a Chinese society fraught with change. Historically, teachers in China have enjoyed high prestige. But there is growing dissatisfaction with teacher preparation as this vast and complex country responds to the demands of its people for political, social, economic, and technological change.

In chapter 9, Torsten Husén sketches the history of the field of comparative education placing special emphasis on developments that have occurred since the 1950s. In particular, he notes the shift from descriptive, travelogue-like accounts characteristic of the early formative period of comparative education to large-scale, empirical studies. Cross-national studies have been made possible throughout by the development of international standards and survey instruments validated by such agencies as the International Association for the Evaluation of Educational Achievement (IEA), The International Council for Economic Development (ICED) and the International Institute for Educational Planning (IIEP).

Professor Husén, for many years a central figure in the development of the field of comparative education, has long advocated a two-pronged approach to cross-national studies that includes both survey technologies and supplemental qualities and ethnographic methodologies. Noting the recent Maästricht Treaty, flaws and all, the creation of the European Union, and recent educational developments in the Third World, Husén concludes that a new and exciting era for educational comparativists is about to begin.

In chapter 10, John Keeves relates how scholars concerned with the inadequacies of cross-national comparative studies in education assembled in 1959 at the UNESCO Institute for Education in Hamburg. He indicates that the major objective of these representatives of twelve nations was to improve a process, not to make invidious comparisons between and among national educational systems. Many of those assembled speculated that it was possible to see the world as a laboratory in which different school systems experimented with ways to obtain the best educational results for children. One of the major outcomes of 1959 was the creation of the International Association for the Evaluation of Educational Achievement (IEA). Today, more than fifty educational systems have participated in one or more of the IEA studies.

To make the case for international comparisons, Keeves offers ten key findings based on IEA research. These findings range from the effects of student retentivity to the effects of classroom time on task in various subject matters and from textbook effects to sex differences in educational achievement. Each major finding is presented together with its implications for educational planning. Keeves suggests that international comparisons yield a wealth of useful information to those prepared to receive it.

In chapter 11, Gerald W. Bracey states his case against international comparisons, arguing that they generate more heat than light. Bracey, who has reported annually since 1991 in the *Phi Delta Kappan* on the condition of public education in the United States, finds fault with international comparisons for three major reasons. First, many countries do not have the traditions of educational testing and social science research so common in the United States. He believes that merely developing sophisticated sampling techniques to overcome the effects of these traditions is inadequate. Second, he finds that a constellation of cultural factors affects outcome measures such that international comparisons are nearly always flawed if not totally useless. Finally, he argues that the results of flawed international comparisons seem invariably to be used to demonstrate that schools in the United States have failed.

To support his contentions he turns to some of the recent major comparative studies pointing to their philosophical and methodological shortcomings. He is especially concerned that, for all the time, money, and effort expended on comparative studies, they offer, in his view, little or no guidance about how to improve educational systems.

A new world order is in the making, and education is a major force driving the process. Even the least developed countries of the Global South pour larger and larger amounts of their scarce resources into schools where enrollment rates continue to rise. Understandably, no two nations are at the same point in the development of an educational system. While some nations struggle to provide their citizens with their first public primary and elementary school system, others work to renew centuries old elementary-through-university educational systems. One thing is certain. Everywhere around the globe there are exciting and challenging educational initiatives—ferment—underway from which it is possible to learn a great deal.

Contributors to this book offer perspectives on the nature of a few key educational initiatives, but they also raise timely and important questions for educational researchers, practitioners, and policymakers both here and abroad. Among these questions are the following: Are policymakers in developing nations creating policy based on flawed data? Is it possible to reform a nation's educational system without first reforming its teacher education programs? Also, what is the current status of education in developed nations like Japan whose highly touted educational programs were widely regarded as ideal models in the 1980s? How do social, political, and economic conditions influence a nation's educational system? And, finally, what purposes are served by international comparisons of educational achievement?

REFERENCES

Armstrong, David G.; Henson, Kenneth T.; and Savage, Tom V. *Education: An Introduction*, 3rd ed. New York: Macmillan, 1989.

Heyneman, Stephen P. "Quantity, Quality, and Source," *Comparative Education Review* 37, no. 4 (1993): 372-388.

Psacharopoulos, George. "Comparative Education: From Theory to Practice, or Are You A:/neo.° or B:/°.ist?" *Comparative Education Review* 34, no. 3 (1990): 369-380.

Chapter 2

THE RECONSTRUCTION OF SCHOOLING IN AFRICA

Joel Samoff

Often regarded primarily as a lending institution, the World Bank has increasingly emphasized its role as a development adviser. Few, if any, other international institutions have a comparable concentration of development expertise and experience. Its investment in research surely exceeds that of most African countries and perhaps all of them combined. In some domains—education is a prime example—the World Bank's development advice may have as much influence on programs and policies as its loans. As it plays this role, the World Bank becomes more than a broker of relevant information. Directly and indirectly, it seeks to guide and manage the creation of knowledge and, in doing so, to set the standards for what has come to be called knowledge production.

Implicit in the provision of foreign assistance to African education are several broad propositions about the relationships among research, knowledge, and public policy. Generally accepted uncritically, these propositions seem unexceptional, so obvious that they hardly require systematic presentation and supporting evidence. Embedded in these propositions is an increasingly influential conjunction of funding and research that has far-reaching consequences for African education and for African development in general.

The understanding implicit in the assistance relationship begins with two related assumptions: education is essential for development, and education in Africa is currently in such disarray that it cannot fulfill its developmental role. From that starting point comes a third widely accepted proposition: foreign assistance is required to support new initiatives in education, to rehabilitate African education systems that have deteriorated in recent years, and to meet recurrent expenditures. A second set of propositions informs the determination of what sort of assistance is to be provided. Although foreign assistance is of course negotiated and thus subject to the exigencies and vagaries of politics, priorities and targets for foreign aid should be determined, it is generally assumed, on the basis of careful research on education and development. That is, reliable knowledge about education, both in general and in its role in African development, ought to be the primary standard against which specific proposals and projects should be assessed. Finally, it is taken for granted that the most reliable knowledge is the product of research undertaken according to the canons of Western social science by individuals educated and socialized in the universities of the North Atlantic.[1] What insiders have come to refer to as "Jomtien" provides a useful case in point.

WHY INVEST IN SCHOOLING?

With appropriate substance and ceremony, a distinguished group of educators and political leaders met in Jomtien, Thailand, in March 1990 to declare their support for making education available to everyone on the planet. At the World Conference on Education for All, sponsored by the UN Development Program, Unesco, Unicef, and the World Bank, some 1,500 participants from 155 governments, 20 intergovernmental bodies, and 150 nongovernmental organizations adopted by acclamation a World Declaration on Education for All and a Framework for Action. As the conference title suggests, the central tenet of the preparatory documents and the resolutions adopted by acclamation is that it is the imperative that all people have access to basic education, both because

---

[1] My concern here is not to explore all the assumptions that inform the provision of foreign assistance to African education, nor to address all of their defects, but rather to highlight the generally unchallenged propositions that both reflect and reinforce the conjunction of funding and research. As is always the case, generalizations that focus attention on major relationships and the trajectory of change at the large scale necessarily omit and distort at the small scale. For the purposes of this discussion, it is reasonable, I think, to consider shared orientations while recognizing the diversity and disagreements among scholars and practitioners concerned with African education and development.

(basic) education should now be considered a right of citizenship and because development, however conceived, requires an educated populace. The language is unequivocal and dramatic:[2]

Therefore, we participants in the World Conference on Education for All, assembled in Jomtien, Thailand, from 5 to 9 March 1990: [recall] that education is a fundamental right for all people, women and men, of all ages, throughout our world . . . [know] that education is an indispensable key to, though not a sufficient condition for, personal and social improvement . . . [recognize] that sound basic education is fundamental to . . . self-reliant development. [Pp. 2-3]

Every person—child, youth and adult—shall be able to benefit from educational opportunities designed to meet their basic learning needs. [P. 3]

Basic education should be provided to all children, youth and adults. [P. 4]

National, regional, and local educational authorities have a unique obligation to provide basic education for all. [P. 6]

Meeting basic learning needs constitutes a common and universal human responsibility. [P. 8]

Noble goals, with which few would disagree, though of course many countries do not have the means to achieve them rapidly.[3] But why? Why should everyone be educated? And to achieve that goal, why assign the highest priority to basic (primary) education rather than, say, adult education or teacher education? If basic education is a fundamental human right, then other rationales are unnecessary. If, however, universal basic education is an instrumental goal—a necessary if not sufficient foundation for some other important goal(s)—then these *why* questions must be addressed.

There are many answers to those *why* questions, but the answer that seems the most important as we enter the 1990s, especially to those who disburse funds to support African education, is that research shows that investing in primary education yields the best return. That is, support for

---

[2] The quotations, with original emphasis, are from the *World Declaration on Education for All and Framework for Action to Meet Basic Learning Needs* (Jomtien, Thailand: Inter-Agency Commission [UN Development Program, Unesco, Unicef, World Bank] for the World Conference on Education for All, 1990).

[3] Indeed, although the World Bank was a principal sponsor of this world conference, its own projections for Africa have been far less optimistic. See, e.g., World Bank, *Education in Sub-Saharan Africa: Policies for Adjustment, Revitalization, and Expansion* (Washington, D.C.: World Bank, 1988), p. 19.

this focus on primary education rests on the claim that research has persuasively demonstrated that investing in primary education promises the greatest progress toward development (however defined).

What is most striking here is not the substantive conclusion, for its life span is likely to be short. Like other general understandings that are characterized as definitive and unimpeachable and that are for a moment passionately presented and defended, this one will be revised and displaced by a new truth, advocated just as ardently. Rather, it is the implicit consensus on research as the principal determinant of education policy that is remarkable. The Jomtien resolutions are but a single example of the privileged position of research or, more accurately, of claims about research and its findings, in the discourse on education policy. Whether research in fact informs and guides policy or rationalizes and justifies policies adopted for other reasons, assertions about what research shows constitute the core of the discussion. Without the claim of research support, policy proposals lose credibility. Similarly, policy critiques that do not cite supporting research are easily ignored. Prospective participants in the policy debate must demonstrate an adequate supply of relevant research simply to enter.

This formulation—"research shows that . . ."—and its synonyms are ubiquitous. Among the large number of possible examples are several drawn from the World Bank's basic policy document for African education:[4]

Substantial *evidence from research* supports the proposition that within broad limits (between 25 and 50 pupils) changes in class size influence pupil achievement modestly or not at all. [P. 40]

The *increasing body of evidence* on the payoff in various amounts and kinds of teacher training indicates that for primary school teachers preservice training that consists of more than general secondary education and a minimum exposure to pedagogical theory is not cost effective. [P. 40]

There is strong evidence that increasing the provision of instructional materials, especially textbooks, is the most cost-effective way of raising the quality of primary education. [P. 42]

The very ubiquity of the "research shows . . ." claim reflects a very striking contemporary phenomenon: the conjunction of foreign assistance

---

[4] Ibid. (emphasis added).

and research accompanied by an entrepreneurial and expanding development business.[5]

EXPANSIVE GOALS, LIMITED RESOURCES

Nearly everywhere in Africa, schooling expanded rapidly after the end of European rule. Although the mix of pressures for expansion differed among countries, three were generally of particular importance. First, expanded access to education was both a premise and promise of the nationalist movement. Once in power, the new leadership assumed an obligation to build more schools. Indeed, in part their legitimacy and the legitimacy of the state depended on that construction process. Combined, obligation and demand elevated education to a basic right of citizenship.

Second, the intensity of popular demand reflected not only the promise of the nationalist era but also the widely shared understanding that schooling was the single most important route to individual and social benefits: secure employment, influence, prestige, affluence, status, and authority. Social mobility and political recruitment are of course far more complex than this suggests. It was clear to everyone, however, that schooling mattered and that, for improving one's own or the community standard of living, it mattered a great deal.

That perception of the role of schooling in determining individual life chances was reinforced by the image of meritocracy. In the developmentalism that washed over Africa, reliance on ascriptive criteria was

---

[5] Providing development advice is a burgeoning business that has come to constitute the setting within which both goals and projects are considered and that warrants a detailed critical analysis in its own right that is beyond the scope of this discussion. It is important to note here, however, that (1) the community of development consultants-for-hire is transnational in its constitution; (2) although many, perhaps most, consultants are formally employed by universities or research institutes, they derive significant, and for those from Africa perhaps their most significant, income from their advisory services; (3) in some, perhaps many, Third World countries, the agencies that hire consultants have thereby become principal employers of a large segment of the highly educated personnel in particular disciplines, especially economics; and (4) development consultants' advice, though presented in very different ways to very different agencies and governments, functions to disseminate globally a particular worldview and a particular understanding of development. For a critique of one branch of this business (it seems preferable to reserve "industry" for settings where what is produced is more tangible), see Patricia Maguire, *Women in Development: An Alternative Analysis* (Amherst: University of Massachusetts, Center for International Education, 1984).

associated with the backwardness that was to be overcome. Modernization was assumed to require meritocratic advancement, which thereby
became a principal indicator of a society's modernity.[6]

Third, schools were needed to develop the pool of educated and
skilled personnel that progress required. That is, education was, and is,
widely presumed to be a requisite for development:

Greater investment in education can, at this time in Africa's history, be expected to
yield broad economic benefits. . . . The stock of human capital in Africa will determine
whether Africans can harness the universal explosion of scientific and technical knowledge for the region's benefit, or whether Africa will fall farther and farther behind the
world's industrial nations.[7]

Increased investment in education can accelerate growth in several ways. . . . Education is intrinsic to development in the widest sense; empowering people, especially the
poor, with basic cognitive skills is the surest way to render them self-reliant citizens.[8]

Reliance on Foreign Funding

With a sorely limited legacy, the task was enormous. Pulled by popular demand and pushed by the need for highly educated and skilled personnel, schooling became an inexhaustible sink for capital. Since there
were other pressing claims for available funds, and especially as economic crises succeeded the initial developmental optimism, the common
recourse was to foreign funding.[9] For many, perhaps most, African countries, the external provision of assistance funds has become the center of

---

[6] Though it is beyond the scope of this discussion to develop this point fully, it is
important to recognize here (1) the deep psychological and social roots of the ideology of
modernization, (2) the we/they (modern/primitive) duality embedded in that ideology, (3)
its incorporation into the languages of both daily discourse and academic research, (4) its
institutionalization in schools and schooling, and, for all of those reasons, (5) its pervasive-
ness and durability.

[7] World Bank, *Education in Sub-Saharan Africa*, pp. 6-7.

[8] World Bank, *Sub-Saharan Africa: From Crisis to Sustainable Growth* (Washington:
World Bank, 1989), p. 77.

[9] I am not concerned directly here with the motivations of the external agencies, both
national and transnational, that provided and provide support to African education.
Although there is no lack of carpetbaggers and opportunists, I presume most individuals
involved in the provision of that support to be genuinely committed to improving the standard of living and the quality of life in Africa. At the same time, it is also clear that investors
in African education acquire a structural capability to influence both the content and the
orientation not only of schooling in the present but also of fundamental values, world views,
and ways of knowing far into the future.

gravity for education and development initiatives. Over time, it has come to seem not only obvious but unexceptional that new initiatives and reform programs require external support and, therefore, responsiveness to the agenda and preferences of the funding agency(ies).[10]

Sometimes that relationship is aggressively manipulative. The funding agency may make the provision of support conditional on the adoption of specific policies, priorities, or programs. Or to secure support for a preferred program, the leadership in an African country may mobilize support and bring pressure to bear on the funding agency in its home. At other times the influence is less direct. The funding agency may, for example, finance research intended to support its preferred programmatic orientation. Or African educators may tailor their requests, more or less explicitly, to fit within the funding agency's agenda. The paths of influence may also be circuitous. A desire to win support for a high priority goal in one project may promote a willingness to accommodate to a low priority goal in another.

Having concluded that local decision makers have fundamentally mismanaged their responsibilities, the external agencies offer general and rapidly disbursed support in exchange for broad control. This broader form of external assistance impels a demand for broader expert knowledge. The expertise required goes well beyond, say, curriculum development and teacher training. The relevant experts are those who can understand and manage production, finance, international exchanges, and national planning as well as social services. This call for broader expertise comes at a moment of severe economic crisis, precisely the time when African countries are least able to supply expertise and experts at the level and scale and with the credibility and legitimacy the external agencies demand.

External influence on African education policy is not limited to direct links between those who seek and those who provide funds. Even more fundamental patterns of influence may be embedded in other interactions between providers and recipients. Overseas education and training, for example, may involve an intellectual socialization that inclines those who assume positions of authority on their return home to

---

[10] Externally provided funds for African education are of several sorts, involving both national and transnational institutions. Although it clearly matters to the recipient country whether the funding received is a loan or a grant, for the purposes of this discussion I group them together, using the terms "funding" and "assistance" interchangeably.

approach problems, specify relevant factors, and delimit solutions in terms of a particular understanding of development, or economics, or education. That understanding subsequently influences the initiatives and reforms that are proposed.

Note that neither the explicit nor the more subtle insertion of externally specified agendas into African education policy-making is primarily a consequence of external ignorance of or insensitivity to African values, or philosophies of education, or policy preferences (though that distance from Africa and disdain for things African are widespread).[11] Rather, what is most powerful and most insidious in this relationship is the internalization within Africa of world views, research approaches, and procedures for creating and validating knowledge that effectively perpetuate Africa's dependence and poverty. However direct or indirect the influence, the presumption that education reform requires external funding situates foreign assistance and thus a dependent support relationship at the center of education planning. Whatever the initiative, it must accommodate to the nature and content of that relationship.

Many African countries solicit support from several external agencies, seeking to limit their dependence through diversification and diplomacy. Occasionally it is possible to secure funding from one agency for a project that another agency has been unwilling to finance. By the end of the 1980s, however, a remarkable convergence in the orientations and priorities of diverse national and transnational funding agencies became apparent. A review of education sector studies commissioned by a wide range of national and transnational agencies during the last half of the 1980s showed a striking commonality of orientation, approach, and priorities.[12] Increasingly, the World Bank has come to be the lead agency in setting the education and development agenda.

Several factors have contributed to the World Bank's interest in and ability to assume this role. By the end of the 1960s, the World Bank's senior leadership increasingly charged both operations and support staff

---

[11] Kenneth King emphasizes both the increased role of the assistance agencies and Northern ignorance of the educational agendas of countries of the South; see his "The New Politics of International Collaboration in Educational Development: Northern and Southern Research in Education," *International Journal of Educational Development* 10, no. 1 (1990): 47-57.

[12] Reported in Joel Samoff, "Defining What Is and What Is Not an Issue: An Analysis of Assistance Agency Africa Education Sector Studies" (paper presented at the annual conference of the Comparative and International Education Society, Anaheim, Calif., March 1990).

to focus on poverty and the poor and to stimulate and enhance development (formally, of course, the World Bank has always been the International Bank for Reconstruction and *Development*). Drawn from both funds it controls directly and funds it can mobilize from other sources, the World Bank's resources for supporting projects and financing the research that has come to play a critical role in shaping the agenda far exceed the resources available to most other agencies. The World Bank's significantly expanded professional staff enables it to command expertise far more directly and extensively than is possible for other agencies. Indeed, the education level, analytic abilities, and years of experience of the individuals employed directly and indirectly by the World Bank are truly extraordinary.[13] That professional staff also extends the range of settings in which the World Bank can assert the initiative and not simply react to the circumstances. In addition to its command of expertise, the World Bank has become pivotal in the communications among the education policy-makers of other agencies and from different countries. The severity of Africa's economic crises has increased the importance of external funding for nearly all sectors, correspondingly reducing African countries' leverage in their negotiations with the World Bank.

Research and Funding (Education Policy) Decisions

In both national and international discussions of education policy, many competing voices and claims clamor for attention. Advocates of radical innovation challenge the reformers who in turn chastise those who insist on the preservation of what they regard as enduring values, goals, and practices. All participants in these debates point to practical experiences they consider to have confirmed the desirability and utility of whatever program they are advancing. At the same time, in part because nearly all educators are optimistic about the developmental and liberating possibilities of schooling, education policy discussions often reflect and revolve around a pervasive sense of failure. What has education failed to accomplish, and what to do about it? That sense of failure

---

[13] Probably unique in the history of transnational organizations, this concentration of analysts and researchers warrants systematic study in its own right. Were one to consider afresh how best—in terms of serving the education needs and aspirations of the world's people—to deploy this pool of skills, it is not immediately obvious that such a large part of the pool should be located in Washington or primarily responsive to directions from Washington.

and frustration is particularly intense in discussions of African education. The rapid social transformation and improvement in the standard of living that was to have followed decolonization has yet to materialize in most countries. Even worse, the education systems that were to initiate and sustain that transformation by developing new skills and technologies, innovative ideas, and new values in most countries still do not reach all of the school-age population and are unable to provide sufficient teachers and textbooks for those who are in school.

How, then, to choose among alternative policies? Where failures abound, success stories are scarce, and available resources are scarcer still, which policy directions are to be pursued? It is in this process of specifying education strategies, both large and small scale, that the research and funding become principal determinants. The prevailing understanding, indeed, faith that education is a complex undertaking whose organization and management are best left to relevant experts limits popular participation in discussions of education policy and privileges those among the experts who are most successful in characterizing their recommendations as supported by relevant research. In the face of an unmet and in most places still expanding demand, the absolute shortage of funds advantages those who are most successful in attracting external resources to support their recommendations. Together, research and funding constitute control, sometimes challenged and occasionally deflected but rarely rejected or overturned.

The organization, orientation, and rhythm of the funding agencies condition the sorts of development projects and particular roles for research they will support. That the lead agency is a bank is not unimportant. In general, disbursers of funds prefer certainties to tentative propositions, large projects with visible impact to more numerous but far less visible small projects, and projects with clear short-term outcomes to projects whose implementation is likely to be uneven and slow and whose consequential outcomes may be years into the future. Within those agencies, professional advancement is often a function of the rapidity with which projects deemed successful are developed and funded. Even though at the abstract level education reform is understood to be a complex process that may take a long time to come to fruition, project managers who have little concrete to show after a few years' work are unlikely to be promoted very quickly. For similar reasons, while project managers may recognize the advantages of small-scale projects, since they also understand that each small project may require as much preparation time and administrative effort as a single large project, their general inclination is toward the apparent economies of scale. Those project managers who are most successful in moving money relatively quickly may well have other responsibilities when the longer-term consequences of the projects they funded become fully visible.

Quite understandably, project managers want to know what works. Especially in those agencies, like the World Bank, where the dominant perspective is economic, "what works" must be specified in explicit and quantitative terms.[14] The assertion that investment in primary education yields a greater return than spending on higher education provides a relatively clear guide to action. A conditional and situationally specific statement does not. The conclusion that "whether or not investment in primary education yields a higher return than spending on higher education depends on the organization and philosophy of the government, the interests of the particular coalition that is currently most influential in the ministry of education, the support of the party and the teachers union, and the world price of coffee" can be used to support a wide range of alternative, and perhaps incompatible, policies. Although many are aware of local circumstances that distinguish one setting from another, project managers simply cannot do their job if each decision is dependent on a detailed and timely analysis of the political economy of the affected district, or region, or even country.[15]

---

[14] The World Bank is of course not a monolithic organization. Indeed, the divergence of perspectives and priorities of its personnel may be much broader and sharper than the policy and programmatic differences between funding agency and recipient country. At the same time, there do exist official World Bank policies that are influential, if not determining, in every situation. As well, notwithstanding the diversity of perspectives, there are within the World Bank widely, though of course not universally, shared understandings. Those shared understandings include a conception of development and therefore of strategies of development, a sense of the nature of the obstacles to the changes that are deemed desirable and therefore tactics for addressing them, and a vision of the appropriate role of the World Bank itself. The broad agreement on basic premises and fundamental assumptions—though, it is worth stressing again, neither universal nor unchallenged—makes it both reasonable and necessary to treat particular World Bank ideas, roles, and practices in a relatively undifferentiated manner. That sharp critiques of World Bank policies have emerged from among its own personnel and that particular project managers pursue an agenda that diverges in some respect from that of the World Bank as a whole must not obscure the general orientation, trajectory, and consequences of World Bank funding.

[15] My argument here is structural, not personal. Its subject is the set of organization and ideological imperatives and pressures that guide and constrain behavior, not the motivations, preferences, and sensibilities of particular individuals.

The need to know what works both nurtures and is compounded by the tendency to generalize. To address fully the particularities and uniqueness of each setting would make it impossible to develop general principles and priorities to guide funding decisions. Since ultimately a very small group of individuals must approve all projects, adherence to general principles will be persuasive in securing approval more often than appeals to the unique circumstances of particular settings. And since the responsibilities of individual regional specialists and project managers are too broad and their tenure in office too brief to permit detailed familiarity with diverse local settings, they too are inclined to generalize, often on the basis of sorely limited evidence.

The prevailing superrational and utilitarian ethos requires an affirmation in the form of "it [this investment] is [cost-]effective," or "it will work," or "this strategy works best." While the assessment of a senior manager with extensive relevant experience may still occasionally provide sufficient warrant to proceed, most often the affirmation of effectiveness must rest on appropriate research findings.[16] The greater the role in the approval process played by individuals who consider themselves "hard" scientists (a self-description that is common among, but not limited to, economists), the greater the pressure for explicit and unambiguous research findings expressed in quantitative terms.

This demand for research combines with trends in contemporary social science to make the appropriate research relatively expensive to undertake and complex to administer. That in turn leads to an increasingly prominent role for the agencies with the resources and professional staff most able to initiate and support an appropriate research program. In this way, external agencies and especially the World Bank are not only sources of funds for education projects and prominent clients for research. They, and particularly the World Bank, become as well the principal agencies commissioning, undertaking, and managing research on education and development in Africa.

At first glance, that seems to be a healthy situation, not a problem. Researchers have long complained that decision makers pay too little attention to research. Finally they are listening to us, say the academics. In practice, however, that initial view is deceptive in several ways. First,

---

[16] Only some research can play that role. The specification of the sorts of research that can credibly support (or reject) the affirmation of effectiveness in another dimension of the conjunction of funding and research, to which I shall return shortly.

the common understanding that competent policymakers generally base their decisions on a careful review of relevant research is simply inaccurate. Second, policymakers who are largely guided by research focused on the issue to be decided do not necessarily make better decisions. The research that is deemed relevant is generally instrumental and relatively narrowly gauged since it takes the existing patterns of economic, political, and social organization as givens. Yet effective and appropriate public policy cannot ignore interests, preferences, and politics. Making public policy is not, after all, an antiseptic, sheltered, apolitical process. Successfully implemented policies must confront and engage, not avoid, the conflict of interests and the tensions among the organization of production, the structure of power, and patterns of social differentiation. Third, the conjunction of development assistance and research transforms both research and its role in the policy process, to the detriment of both.

My point here is not that research has no role in decision making or that policymakers should ignore research in favor of nonscientific decision rules. Rather, I am concerned with the consequences of a largely uncritical reliance on claimed findings generated by a particular sort of research in a setting where the arbiters of research quality are also the providers of funds. My argument is that both research and funding—and to the extent that research findings can contribute to development, development itself—are poorly served by this marriage.

WHOSE GOALS?

The voluminous studies on education in Africa commissioned or supported by external assistance agencies show clearly one consequence of this conjunction of funding and research.[17] The insistence that the research in those studies emphasize specifying and testing falsifiable

---

[17] The findings and observations reported here are drawn from a survey of recent education-sector studies prepared for the Operational Policy and Sector Analysis Division, Bureau for Coordination of Operational Activities (BAO-PSA), Unesco, in 1989 for the use of the Task Force of Donors to African Education, Action Group on Sector Studies. The studies reviewed reflect the work of a wide range of national and multinational agencies; the majority were prepared by or for the World Bank, both directly and through its cooperative arrangements with other agencies. Of the more than 100 studies reviewed, those published in 1988 and 1989 (44 of them) were summarized in detail to create a database maintained by BAO-PSA. The observations and analysis are of course my own. I report on this review in "Defining What Is and What Is Not an Issue."

hypotheses resulted in limiting the goals for African education to objectives that could (in principle) be measured and tested. Since many of the goals articulated by African leaders were deemed difficult to quantify and therefore impossible to test, they were simply excluded from the agenda. Among those goals, often specified in general education policy statements, are the expectations that education will (1) implant and nurture an inquiring and critical orientation toward the local setting and the world at large and foster the sense of curiosity that makes learning self-rewarding (indeed, there is little explicit attention in these studies to *learning*); (2) promote national unity and especially the national integration of diverse ethnic, cultural, religious, racial, and regional communities; (3) equip and encourage young people to become effective citizens in their society; (4) develop in young people a sense of individual and collective competence, self-reliance, and self-confidence; and (5) reduce the elitist orientations students are inclined to adopt, promote in students a sense of national responsibility, and develop among students a respect for manual labor.

Notwithstanding their ostensibly descriptive charter and character, these education-sector studies in practice define a terrain that is both intellectual and political. Sometimes explicitly, more often implicitly, they specify the core components of education (and development) and the appropriate relationship between education and development. As they do so, they effectively delimit what is to be studied and how studies are to be conducted. As they do that, they function to characterize the important educational decisions as technical and administrative and thus to remove them from the political agenda. Education policy—perhaps the most political of the public policy arenas in contemporary Africa—becomes the province not of politicians but of those with certified technical and administrative expertise.

Viewed broadly, these studies reflect an agenda, an orientation, and a process that is largely externally determined, in which African governments and educators are perhaps collaborators but essentially junior partners. Over time, surely, that agenda, orientation, and process must be Africanized. Consequently, how that transfer of responsibility is to occur warrants systematic attention in the present, as a prominent feature of the current cooperation between education assistance agencies and African governments.

A NATURAL EXPERIMENT?

Let us return now to the earlier query: Why invest in education, particularly the sort of general education offered to all students irrespective of their eventual occupations? As I have suggested, the recurring answer in recent World Bank publications is that

greater investment in education can, at this time in Africa's history, be expected to yield broad economic benefits;[18]

the World Bank has long acknowledged the important relationships between education and economic development;[19]

the evidence that education promotes economic growth, and thus puts other goals of development within reach, is firm.[20]

Indeed, having dealt with "virtually every problem in human capital analysis," recently published research on secondary education in East Africa provides "strong backing for the human capital paradigm: educational expansion is shown to raise labor productivity."[21]

What makes these findings so persuasive? They are the product of a natural experiment, the elusive ideal that methodology textbooks describe but social scientists rarely find! Even better. This natural experiment yields knowledge directly applicable to promoting African development. The logic of this natural experiment is imaginative and innovative. How to assess the consequences of dramatically different secondary school policies? Specifically, which of the two policies studied has had a greater impact in increasing labor productivity and contributing to economic growth? And which policy has been more successful in reducing,

---

[18] World Bank, *Education in Sub-Saharan Africa* (n. 3 above), p. 6.

[19] Ann O. Hamilton, director, Population and Human Resources Department, in the foreword to Marlaine E. Lockheed and Adriaan M. Verspoor, *Improving Primary Education in Developing Countries: A Review of the Policy Options* (Washington, D.C.: World Bank, 1990), p. 6. In fact, this assertion does not accurately reflect the World Bank's orientation during the 1960s, which favored investments in directly productive activities and considered general education a social benefit that could be afforded only after production and productive capacity had been expanded.

[20] World Bank, *World Development Report 1991: The Challenge of Development* (New York: Oxford University Press for the World Bank, 1991), p. 56.

[21] Hollis Chenery in the foreword to John B. Knight and Richard H. Sabot, *Education, Productivity, and Inequality: The East African Natural Experiment* (Oxford: Oxford University Press for the World Bank, 1990), p. v. The companion volume is Arthur Hazlewood, *Education, Work and Pay in East Africa* (Oxford: Oxford University Press, Clarendon Press, 1989).

or at least limiting, economic inequality? The strategy is ingenuous. First, identify two countries that are essentially similar in all fundamental respects but that differ on the policy of interest. Second, study a sample of the adult population constructed to insure that it includes varied secondary school experience. Third, supplement the basic survey with additional measures designed to identify and isolate potentially confounding influences. Fourth, develop modeling and statistical techniques to distinguish and control for factors that were not or could not be measured directly. Finally, draw reasonable inferences about the significance of secondary school policy. Arthur Hazlewood's *Education, Work and Pay in East Africa* and John B. Knight and Richard H. Sabot's *Education, Productivity, and Inequality* are refreshingly clear on both findings and methods, albeit laborious and occasionally pedantic in their presentation. Both address what their authors describe as the natural experiment of secondary education in East Africa. Two fundamentally similar countries, they argue, pursued quite different policies. In Kenya, the preference for market-mediated decisions left relatively unfettered the rapid expansion of private and quasi-public secondary schools. At the same time, the Tanzanian leadership expanded primary and adult education and, in an effort to reduce inequality, restricted the expansion of nongovernmental secondary education. As a result, when the authors surveyed the work forces in these two countries in 1980, Kenya's workers in general had more education and higher pay. Moreover, Kenya's rapid expansion of secondary education was more effective in reducing inequality than controls on both schools and wages in Tanzania.

Out of the complexity of approach and method, Hazlewood and Knight and Sabot develop conclusions that are unambiguous and direct. The human capital perspective is supported: schooling raises labor productivity. Expanded access to education reduces inequality.

The authors' claims are indeed dramatic. Kenya has more and better secondary schools. Why? Because Tanzania's Education for Self Reliance policy restricted secondary school expansion, both to favor primary and adult education and to reduce inequality (by discouraging or forbidding private secondary schools). Better educated, Kenya's workers are more productive. Thus, to promote equality, Tanzania has effectively reduced productivity or limited its increase. Pursuing equality, Tanzania has perpetuated poverty: "The divergence between Kenya and Tanzania in education policies appears to have been an important factor in the divergence of mean earnings and productivity of labor in the two countries in recent years."[22] Equally striking, it is in Kenya, not Tanzania, that education policy has had a greater role in reducing inequality. Essentially, that more young people can proceed to secondary school reduces the significance of family background at that level, thereby enabling more children from poorer homes to reap the individual benefits of extended schooling. For more Tanzanian than Kenyan children of uneducated parents, education ends at primary school. The implication is clear: "The Tanzanian policy regime should move closer to that adopted by Kenya."[23]

Perhaps on closer scrutiny, it turns out that the claim to have studied a natural experiment remains unsupported and probably unsupportable and that the analytic problems at each stage in the argument combine to make the conclusions largely unpersuasive.

Hazlewood's *Education, Work and Pay in East Africa* provides the descriptive report of the surveys conducted in 1980. Though it offers the same conclusion as its companion volume—that the restraints on the expansion of secondary education in Tanzania have retarded development there—the bulk of this book is verbose summaries of extensive tables, with limited comparative observations. An appendix provides the text of the Tanzania survey questionnaire. Reports on workers, their education, and their life experiences need not be so dry and dull. And they ought not to be so uncritical of the data gathering strategy.

Even within the bounds of its limited goals, this report of survey results is seriously flawed. The starting premise, that the fundamental similarities of Kenya and Tanzania, or even of their urban workers, reasonably create a natural experiment, is scarcely supported. After an initial caution that as used in this book the terms "Kenya" and "Tanzania" generally mean "the sample of wage-labor in the major city of Kenya/Tanzania,"[24] the text regularly discusses the findings in terms of workers, sometimes the entire population, in the two countries. Yet, there is no systematic comparison of the survey samples with the populations for which they are taken to be representative (Kenyan and Tanzanian urban workers or adults in the two countries), using either the original survey data or other available information.

Most often, the words add little to the tabular presentations; at

---

[22] Knight and Sabot, *Education, Productivity, and Inequality*, p. 24.
[23] Ibid., p. 51.
[24] Hazlewood, *Education, Work and Pay in East Africa*, p. 45.

times, they confuse rather than clarify. The tables themselves are not unproblematic. Although the strength of this research lies in its systematic comparisons, most often the results of the Kenya survey are shown in one set of tables, the Tanzanian in another. The frequent claims about correlations are apparently based on the distributions of raw frequencies rather than on systematic measures of correlation (which might well require assumptions about the data that are not met). Throughout the numerous cross tabulations, there is no explicit attention to statistical significance. In itself, that need not be troublesome, provided the work addressed clearly the significance, statistical or other, of the observed variations. A demystification of the infatuation with poorly grounded statistics would be welcome. We do not find it here, however.

Even the data taken from other sources are presented uncritically. Early in the discussion we encounter an important assertion based on World Bank data. "Education was evidently given a smaller proportion of a smaller budget, that is, a lower priority in Tanzania than in Kenya."[25] The accompanying footnote dismays as it seeks to disarm: "We assume the authors of this report have done their homework, and have avoided the deep statistical traps which litter the path of such tricky statistical comparison."[26] If the researchers who are systematically constructing a comparative analysis will not assess the baseline data, who will? And if analysts with access to the World Bank's raw data will not address the accuracy of the published summary totals, who can?

For Hazlewood and his collaborators in this volume (including Knight and Sabot), time in East Africa seems to have stopped in 1980. While it is certainly reasonable to focus on the situation as it was then, why not address the particular characteristics of that era? Equally puzzling, why not consider either events or research since then?

Knight's and Sabot's *Education, Productivity, and Inequality* is the analytic book of the pair. Here we find the fruits of the detailed investigation of the 1980 surveys, accompanied by nine explanatory appendices including, once again, the survey of Tanzanian employees. Modeled on the quasi-experimental method, each of the substantive chapters considers one element of the larger argument, focusing in turn on labor productivity, the structure and dispersion of wages, and inequality of opportunity.

---

[25] Ibid., p. 27.
[26] Ibid., p. 27.

After explaining the relevant part of their econometric model and noting the problems in addressing the task at hand, the authors apply their data and draw their inferences. Apparently drafted for similarly trained and like-minded scholars, the text is often dense and daunting. Few nonspecialists will find this thicket easily penetrable. Perhaps. Space limitations permit no more than a brief list of the most important of the analytic problems in this argument.

The two countries, the authors assert, are similar in size, colonial heritage, resource endowment, structure of production, employment, level of development, and the technical conditions and capital intensity of their urban wage economies. Their differences may be even more important. The historical, economic, and political contexts for education in the two countries are far less similar than the authors suggest. Kenya's European settlers, however, did make a difference. Kenya has been and continues to be a more affluent country than Tanzania. At its independence, Kenya had a much higher level of capital investment, a substantially more developed infrastructure, a much larger industrial plant, and better communication and exchange with overseas markets. The economic base permitted a substantially larger investment in education, both public and private, in Kenya beginning well before independence. At its independence, Kenya had more than seven times as many students in primary school as Tanzania (892,000 vs. 121,000) and nearly two and one-half times as many secondary school students (29,000 vs. 12,000). Kenya's population in 1980 was also significantly more urban.

These differences reduce the comparability not only of the two countries in general but of the two samples on which the study is based. For example, employed adults in Tanzania are much more likely to live in rural areas and to work outside of registered (or, if registered, nonindustrial) enterprises than their Kenyan counterparts. At best, then, the findings refer to the industrial work force in the two countries, not to all urban workers and certainly not to all employed adults.

The unstated and undefended but powerfully influential underlying assumption here is the appropriateness of a dual society model. Within the framework of that model, it makes sense to explore the relationship between schooling and productivity in what is commonly termed the "modern sector." Accordingly, the samples for this study were drawn from the employees of urban, primarily industrial enterprises. In the East African setting, however, most economically active adults are neither urban nor wage employees. Hence, who the workers are, how much schooling they have had, and what they are paid in this study all refer to a minority of economically active adults. One consequence: only 14 percent of the workers surveyed in the two countries were female, "too few women for it to be statistically legitimate to show them separately from the males."[27] Yet clearly women constitute more than 14 percent of the adult work force in the two countries.

This orientation may mark the return to legitimacy of the dual economy. The notion of a two-sector economy has its roots in the duality of modernization, the assertion of the critical importance of the distance between the "we" and the "they" and the expectation of incessant individual and collective turmoil fueled by the fundamental incompatibility of the old and the new. This perspective became more widespread and more comfortable to Europeans as they imposed their rule on Africa. Entrenched in various justifying ideologies—the rationalizations of Christian participation in the slave trade as well as the subsequent official philosophies of colonial rule—duality fit quite well with the other baggage Europeans brought with them to Africa. It captured what seemed to Europeans to be an unbridgeable gulf between cultures, and its utility was ostensibly confirmed by the readily apparent differences between rural and urban.

It is not surprising, therefore, that much of the literature of Africa's independence era characterized African economies as dual, constituted by the inherently uneasy cohabitation of modernity and tradition. The modern sector produced for export, included European administrators, company representatives, and educated Africans, and aspired to the values, patterns of interaction, and life-styles of contemporary Europe. The traditional sector produced for local consumption, included the mass of the African population, and struggled to maintain the values, social networks, and daily customs of a distant past.

The duality assumed in that early literature has been sharply challenged. As critics of this perspective demonstrated the extent and solidity of the links between these ostensibly sharply distinct sectors, especially the flows of labor, small-scale commodities, and wages, the popularity of the construct waned. Where dual economy focused attention on separation, incompatibility, and distance, the critics emphasized

---

[27] Ibid., p. 46.

the integration of Africa into a global economy and the incipient homogenization of cultures.

Within the analytic framework that assumed Africa's duality, the economy came to refer to the modern sector: registered firms, wage employment, and tax-paying citizens. In the national statistics, the much more extensive but presumably anachronistic and disappearing exchanges organized around local production and consumption went largely unrecorded. In this regard, attention to the informal sector brought an important corrective to the study of the economies of Africa.[28] The unregistered and unrecorded were accorded a new legitimacy. Their durability and rationality were formally recognized.

That very recognition, however, restored duality to the center of economic analysis. Within education, for example, it is now fashionable to preach the importance of training for the informal sector to compensate for the apparent inability of the modern sector to generate employment at the rate at which young people finish school. Yet this usage is in part a process of labeling that characterizes as qualitatively different and often of lesser significance those economic activities that economists and other social scientists for many years did not study carefully and still find difficult to study systematically and that governments found, and find, more difficult to regulate and control.

In fact, as is increasingly widely acknowledged, the economy of the informal sector is neither very informal nor invisible. Patterns of employment are reasonably clearly structured and supported by a rich institutional network. There are hierarchical chains of authority, functional specialization, reliable sources of credit, and often even small-scale bureaucracy. Nor are these activities marginal to the national economy. In many, perhaps most, African countries, the majority of employment is in activities labeled "informal," and those activities are integrally connected to the rest of the economy through wages, purchases, credit, labor deployment, and the like.

In Knight and Sabot's study, the dual economy model leads to the assumption that the majority of adults who have completed secondary school are likely to be found in wage employment and therefore reasonably sampled through a survey conducted among the workers of urban industrial enterprises. That assumption, too, may be unwarranted in

---

[28] Several terms other than "informal sector" have also been used to label this phenomenon, including "parallel," "invisible," "hidden," "subterranean," "underground," and "second economy."

East Africa, where it is certainly possible, perhaps likely, that a significant percentage of adults with secondary education are not found in
urban wage employment. Indeed, in 1980 Kenya and Tanzania may have
been quite different in this regard.

In short, whatever the findings about urban wage workers in Kenya
and Tanzania in 1980, there is no solid ground in this study to generalize
those findings to the larger populations of the work forces or to adults
with secondary education in the two countries. There are similar problems in using the wages of the workers in the two samples to indicate
productivity in the two economies. Assuming that wages are a reasonable indicator of productivity is problematic, though common. To use
urban industrial sector wages as a measure of the economy's overall productivity, however, requires an even greater leap of faith.

Similarly troubling are several of the other measures on which this
study relies. In order to make their case, the authors need to find support for the human capital thesis (higher wages correlated to years of
schooling reflect greater productivity developed in school and therefore
a link between individual and social benefits) in order to reject what the
authors term the "screening hypothesis" (schools identify and certify students of higher ability but do not directly increase their skills) and the
"credentialist hypothesis" (wages are associated with certificates, not
productivity, so that more schooling leads to an increased individual
reward but no direct social benefit). To do that, the authors employed
independent measures of reasoning ability and cognitive skill. Their conclusion: "Whereas the direct returns to reasoning ability in the labor
market are small and the returns to years of schooling are moderate, the
returns to cognitive achievement [i.e., what students improve through
schooling] are large."[29]

Knight and Sabot used Raven's Coloured Progressive Matrices to
assess reasoning ability ("a measure of predetermined natural ability")[30]
and literacy and numeracy tests designed by the Educational Testing
Service to measure cognitive skill (cute). Though they ostensibly do not
depend on acquired literacy and numeracy skills, the graphic puzzles of
the reasoning ability measure do require a common perception of space
and competitive motivation—that is, ways of seeing and behaving that

---

[29] Knight and Sabot, *Education, Productivity, and Inequality*, p. 17.
[30] Ibid., p. 58.

may well be more learned, probably in school, than innate. Critiques of the cultural biases inherent in the Scholastic Aptitude Test and its other products are numerous within the home country of the Educational Testing Service. Since the results of this test carry so much weight in the study, its validity and reliability as a measure of learning in school need to be examined systematically and skeptically, not assumed or taken for granted. As the authors note, rarely do economists use tests of this sort. And they are to be commended for including an appendix that explains and provides samples of the two tests. Still, the basic argument strains credulity. Two tests were administered by university students in 1 hour to a 10 percent subsample of the workers surveyed. The scores of the 200 workers in each country were then used to distinguish between innate ability and school learning. That distinction, in turn, permitted differentiating labor productivity in the two countries. Linking the differential productivity of labor to the larger number of secondary schools in Kenya, the authors find convincing support for human capital theory and confidently proclaim the advantages of Kenya's education policy.

At a minimum, recognizing the difficulty of measuring and distinguishing reliably innate ability and school learning in one's own culture requires that we remain skeptical about the heavy weight to be born by these two tests. If the results of either of those tests are significantly flawed, or even have a wide margin of error, the basic argument of this study becomes untenable.

Wages are not entirely satisfactory as measures of either productivity or inequality. There are two different problems here. The first concerns relying on wages to indicate productivity and inequality among the population surveyed. Reservations about the wage-productivity relationship have been and continue to be widely debated. The wage-inequality relationship is more complex in the East African setting. Inequality may be perceived as a collective (household, or perhaps larger grouping) rather than individual phenomenon. Even for urban workers, wages may constitute a small part of household income and may therefore have no linear relationship to the household's standard of living or quality of life. Securing medical care, for example, may depend less on disposable income than on the proximity of a clinic or dispensary. General health, including infant and maternal mortality and adult longevity, may depend less on what individuals can purchase than on the community's clean water. Thus, for many people the most troubling and politically significant inequality may be more a function of differential access to social services like health and education than unequal incomes. To focus on individual incomes is to treat as natural and universal a particular pattern of social organization and thereby to consider unimportant both how it got that way and its unique characteristics.

Second, as I have suggested, the characteristics of the East African setting also make it difficult to generalize to the entire work force whatever the wages are of the sampled population are taken to show. Urban industrial workers are a small and surely atypical segment of economically active adults. Even if we could speak confidently about productivity and inequality among them, that would permit at most informed speculation about productivity and inequality in the larger society.

Another set of problems has to do with the location of causality. For example, the authors take the greater cognitive skills of the sampled Kenyan workers to be a function of the higher quality of the Kenyan schools. Perhaps. But from the data presented, we simply cannot tell. Here, a plausible assumption is presented as if it were a well-founded inference.

More troublesome is the authors' major conclusion about the source of the difference between the experiences in the two countries. The authors argue that "The difference between Kenya and Tanzania in secondary enrollment rates and in the stock of secondary school graduates in 1980 can be traced to these changes in education policies in Tanzania in the late 1960s."[31] There are two important misunderstandings here. The first concerns the pace of education reform. Changes in education policy adopted in the late 1960s began to appear only in the 1970s. Indeed, restraints on secondary school expansion in Tanzania were not effectively imposed until the 1980s, that is, after the period studied. While government secondary schools in Tanzania increased from 61 to 83 between 1962 and 1980 (approximately 1.2 new schools per year, or a 2 percent annual increase over the 18 years), private secondary schools increased from 1 to 71 during the same period. Thus, the policy that is ultimately deemed responsible for slower growth in Tanzania had not yet been implemented. More generally, the time studied is too short to permit an effective comparison of secondary school policy. Even had a significant policy change been implemented in Tanzania following the

---

[31] Ibid., p. 22.

national policy reforms of the late 1960s (articulated in the Arusha Declaration and related papers), relatively few of the sampled adult workers would have been in secondary school between 1970 and 1980. For most of the sample, then, the quality of their secondary schooling was affected by something other than late 1960s education policy.

Second, articulated secondary school policies in the two countries were more similar than the basic organization of this study suggests. In the early 1960s in both countries, what was termed "manpower planning" guided post-primary-school expansion. In both countries, educators and political leaders sought (as the authors note, with strong support from the World Bank) to control the growth of general secondary education. What differed was the commitment to and the ability to implement the announced policy.

The new Tanzanian education policies of the late 1960s effectively rejected the priority accorded to the carefully managed development of higher-level skills in favor of a commitment to universal primary education and the eradication of adult illiteracy. Although they were sometimes described in humanpower planning terms, efforts to restrict private secondary schools—always uneven and with limited success until the end of the 1970s and early 1980s—reflected limited resources (even private schools generate public expenditures) and an attempt to reduce regional inequalities.

Contrary to the authors' claim, then, the differences in the availability of secondary education observable in 1980 were more a function of Kenya's relative affluence than of Tanzania's socialism. Without a systematic comparison of the sample with the larger population and in the absence of data on access to social services, it is impossible to reach confident conclusions about which arrangement was more successful in reducing inequality.

In some ways, this study is strikingly innovative and iconoclastic. At critical junctures the authors self-consciously distance themselves from the ways economists commonly understand things (e.g., pointing to the individual characteristics of workers, rather than their specific jobs, to explain differences in earnings). They are painstakingly detailed as they unfold their case, regularly identifying and then addressing counterarguments. They do not hesitate to challenge conventional wisdom.

Yet overall, this study is problematic in several fundamental respects. The significant differences between the two countries weaken the natural experiment. The general findings depend on heroic assumptions and on a very high level of confidence in what may be seriously flawed measures of the basic factors. Statistical association is regularly described as correlation. Identification of the prime cause rests at least in part on a shallow understanding of national education policy and its implementation. Findings about the sample actually studied are frequently overgeneralized to larger populations that it does not adequately reflect. And notwithstanding the decade that has passed since these data were collected and the major conference at which these findings were initially presented, there is hardly any attention to subsequent research or later events. Yet Knight and Sabot commonly argue their case in the present tense, suggesting the contemporary value of their inferences and recommendations. Recall their advice: "The Tanzanian policy regime *should move closer* to that adopted by Kenya."[32]

It is useful that studies of this sort be undertaken. It would be even more useful if the research had its center of gravity within East Africa, where challenges to and refinements of the findings could be the ordinary business of students of education and development.

IMPLEMENTING EDUCATION REFORMS

There is also in this work a striking critique of the contemporary emphasis on investing in primary education. As Knight and Sabot argue their human capital case, they criticize the alternative and currently popular perspective based on the rate of return to investments in education. The current wisdom in this regard is that investments in primary education yield a higher social rate of return than investments in secondary education. But, the authors argue, the failure to recognize the gap between the average and marginal rates of return leads to overestimating the returns to education. As well, because the gap is not the same at primary and secondary levels, the order of benefits may be reversed. That the wages of particular occupations may change over time further confuses the analysis. In Kenya, it seems, it is secondary, not primary, education that has the higher rate of return. As they respond to "Why invest in education?" Knight and Sabot question the global agreement on the level to which that investment should be directed.

How, then, should education funds be allocated? One potentially useful approach is to explore allocations in several countries. A recent

---

[32] Ibid., p. 51 (emphasis added).

series of World Bank discussion papers seeks to provide a comparative overview of education reform efforts in eastern and southern Africa. Eight case studies (Ethiopia, Lesotho, Swaziland, Kenya, Tanzania, Uganda, Zambia, and Zimbabwe) are complemented by a brief general overview by the series editor and a literature review.[33] Unlike the study of education and labor productivity in East Africa, these papers do not report on their authors' original research but rather summarize what is known on their respective topics. As they do so, these papers provide another vantage point on the World Bank's role in knowledge creation and in policy production and analysis. In particular, they highlight the regularly reiterated insistence that only hypothesis testing research yields reliable knowledge on which to base policy, the global dissemination of a particular analytic framework and its key constructs, and at the same time the publication of insubstantial scholarship.

John Craig undertakes a broad literature survey, considering some 300 articles from 147 periodicals. He organizes the findings from these studies in terms of six sets of factors that explain unsuccessful implementation. Most important, he argues, is the policy process itself (what he terms the "policy message"), including the substance of the policy, the implementation strategy, and communication about both policy and implementation. Of somewhat lesser importance are political factors and

---

[33] The case studies are by Paul W. Achola, *Implementing Educational Policies in Zambia*, Discussion Paper no. 90, Africa Technical Department Series (Washington, D.C.: World Bank, 1990); G. S. Eshiwani, *Implementing Educational Policies in Kenya*, Discussion Paper no. 85, Africa Technical Department Series (Washington, D.C.: World Bank, 1990); C. J. Galabawa, *Implementing Educational Policies in Tanzania*, Discussion Paper no. 86, Africa Technical Department Series (Washington, D.C.: World Bank, 1990); Fassil R. Kiros, *Implementing Educational Policies in Ethiopia*, Discussion Paper no. 84, Africa Technical Department Series (Washington, D.C.: World Bank, 1990); Cisco Magalula, *Implementing Educational Policies in Swaziland*, Discussion Paper no. 88, Africa Technical Department Series (Washington, D.C.: World Bank, 1990); O. E. Maravanyika, *Implementing Educational Policies in Zimbabwe*, Discussion Paper no. 91, Africa Technical Department Series (Washington, D.C.: World Bank, 1990); Cooper F. Odaet, *Implementing Educational Policies in Uganda*, Discussion Paper no. 89, Africa Technical Department Series (Washington, D.C.: World Bank, 1990); T. Sohl Thelejani, *Implementing Educational Policies in Lesotho*, Discussion Paper no. 87, Africa Technical Department Series (Washington, D.C.: World Bank, 1990). The overview is by George Pschacaropoulos, *Why Educational Policies Can Fail: An Overview of Selected African Experiences*, Discussion Paper no. 82, Africa Technical Department Series (Washington, D.C.: World Bank, 1990), and the literature review is by John Craig, *Comparative African Experiences in Implementing Educational Policies*, Discussion Paper no. 83, Africa Technical Department Series (Washington, D.C.: World Bank, 1990).

bureaucratic and administrative factors. Relatively unimportant in explaining unsuccessful policy implementation, he concludes, are teachers, client populations, and resource constraints. Much of this paper, however, is a lament. No study of policy implementation in Africa has the theoretical and methodological sophistication, the familiarity with relevant literature, and the systematic comparisons that are found in the U.S. policy literature. Because essentially all research on policy implementation in Africa is in the form of case studies, he concludes, more research, with explicitly comparative and testable hypotheses, is needed.

Here we have the assertion of the positivist faith. Explanation means establishing cause-and-effect relationships by generating testable hypotheses and using them to organize both the research and its presentation. Studies not principally concerned with testing hypotheses—indeed all other approaches to knowledge and understanding—are fundamentally flawed. At best, they can lay the foundation for and perhaps illuminate experimental designs in which the phenomenon or relationship of interest varies across a specified range while potentially obscuring or confounding influences are excluded, held constant, or minimized. The appeal of the natural experiment is especially visible here since social scientists' research terrain rarely permits the tight control of laboratory experiments (a degree of precision that social scientists often exaggerate), and quasi experiments are always defective in some respect.

The series editor is even more direct, restating in his paper the perspective he has articulated in many of his other publications. George Psacharopoulos begins with a very brief overview of African education policies and a summary of policy goals articulated by national and international agencies. Fortunately, his own extensive experience in this arena affords him a broader base than that provided by the generally superficial and uncritical reports in this series' case studies. He argues that most African education policies have failed. Why? Policy outcomes do not fulfill the initial expectations because the policies have not been implemented or have been poorly implemented. Why is that? Implementation fails because policies are vaguely stated and because their financial implications are not adequately addressed. Most important, policies fail because they are based on assumptions ("theories") about the relationship between instruments and outcomes that cannot be sustained empirically. Psacharopoulos concludes with a call for better policy-making, that is, explicit statements of desired outcomes and reliance on empirical evidence: "Perhaps the safest course of action for the policy maker would be to abstain from educational policy fireworks, and concentrate on the documentation of cause and effect relationships—the only activity, in my opinion, that can lead to successful school reform."[34]

Here, the conjunction of funding and research becomes the vehicle for imposing orthodoxy. One approach to knowledge is characterized as social science itself. Detached from its content and shorn of its ideology, the scientific method is transformed into an atheoretical straitjacket. Positivist proselytizing parades as injunctions for good research, and only good research should guide the allocation of funds and the specification of activities to be supported.

For the most part being descriptive summaries of major colonial and postcolonial education policies, the eight case studies vary from detailed to shallow. Fassil Kiros, for example, sketches carefully the increasing importance of education policy during Ethiopia's imperial era and its reorientation after 1974. Other papers do little more than list policy pronouncements; some do not even manage to do that well. None develops a substantial analysis. While a few papers provide basic quantitative information (again, Kiros's paper stands out), in many the numbers limit the view of change over time to the expansion of schools and enrollment. Inconsistencies and inaccuracies are far too frequent.

For whom was this series produced? Informed readers will find the case studies superficial. Readers with little background on African education will find the jargon frustrating and confusing. Policymakers are not likely to find these papers much more useful. Other sources provide clearer concise summaries and more substantial analyses. Nearly all of the authors have published more insightful, better supported and documented, and more rigorous and stimulating analyses elsewhere. Yet reading these papers does prove instructive. They reflect both the World Bank's willingness to accept insubstantial work from competent Third World scholars and its effort to institutionalize a particular set of understandings and constructs in research on education. Although those constructs do not significantly enrich these papers, their uncritical acceptance is striking.

While there is a good deal of variation from one paper in this series to the next, apparently they were all to include a critical appraisal, based on four sets of criteria: internal efficiency, external efficiency, equity, and

---

[34] Psacharopoulos, *Why Educational Policies Can Fail*, p. 21.

nonquantitative criteria. These categories, which have come to be standard in World Bank and other agency commissioned research, ought to be particularly disturbing to educators since they insist on treating some important dimensions of education solely quantitatively, while relegating much that is deemed important to a catchall nonquantitative category.

Here we find another consequence of the conjunction of project support and focused research within a single institution. Access to its funding requires requests and rationales to be formulated according to its standards, which effectively structure the education and development discourse. Within the legitimate terminology are embedded particular conceptualizations, conceptions, orientations, prejudices, and policy preferences. That terminology treats as part of the environment—what is "given" and therefore does not require explicit justification and is not subjected to critical attention—important issues that ought to be the focus of policy discussion. As well, that terminology obscures important issues and, thereby, far too frequently misdirects the search for understanding.

This discourse-structuring terminology is prominently visible in this set of papers. For many students of education, these constructs have been so deeply ingrained in assistance-agency thinking and documents that only their absence would be noticed. Space permits only a few examples here.[35]

Wastage

Wastage refers to those who begin but do not complete an education program. Understood in this way, wastage is often identified as one of the most serious problems in African education. Where resources are limited, they are surely wasted when they are spent on projects that are never completed and when they are invested in highly inefficient training programs whose students fail to finish and whose graduates are poorly trained.

Yet since most students in Africa who do not complete their schooling are pushed out (rather than drop out), a high attrition rate is a normal

---

[35] My concern here is not to develop a detailed analysis of each of these terms and its usage. Rather, my point is that the generally uncritical use of these terms not only directs attention toward some issues and away from others but also privileges a particular way of understanding with the result that some ideas and perspectives remain unnoticed and unevaluated. That, after all, is the point of theories and constructs: to assign higher priority to some ideas and to exclude others. What is problematic is that one such filter is deemed universal, discrediting and displacing all the others, in a setting that discourages rather than nurtures the contestation of ideas.

feature of the education system, not an unexpected, or abnormal, or even avoidable waste. That is, decisions about the number of places available at each higher level and the intentional design of selection and promotion procedures effectively determine the number of students who will advance. Examination results and perhaps other criteria may specify who among the students will proceed. But the threshold for promotion is a function of education policy, not individual achievement. Indeed, there may be many students who pass (score high on the examination) but do not proceed. What occurs is eviction, not dropping out. In these circumstances, if attrition is considered problematic, it needs to be addressed as such. That some students are afforded additional time to complete their courses is reasonably understood as an issue of education policy, not a measure of inefficiency. Automatic promotion might well reduce repetition and attrition, but to consider it less wasteful is a distortion of common meanings. The terminology matters. Where concern with wastage directs attention toward individual motivation and the quality of instruction, concern with attrition requires attention to the basic assumptions and organization of the education system. To focus on attrition also requires attention to which students are not permitted to proceed. Are females, or students from a particular region or religion or socioeconomic stratum, more likely to be excluded?

Efficiency

Internal efficiency is concern with student progress through school, teacher-student ratios, use of physical facilities, and measures of achievement, commonly all summed in the unit cost per student; external efficiency is concern with the relationship between schooling and the labor market, commonly assessed in terms of the percentage of students who pass, graduate, and secure employment. Like cost-benefit analysis, notions of efficiency focus on achieving particular goals with the smallest expenditure. Schools with low spending per pupil (or, per student who completes the education cycle) are considered to be internally more efficient than schools with higher per pupil expenditures. In this example, internal efficiency may be improved by either spending less per pupil or reducing dropouts and repetition, or both. Increased employment rates among graduates are the principal indicators of greater external efficiency.

In two important ways the constructs internal efficiency and external efficiency focus policy attention in the wrong direction. Concern with reducing the unit cost per student is likely to be far less fruitful than focusing on increasing the effectiveness of each unit of expenditure. As the World Bank itself regularly points out, African countries currently allocate far less of their national budget and spend far less of their gross domestic product on education than do countries in much of the rest of the world. Second, since pass and graduation rates are largely the consequences of general education and national policy and therefore not of either student or school achievement, it seems particularly obfuscating to characterize as internal inefficiency the decision to promote few students. Recognizing that the charter of schooling is far broader than, and may not even include, vocational preparation, requires discarding efforts to assess education's external efficiency from rates and types of employment. And since it is far from clear that in-school and skill-specific vocational training make better employees, unemployment rates cannot provide even a rough measure of a more limited notion of employment-preparation efficiency. Note that while efficiency might be assessed in terms of learning rather than expenditures, that is rarely done. The pressure to quantify is easily frustrated by the problems in measuring learning.

Put simply, if the primary goals of schooling are to develop literacy, numeracy, and social consciousness and to foster curiosity, creativity, and critique, if educators know relatively little about the sort of early in-school training that leads to better mechanics, or managers, or teachers, and if it is likely that adults will work in several different occupations, then there is little point in evaluating schooling with a rate-of-employment yardstick. From this perspective, to focus on internal and external efficiency as commonly defined is to undermine education's efforts to achieve the broader goals with which it has been charged. It is also important to note here that to use this terminology—"internal and external efficiency"—is to cast as problems of administration and management, presumably amenable to technical solutions, what are fundamentally issues of public policy.

My concern here has been to highlight the ways in which the conjunction of funding and research, through its common and officially sanctioned terminology, structures the education and development discourse. In these illustrative examples, I have not attempted either to develop fully the critiques of quasi-official terminology or to make a strong case for particular alternatives. My point is simply that the quasi-official status of these constructs in a setting where the same agency oversees both funding and research effectively diverts attention from and often precludes consideration of alternatives that warrant serious exploration, systematic elaboration, and critical evaluation.

CERTIFIED KNOWLEDGE

A second consequence of the integration of project funding and development research is to legitimize poorly supported propositions. Project managers are often prepared to accept as valid findings whose relatively weak foundations would lead most academic researchers to present them tentatively and conditionally. That weaker confidence standard may be satisfactory in an operation setting, where the pressure for prompt decisions exceeds the demand for very high levels of confidence. The conjunction of funding, project management, and research, however, functions to obscure the caveats that were (or should have been) attached to the original research.

This process of legitimizing weak propositions by granting them official sanction and ignoring their tentative or conditional character is especially clear in the use of quantitative data.[36] As I have suggested above, the need for certainty combines with the influence of economists and the premises of contemporary behavioral science to demand quantitative data wherever possible. Data (or what the data are claimed to show) provide the most compelling support for particular policies and the grounds for rejecting others. Careful scrutiny of the reported data, however, often reveals that the variation from one period to the next is smaller than the margin of error.[37] For example, a 1 percentage point change in

---

[36] That many funding agency documents do not indicate clearly the sources that support their claims about what research shows compounds the problem: even careful and critical readers find it difficult or impossible to locate and assess the reliability and validity of the relevant research.

[37] Both the problems with the reported data and their major causes are well known. The basic data deficiencies are often compounded by careless use of what is available (e.g., assuming that budgeted allocations are approximately the same as actual expenditures, or comparing budget data in 1 year with expenditure data in another). Unfortunately, far too often the relatively wide margin of error in the base data is ignored. Even authors sensitive to the data problems frequently note those difficulties at the beginning of their reports and then dismiss their own caveats as they proceed with their analyses, on the grounds that whatever their limitations, these are the best data available: "The limitations of the quality of data and aggregative analysis were fully recognized" (World Bank, *World Development Report*, 1991 [n. 21 above], p. 65). I have addressed this problem more fully in "The Facade of Precision in Education Data and Statistics," *Journal of Modern African Studies* 29, no. 4 (December 1991): 669-89.

the portion of the national expenditures allocated to education may be reported as evidence of the government's increased commitment to education. Yet in practice, the margin of error in both the total and education spending is generally much greater than 1 percent. In those circumstances it is impossible to be sure that any change has in fact taken place. A careful researcher will say precisely that. Project managers, however, may be willing to discount the data problems in order to have a clear finding that will support a particular decision. When that research is filtered through the project process and combined with other research in a general policy document—that is, when the project funding process subsumes the research—a finding of no clear relationship is transformed into a confidently presented and unqualified assertion about the direction of change. The tenuous becomes a certainty. Having been legitimized and disseminated, the assertion becomes a guide to, and not infrequently a constraint on, subsequent research.

In a similar way, research in different settings that may vary widely in orientation, assumptions, methodology, and quality is cumulated to support particular propositions:

Perhaps the most influential fact to emerge from twenty-five years of studying rates of return in developing countries concerns the relative returns to primary and secondary schooling. Most studies, including most of those conducted in Africa, have reported substantially higher rates of return at the primary level.[38]

A diverse body of literature demonstrates . . .[39]

A disarming entry into the discussion! Who would not find persuasive what extensive research has found? But a hundred bullets are no more effective than one if they miss their target. The findings of six seriously flawed research projects are surely no more persuasive than the results of a single study that is especially well done. The dilemma here is that we have no good way to determine whether the cumulated studies are compelling. There are two related problems. First, often it proves impossible to determine exactly which studies constitute the "diverse body of literature." Hence, we cannot assess the basis on which the claim rests. Second, the studies may not be comparable in important respects. Some may rely on

---

[38] World Bank, *Education in Sub-Saharan Africa* (n. 2 above), p. 23. Recall Knight's and Sabot's rejection of this "stylized fact."

[39] Lockheed and Verspoor, *Improving Primary Education in Developing Countries*, p. 1.

direct observations while others have used surveys. Some may have large samples or many observations, while others may draw inferences from very few. Some may be systematically comparative, while others are exploratory or focus on unique situations. Some may include external measures of validity and reliability (and perhaps still be quite superficial), while others are entirely dependent on the expertise of an individual scholar (and thereby offer incisive insights). Precisely because of these problems, scholars fashioned standards to be used in such metacomparisons. Yet rarely, if ever, are those standards, or any others, applied in this setting.

It is quite reasonable to assert that the bulk of the research that has been undertaken supports a particular argument. Skeptics can consult the original research and attempt to demonstrate that it does not support the claim made or that combining it obscures poor quality and inconsistencies. Within the financial-intellectual complex, however, it is frequently impossible to identify the original research. Even when cited, that research may have sharply restricted circulation, precluding effective access and assessment. Again, the possible becomes probable and the reasonably likely is transformed into a certainty. As it officially certifies particular perspectives, the process stymies scrutiny.

A third consequence of the strong connections between providing funds and conducting research is to accord legitimacy and international sanction to approaches and understandings that are at best partial and at worst simply wrong. Misunderstandings are entrenched. The official overview publications of the World Bank currently have such a commanding presence in the academic arena that few authors address the issues of African development without referring to them.[40] Even authors who reject both the approach and the conclusions of those publications seem to feel obliged to refer to them. Thus, documents commissioned by the World Bank to guide its lending operations and to present a coherent programmatic perspective to the representatives of recipient countries acquire the status of standard references in the academic arena.[41]

---

[40] Including, among others, World Bank, *Accelerated Development in Sub-Saharan Africa: An Agenda for Action* (Washington, D.C.: World Bank, 1981), *Financing Adjustment with Growth in Sub-Saharan Africa, 1986-90* (Washington, D.C.: World Bank, 1986), *Sub-Saharan Africa: From Crisis to Sustainable Growth* (see n. 8 above), *Education in Sub-Saharan Africa*; Lockheed and Verspoor; and the annual *World Development Reports* and the periodic *World Tables*, also by the World Bank. Many of the large number of more narrowly focused studies and reports on which these publications draw are little known outside the sponsoring agencies.

[41] That a bank commissions and publishes studies of African development is not in itself problematic. Nor is it necessarily problematic that those studies are widely cited.

As I have suggested, one example of the entrenchment of (mis)-understandings is manifested in the current resuscitation of moderniza-tion theory, which insists now, as it did 25 years ago, that the causes of Africa's problems are to be found within Africa: its people, resources, capital, skills, psychological orientation, child-rearing practices, and more. That analytic framework is seductive and often assumed uncriti-cally. Just as poverty is to be explained by the characteristics and (in)abil-ities of the poor,[42] so the explanations of problems of African education are to be found within and around African schools. The funding and research agencies of the development business—a veritable financial-intellectual complex—institutionalize this fundamental misunderstand-ing in the centers of financial, industrial, and academic authority, entrenching it against the challenge that the primary sources of contem-porary problems are to be found in the process by which African coun-tries have been incorporated into the global economy. The international relationships are acknowledged and at the same time treated as part of the policy environment. As normal and largely unexceptional features of the structure of international interactions, those relationships are assigned a low priority in the search for explanations and strategies for change. The resulting explanatory framework and research agenda thereby largely exclude from active consideration the analytic perspec-tive that emphasizes global integration, instead directing attention to things African.

Rather, my argument here is that it is important to recognize the power, influence, and aca-demic and developmental consequences of this historically unique combination of funding development projects and development research. (Note here the echoes of the early imper-ial era, when the metropolitan governments funded learned societies that in turn supported the field work of missionaries and adventurers—who also saw themselves as geographers, anthropologists, and historians—like Livingston.) In this setting, it is appropriate, indeed imperative, to understand the World Bank not simply as a bank but also as an institution whose basic policies are largely determined by the interests of a few affluent countries, whose lending program is justified by the extensive research it commissions, and whose own analyses and development agenda have come to constrain and shape the entire develop-ment discourse.

[42] At its root, identifying the nature, characteristics, and behaviors of the poor as the causes for poverty necessarily devolves to a genetic explanation. If the circumstances in which they live lead the poor to behave in ways that perpetuate their impoverishment, then it is those circumstances—local, national, global—that cause poverty, not something inher-ent in the poor. To insist that the poor are poor because of who they are, however disguised, sanitized, beautified, and situationally conditional that claim may be, is to assert a genetic basis for differences in wealth and their consequences.

The amalgamation of funding and research also nurtures an intense but usually ephemeral fixation on a particular understanding or strategy. Decisions in this environment require not only clarity but also simplicity. To ask, "What is *the* problem?" calls for *the* solution, which in practice becomes a succession of solutions, each proffered as definitive (or nearly so) and each ostensibly supported by unimpeachable research. This faddishness in education and development is fostered by the centralization of communication and the antipathy to the tentative, the uncertain, and the condition within this setting. Periodic fads flourish in an environment that regards what works as more important than understanding why it works, that emphasizes relatively rapid tangible outcomes at the expense of attention to the quality and consequences of process, and that prefers technical-administrative to social-political explanations and solutions.

A new insight, or perspective, or approach that captures the attention of the major funding agencies is quickly communicated to their principal consultants and African collaborators, who in turn disseminate it more widely. For a moment, often a very brief moment, it acquires extraordinary visibility and influence. It may even be enshrined as a guiding principle for particular projects. Complex problems, however, are rarely amenable to simple solutions, notwithstanding the preference for uncluttered and unencumbered understandings. New evidence is collected, new objections are lodged, new personnel assume responsibility, and disenchantment sets in. The successor to the current fad is already emerging. Acknowledging that their confidence in the previous approach was misplaced seems not to make the advocates of its successor any more reserved or cautious in their enthusiasm. We were wrong before, they say, but this time we are sure.

Hence, there is a continuing search for a prime cause for whatever problem happens to be currently specified as the most important. Periodically, it is announced that a prime cause (or its mate, a prime solution) has been identified. For example, relevant research shows clearly, it is claimed, that the quality of instruction depends heavily on the availability of textbooks and very little on class size. The canons of social science research disappear in the push for clarity and certainty. As the marketing of the new understanding proceeds, few of its distributors are aware of the setting or the limitations of the initial research on which it rests or of the context, orientation, and deficiencies of the interpretation of that research. Subsequent research, however, generally shows that the purported prime cause is at best partial, and perhaps neither primary nor a cause. The old prime cause is discarded in favor of its successor.

As the fascination with a particular understanding peaks and wanes, it is not uncommon to find complete reversals in recommended policies. The assertion a decade ago that it was desirable to introduce some vocational curriculum in all schools has apparently now been succeeded by the equally ardently articulated assertion that vocationalization of that sort is far too expensive and yields far too few benefits for most countries to undertake.

Another consequence of the integration of education and development funding and research is the pervasive treatment of education as technique and administration. Again, the common terminology is revealing. Policy-oriented research is more likely to talk about delivery systems than learning, about inefficiency than the realization of human potential, and about returns on investment than nurturing curiosity or encouraging innovation or the creative expression of ideas and insights.

How, though, will Africans overcome their dependence on external intellectual leadership and standards if learning and creativity are not the central focus of education and development initiatives? How will assessing its schools in terms of efficiency and productivity fortify a new generation to criticize and risk departing from received wisdom? Who is best served by regarding the improvement of education largely as another of the development tasks to be organized and managed and thereby relegating to the status of by-product—for both the youngest and oldest learners—the intrinsic excitement and self-regenerating dynamo of learning?

More generally, the financial-intellectual complex not only consumes and commissions research, but it also specifies the types of research that it will regard as legitimate and able to generate valid results. As should be clear from the discussion thus far, it is the behavioral science mainstream that is preferred, especially studies that seek to test hypothesized relationships through the analysis of quantitative data. Beyond its role in project proposal, specification, assessment, and approval, it is not uncommon for that preference to be employed in the evaluation of research proposals that address topics of particular interest to the development business even where those proposals envision little or no direct connection with that business.

In that regard, it is striking that individual scholars may orient their work very differently in the academic and development business spheres of operation.[43] In the former, the relevant audience is institutional and disciplinary academic peers and university chairs and deans, while in the latter, the officials of the employing agency constitute the audience that matters. Much more easily than is possible at most universities and research institutes, funding agencies can readily terminate their relationship with a particular scholar.

One result of this process is that research, or rather claims about what research shows, elevates to the pedestal of fact what on closer examination often turn out to be limited, tentative, and partial findings. Conditional conclusions become generalizations legitimately employed to influence major public policies, both directly and indirectly by providing or withholding funding. In the conjunction of funding and research, scholarship becomes a proprietary process. The investors have the determining voice in the selection of topics, researchers, and methods, limit access to source materials, and often control the dissemination of findings. Consequently, the process of knowledge creation is obscured, mystifying the power relations embedded in the research and thereby in the programs it supports. Perhaps not entirely aware of their own role, scholars become advocates not only for particular understandings of development and underdevelopment but also for a particular sort of global order.

ORTHODOXY AND CRITICAL INQUIRY

Equally corrosive of innovative, thorough, and reliable research is the absence within the financial-intellectual complex of the critical review and peer scrutiny of academia. Notwithstanding analysts' own experiences in higher education and the regular recruitment of academic consultants, little of the research that provides the foundation for broad analyses, general policies, and specific projects is reviewed critically and publicly by scholars with relevant expertise. That is especially problematic in the social sciences since, unlike the chemists and physicists intrigued by the claims about low temperature nuclear fusion, skeptical academics cannot attempt to replicate the original results of development initiatives in their own laboratories.

---

[43] Indeed, my review of education-sector studies ("Defining What Is and What Is Not an Issue," n. 12 above) found that academic authors and education funding agency consultants—often the same people working in the two settings—rarely referred to the work of the other. The primary source materials generated by the development business are frequently unavailable and generally little known in academic settings.

The external assistance agencies fund a vast amount of research in the Third World, an investment that certainly exceeds the expenditures on development research by universities and research institutes. Yet, much of that research is heavily discounted, regarded by decision makers as incomplete, irrelevant, or of insufficient quality. For example, the World Bank alone supported 272 studies of education from 1972 to 1982, and, notwithstanding a decline in the percentage of total education project funding expended on research between 1982 and 1989, it allocated $98.5 million to support 436 studies in that period.[44] Most of those studies, however, were never completed: only 27 percent between 1972 and 1982, and 42 percent between 1982 and 1989. According to a senior World Bank researcher, little of this extensive research investment yielded results that could be used to inform and guide policy-making.

What consultants report and recommend is rarely exposed to critical review by other people with relevant expertise. In this regard, it is striking that most consultants are associated with academic institutions, where various forms of peer review are the norm. Scholars expect their work to be assessed by colleagues, both informally and formally. When that process works well, new ideas are encouraged, analytic perspectives and strategies are continually refined, and unsupported and superficial claims are discarded. Sometimes, of course, that system works poorly. Surely peer review is periodically ignored, distorted, and misused in academic settings. In the development business, however, it takes place only by accident. Instant wisdom, which has a role, becomes entrenched wisdom, resistant to scrutiny, critique, and revision. The situation would be even worse than it is, were it not for the periodic emergence of new understandings that, however unsubstantiated they are themselves, become grounds for discarding whatever preceded them.

Consequently, research that would not withstand broad exposure and critical examination entrenches selected approaches and methods, filters

---

[44] The data on World Bank support for education research are from Marlaine E. Lockheed and Alastair G. Rodd, *World Bank Lending for Education Research, 1982-89*, World Bank, Population and Human Resources Working Paper no. WPS 583 (Washington, D.C.: 1991), which relies for the 1972-82 data on J. P. Tan, *Research Components in World Bank Education Projects* (Washington, D.C.: World Bank, Education Department, 1992). Note that, since World Bank allocations are in the form of loans and credits, these figures in fact reflect spending by the recipient countries. Note also that these figures understate the total expenditure on education research associated with World Bank projects since studies undertaken by institutions within the recipient countries are categorized as technical assistance.

explanations, and legitimizes particular courses of action. Orthodoxy masquerades as pluralism. Enmeshed in the techniques and administration of proprietary research, perceptive and well-meaning individuals lose sight of the larger issues at stake. Obliged to cast their comments in the language and form of this special sort of research, even critics are distracted. Much of the research that is conducted in the Third World, even a good deal of the research supported by the external agencies, is discounted, discarded, or too narrowly disseminated to have significant influence.

THE FIXATION ON FINANCE

Much of what the World Bank writes about education has to do with finance. Currently, it calls for increased allocations to primary education and smaller expenditures at other levels, especially higher education. The recurring refrains are to reduce spending and increase fees: "In postsecondary education, the immediate priority is to reduce the public costs per student. Governments . . . should close or consolidate small or low-priority programs . . . spend less on arts and humanities . . . institute tuition charges and provide fewer subsidized services and student stipends."[45] It is not surprising that in documents prepared by and for a bank the analyses and recommendations are generally phrased in terms of preferable investments, reduced unit and cycle costs, greater efficiency, and the like. It may well be salutary to insist that educators be more aware of the cost implications of their decisions. Unfortunately, the concern with costs and finance often becomes the exclusive focus of studies of education in Africa.

When that occurs, schools as community-based institutions, teaching as an interactive process, learning as something more than memorizing selected facts, and even the learners themselves disappear from view. Or rather, the recommendation to pursue or not pursue a particular course of action comes to be justified in terms of its costs and financing, with little attention to its overall contribution to education or to related national goals and aspirations.

When the stress on resources is particularly severe, as is the current situation for most of Africa, many education studies focus almost exclusively on the reduction of spending. In addition to relegating learning

---

[45] World Bank, *Financing Adjustment with Growth*, p. 30.

and teaching to a marginal role, that orientation also favors those objectives of education that can be quantified and explicitly valued and often ignores those that cannot. At the level of theory, nearly everyone agrees that education's value to society goes beyond preparation for employment. In practice, however, when the focus on finance becomes a fixation, the bulk of education's contribution is effectively devalued.

As well, reliability and sustainability may be sacrificed at the altar of efficiency. While there are clearly circumstances where efficiency is appropriately the highest priority goal, there are also circumstances in which reliability and sustainability are more important. Consider, for example, adult education. It is not uncommon to find in Africa that several organizations sponsor adult education programs, perhaps each with its own copying machine or printer and newsletter. An efficiency expert might point to the duplication of facilities and suggest creating a single printing facility to service all of the programs. On first view, that would seem to be the best use of the capital investment. In practice, however, a problem in the printing facility (say, mechanical breakdown, or shortage of paper or ink) would halt all newsletter production. Where such breakdowns and shortages are common, few newsletters would circulate. The duplication of facilities—each organization with its own printing capacity—increases reliability. When one printer has broken down, the others continue to work, perhaps even producing materials for the organization whose own equipment is not functioning. Indeed, on balance the duplication may turn out to be more efficient as well as more reliable, at least as measured in terms of the number of newsletters circulated per month.

The point here is straightforward. To fail to consider costs and financing may promote inefficiencies and cripple promising initiatives. To focus single-mindedly on costs and financing may prove even more disastrous. Seeking to increase efficiency by ignoring learning cannot improve the quality of education.

THE RECONSTRUCTION OF THE STATE

As I have indicated, for much of the World Bank's writing on African education, the starting point is the presumption that state education policies have been fundamentally defective and that the state is institutionally incapable of guiding and managing the education establishment. The corollary is to blame schools and teachers for whatever decline in quality can be observed. If it is in the public sector, the argument goes, it must be incompetent and inefficient.

Accordingly, many of the proposed remedies involve reducing the role of the state in providing education. The clarion call is to privatize. Ministries and other government offices are seen as obstacles. Rather than working with their personnel to reform those institutions, the World Bank often prefers to create special program implementation units or other extragovernmental structures or even to install foreign personnel, to oversee and carry out the projects it supports. In part in response to criticisms of that strategy, the World Bank has turned to nongovernmental organizations, both foreign and local, to implement its programs and disburse its funds. Responsibility for education can be so widely diffused that even the state officials themselves are confused about what is to be their own role.

Yet the World Bank and the other external agencies in fact need the state. Nearly all of their programs envision a central point of authority and control accompanied by a strong measure of central planning, monitoring, and evaluation. Hence, it is useful to understand the current era as a transitional period. First, the state is to be marginalized and the power and authority of its officials reduced. Then, state organizations are to be dismembered and dismantled, with the parts recombined into new forms under the control of a different set of leaders. Once that has been accomplished, the state can be reconstituted. The reconstructed state will be less able to pursue national policies at odds with the international system. Superficially it will be more democratic, but in practice it is likely to be less responsive to the situation and needs of the least affluent and most disadvantaged. The dependent liberal capitalism that the Europeans envisioned when they ended direct rule over Africa will finally have been installed.

Two manifestations of this need for a strong central authority are especially striking. First, in their interactions with national authorities, the external agencies expect to find a sharply delineated hierarchy, clear lines of authority, functional divisions of responsibility, and reasonably direct paths of communication. They expect consistent responses to their queries and proposals and continuity in implementing the agreements that have been reached.

For much of contemporary Africa, however, coping rather than centralized direction has become the order of the day. The institutional model is not the military general headquarters but the flea market where everything is negotiable. The prices, terms, and forms of exchange are always in flux. Even the goods to be exchanged are regularly revalued. No response is ever definitive. Alliances and partnerships are rarely permanent, more often quite short-lived. There is little point in rejecting an offer or proposal—except as a bargaining ploy—since one may always hope that the terms will improve.

I exaggerate, of course. But caricatures are useful in highlighting underlying patterns. Foreign agencies act as if their national counterpart were a tightly knit bureaucracy with clear and fixed lines of authority. The foreigners spend a lot of time trying to figure out where power really lies. They are profoundly frustrated when they get different answers to the same questions. And they immediately assume there has been willful duplicity when supported activities seem to wander off the agreed path.

But, in much of Africa, it has been shifting coalitions, not fixed institutional locations, that have mattered. That is even more so in the flea market spawned by economic crisis and structural adjustment. What appears to outsiders as inconsistency and duplicity is probably the reflection of a shifting balance of power. In the current circumstances, the clear answers and definitive commitments that the outsiders seek may be impossible, for to commit firmly to one course of action today may preclude pursuing a direction that seems essential tomorrow. The negotiating mode may also be an effective strategy that the weaker and poorer party employs to improve its leverage and enhance its influence. When facing a stronger opponent, diplomacy is often preferable to war.

Both hierarchical decision making and negotiation have their place. Neither is universally more appropriate or best. But both the external agencies and Africa are poorly served when the foreigners insist on treating the flea market as if it were a military general headquarters.

Second, the World Bank and other external agencies insist on authoritative central planning for African education. For the past few years, however, the international financial institutions have regularly and loudly asserted the failure of centralized planning. Experiences in eastern Europe and elsewhere, they argue, make a persuasive case for decreasing the role of the state and increasing the role of private enterprise, nongovernmental organizations, and other groups outside the state. Yet many of those same international financial institutions, in their role as providers of assistance to African education, insist on a very high order of central planning and direction. On the one hand, they declare that centralized authority institutionalizes incompetence, discourages innovation, insures inefficiency, and impedes implementation. On the other hand, they say to prospective recipients of education assistance: to receive our support, you must have a clear plan that indicates exactly what you will do, both now and for some years into the future.

It is understandable that the assistance providers prefer clear and detailed plans. It is less clear that proceeding in that way makes the most sense for those responsible for education in Africa, where the demand for high-level planning and managerial skills will exceed the supply for some time to come and where many of the critical contextual factors are beyond local control. Indeed, contemporary conditions in Africa suggest the importance of flexibility, responsiveness to changing circumstances, and the ability both to reorder priorities and to modify implementation at short notice. Although central planning is assumed to rationalize and maximize the impact of scarce resources, in practice, where circumstances limit central direction to statements of intent rather than systematic control over relevant resources and behaviors, centralized planning and direction may well prove more, not less, costly and less, not more, efficient. Once again the appropriate decision-making model may be more the apparent chaos of the stock market or even the overlapping alliances and ambiguities of academic governance than the order and fixed lines of authority of the military general headquarters. Education's administrative apparatus is not tightly compartmentalized and only partially functionally specialized. Rather, it is loosely coupled and regularly operates by muddling through.

To put that point somewhat differently, for most African countries the institution is likely to be more important than the plan. An institutional apparatus sufficiently resilient to respond effectively as events require, to seize opportunities as they occur, to build on successful strategies, and to discard those that do not work will contribute more to education and development than a clearly articulated plan and authoritarian decision makers. Accordingly, policy attention in the present may be more fruitfully directed toward developing the institutions of education planning and management than toward preparing and elaborating plans in fine detail.

INSTITUTIONAL IMPERATIVES AND THE STRUCTURE OF POWER

I have been concerned here with the increasing importance of the conjunction of funding and research and especially with the dominating

role a single agency, the World Bank, has come to play within that financial-intellectual complex. By offering another glimpse into its inner work-
ings, two recent but very different sorts of publications prompt us to
reflect critically on the current state of scholarship on education and
development. Both the detailed study and the superficial summaries
highlight the process of reconstructing schooling in Africa. Education is a
commodity to be delivered and dispensed. Schools produce and form
their students. The appropriate standards for assessing education systems
have to do with costs and efficiency. In this digital age, those standards
must have exclusive categories that are readily quantifiable. Learning as
an interactive process nearly disappears from view. It is lamented and
protested rather than prized that education is the most intensely con-
tested of public policies.

Against the grain of both the political and methodological individual-
ism of the contemporary intellectual environment (and of the liberal tradition), my argument here has been about structures and process, not
particular people. What is problematic about this conjunction of funding
and research is not the incompetence of its scholars. Not at all! As I have
suggested above, the World Bank and other agencies have recruited, and
will continue to employ and commission, particularly insightful, incisive,
and accomplished scholars. Nor is it the case that those scholars are fundamentally more conservative or more insensitive to poverty and its consequences than the academic community in general. Indeed, some of the
critiques of World Bank policies from within its domain are as pointed
and devastating as those articulated outside that arena.[46]

Focused on the structure of power and not its agents, my discussion
has not sought to identify good guys and bad guys. It is certainly the case
that in particular settings the World Bank articulates policies that are far
more liberal and democratic than those of the governments with which it
deals. Indeed, as the liberals within the financial-intellectual complex
increasingly point out, in specific cases they support the challenge of
impoverished and disenfranchised citizens against their own authoritarian and repressive government.

What is problematic, however, is that the conjunction of funding
and research functions to privilege particular approaches, methods, and

---

[46] What does differ, of course, is the extent to which those critiques are circulated
broadly.

constructs and to shelter them from the crossfire of the contestation of ideas by dismissing critical voices as nonscientific. Notwithstanding occasional manifestations of humility and human frailty, this conjunction fosters a sense of definitive correctness. Stimulated by a banker's need for precision and certainty and nurtured by a gleeful triumphalism at the collapse of the major political platforms for critical perspectives, understanding development becomes an overbearing sense of seeing the truth more clearly and knowing it more fully. Those who believe they have the truth in hand, or at least more so than anyone else in sight, can have no equals.

What is particularly dismaying in this regard is that the current sense of confidence is unshaken by a frank recognition that a comparable conviction at an earlier moment led to the intransigent insistence on policies and programs that subsequently proved disastrous. Once again the institutional imperative and the absence of public scrutiny and expert review overwhelms the humane reasonableness of particular individuals. Often, the clearest analysis of those disasters is to be found in the World Bank's own documents. Yet, the current certainty remains unshaken.

Equally disturbing is the condescension and paternalism bred by the combination of holding the purse and controlling the knowledge. A particular program may well reduce infant mortality or expand girls' access to schools more rapidly than a country's leadership would have done on its own. But when these positive gains are orchestrated externally and often even implemented by a special unit that is more responsive to external direction than to its local political setting, how are those gains to be sustained? Force-feeding may be desirable in an emergency, but it cannot develop local knowledge and skills, promote local interchange and cooperation, foster self-reliance, or enhance the local ability to evaluate, refine, and implement a locally set agenda.

ACCOUNTABILITY

The financial-intellectual complex erects an imposing edifice. The integration of funding and research is seamless. Analyses, explanations, and remedies are all supported by an impressive foundation of research conducted by respected scholars and synthesized in systematic, carefully presented, and widely disseminated overviews of the state of knowledge in particular domains. The reported findings occupy center stage in academic as well as operational settings.

The insistence on clear results, unambiguous inferences, and unimpeachable evidence is neither liberating nor rejuvenating. The cascades of certainty that constitute research on education and development neither wash away ignorance and confusion nor irrigate the seedbeds of local imagination and initiative. Instead, as it becomes a set of largely externally defined rules specifying acceptable courses of action, research disorients and imprisons. Even worse, the prisoners themselves become the warden and jailers.

When pressed, the academics and even at times the operational personnel acknowledge the limitations and inconsistencies in the research. When pressed further they acknowledge that the research foundation is far less solid than it appears. The defects are not minor. Yet few in either group are prepared to distinguish themselves by characterizing that foundation as hollow and the edifice it supports as a fundamentally weak structure, more like the storefront facades erected on a movie set than a keystone arch or the internally braced and self-supporting construction of a long-enduring building. The conjunction of funding and research maintains the vitality of the entire project proposal, evaluation, approval, and support process. In doing so, it effectively obscures its basic inadequacies and less consequential defects.

Two conclusions seem warranted. First, the conjunction of development funding and research casts research in a particular role. Claimed research findings become the required language for proposing and evaluating development projects. Approved methods delimit the legitimate participants in the research process and the legitimate interventions in development discussions. The research deemed acceptable legitimizes particular courses of action and at the same time obscures the politics of excluding others. Second, although a vast amount of research is undertaken in this setting, the research that fulfills this role is limited in perspective and approach and little subject to critical review by people with relevant expertise. Combined, these two results displace the healthy skepticism of scholarly inquiry and the increasing recognition of discontinuities and uncertainty in favor of a frequently unqualified certainty. Both research and development are poorly served.

Several implications follow. First, humility. We need a much clearer sense of the limitations of our understandings and of their partial and conditional character. Second, we need to discard the model of understanding as the result of an incremental accumulation of discrete knowledge in favor of a recognition of a world characterized by discontinuities and small results with large consequences. Third, we need to reject the current model of cloistered or proprietary research in favor of an openness both to alternative approaches and methods and to critical scrutiny. For that to be fruitful, fourth, we need self-consciously to protect and nurture the critics. And fifth, in this era of political democratization, we need to institutionalize the accountability of those who provide development advice to those who are expected to benefit from it.

Some of the ideas developed here were presented at the 1990 annual meeting of the African Studies Association, the 1991 conference of the Comparative and International Education Society, and the fifteenth World Congress of the International Political Science Association, 1991. I am grateful to many colleagues for their critiques, challenges, and advice.

Chapter 3

JAPANESE EDUCATION: MIRACLE RE-EXAMINED

Nobuo K. Shimahara

Japanese education is now at a crossroads. For more than a decade reformers have been trying to overhaul it. Today's education reform movement began in the early 1980s as a national and politically initiated campaign. Orchestrated deliberations on school reform gained momentum in 1984 when the national legislature approved the establishment of the National Council on Educational Reform (NCER). Over a period of three years NCER issued four reports to recommend a broad range of change in the school system, based on its findings regarding the state of schooling. These reports stimulated further reform initiatives in the 1990s. School reform is not fast and drastic in Japan, as in some other nations. Although reformers' rhetoric is expectedly bold and far-reaching, the implementation of school reform is slow and cumulative. This explains why Japan's school reform movement still continues.

In this chapter I will discuss Japan's school reforms with particular attention to upper secondary education, the most critical stage of schooling in terms of transition to college and employment. High school education in Japan has a striking and lasting impact on adolescents because the most pivotal element of that education is preparation for intense university entrance examinations. Americans became acquainted with Japan's educational accomplishments through a variety of publications and the mass media in the 1980s when Japan's economic competitiveness steadily challenged the United States (see, for example, Cummings, 1980; Duke, 1986a; Rohlen, 1983; U.S. Department of Education, 1987). Why are school reforms still urgent in Japan today? Where are they heading?

EDUCATIONAL ACCOMPLISHMENTS IN JAPAN

One of the unique features of Japanese society is that it owes its shape, in very large measure, to education. As an American anthropologist put it, Japanese society is "a meritocracy shaped by an educational competition that enrolls nearly everyone" (Rohlen, 1986, p. 30). Educational credentials and skills are keys to employment, social status, and promotion. This accounts for the paramount importance the Japanese attach to education, as well as to the demanding entrance examinations for high school and university. Japanese students' educational achievement, however, is only partially promoted by the school system. The infrastructure of education in Japan is supported not only by the school system, but also by extensively developed and privately organized schools existing independently outside the standard structure of schooling. These schools, totaling at least 35,000 scattered throughout the nation (U.S. Department of Education, 1987), normally include *yobiko,* or preparatory schools, and *juku,* which are often categorized into schools for exam drill, enrichment, and remediation. *Yobiko* and *juku* vary in size and programs from large *yobiko* with state-of-the-art equipment, enrolling more than 15,000 students to small tutorial facilities with a dozen students. Moreover, parents more often than not procure private tutorial services, usually rendered by university students and retired teachers, to enhance their children's preparation for entrance examinations. Besides, an extensively developed and examination-focused educational industry provides students at all levels with materials for drilling and mock tests, filling many bookshelves in local bookstores. All in all, Japan's educational achievement is promoted by a broad, societal educational infrastructure, of which formal schooling is just a part.

A brief review of the development of the meritocratic ethos in the Meiji era (1868-1912) would shed light on the ardent interest the Japanese take in education. A revolutionary shift in the pattern of social mobility followed as Japan ushered in the era of modernization in the latter half of the nineteenth century. In the Meiji era the ascribed status system in the Tokugawa feudal period (1603-1868) was swiftly replaced by a system of mobility determined by achievement. Part of this modernization campaign was the development of a comprehensive school system, which was initially laid out as early as 1872, only five years after the Meiji Restoration. And by 1890, the system was completed, including imperial universities.

There were two pivotal institutional initiatives in Japan that enhanced achievement orientation. One was the government's hiring practice, instituted as early as 1887, which placed priority on recruiting imperial university graduates to fill middle- and high-ranking positions, and civil service examinations (Amano, 1982, 1986a). Thus educational credentials and competitive examinations were introduced as primary criteria for hiring government officials. Because government positions conferred much prestige on their holders in Japan, as in Europe, the new system inspired young men to compete for better educational credentials. Another institutional initiative, which had a far greater influence on the popularization of educational "credentialism," came from the private sector early in the twentieth century, when companies emphasized educational credentials as a major criterion for hiring (Amano, 1982, 1986a). Companies rewarded graduates of higher education with opportunities leading to managerial positions, better pay, and promotion. As a Japanese sociologist points out, a survey conducted in 1930 indicated that "72 percent of the middle- and upper-level managers in private companies and 57 percent of the engineers were graduates of higher educational institutions" (Amano, 1986a, p. 4). It is evident that the belief that educational credentials provided access to power, wealth, and social status filtered into the people's collective mind in the late nineteenth and early twentieth centuries.

Further, that belief was coupled with the fact that Japanese aspirations for social success were growing apace during the Meiji period (Kinmonth, 1981). The self-help theme was distinct among ambitious young men who aspired to avail themselves of the loosening Japanese social structure. In fact, Samuel Smile's *Self-Help*, translated into Japanese in 1871, and Fukuzawa Yukichi's *Encouragement to Learning*, published in 1872, became the nation's best sellers reflecting the fledgling success ideology of the early Meiji years (see Hirakawa, 1984). That ideology of self-help was preceded by a folk model such as the one illustrated by Ninomiya Sontoku, an exemplar of Japanese nineteenth century morality that stressed self-discipline, a willingness to work hard, and a drive to learn (White, 1987).

After World War II, the Japanese social structure opened to further social mobility as the occupation-initiated sweeping land and corporate reforms broke up the monopoly of wealth and power. By 1948, a single-track school system emphasized equal access to schooling. It was under

this new system that youths' enrollment in secondary and higher education grew phenomenally as their rising aspirations for mobility were translated into employment in an expanding national economy. For example,
the 1960s witnessed industrial and economic expansion unparalleled in
Japanese history. Personal incomes tripled, as did international trade.
Industry was desperate for ever greater numbers of better trained people,
and it demanded that education be upgraded. Reflecting the tenor of
those times, enrollments in high schools and four-year colleges increased
from 57.7 percent and 9.2 percent, respectively, of all youths in 1960 to
82.1 percent and 20 percent in 1970, a spectacular change within a single
decade. In 1975, youth enrollment reached 93 percent and 34.2 percent
at the high school and college levels, respectively (Shimahara, 1992).

Japan enjoyed an enviable position in the world in terms of both its
unparalleled growth of secondary and higher education and its level of
academic achievement. The International Association for the Evaluation
of Education Achievement conducted the first large-scale study in 1964
and a similar study in the early 1980s. Both studies tested mathematical
knowledge and skills at the eighth and twelfth grade levels, and Japanese
students ranked at the top (Husén, 1967; LaPointe, Mead, and Phillips,
1989). Likewise, other studies, such as Stevenson and Stigler's (1992)
sustained comparative research on elementary student achievement,
support the high performance of Japanese students. Rohlen (1983) characterized Japanese high school students' knowledge in mathematics and
science as equivalent to that of American college graduates:

[T]he more I looked at the fundamental facts, the more convinced I became that the
majority of high school graduates in Japan would compare well with the majority of
our university graduates in terms of basic knowledge in all fields and mathematics and
science skills. [P. 160]

Although his sweeping generalizations based on observations made in
the 1970s is probably disputable, his comment appropriately suggests
that the Japanese high school curriculum is condensed and maintains
high standards.

WHAT IS WRONG WITH JAPANESE EDUCATION?

Japan has now surpassed the West in many aspects of technological
and economic development. For example, in 1991 Japan obtained

76,984 patents, in contrast to 104,541 for the United States, 17,643 for Germany, and 8,795 for the UK (*New York Times*, 28 May 1991). The nation was ranked first in the 1993 human development report issued by the United Nations, followed by Canada, Norway, Switzerland, Sweden, and the United States (United Nations Development Programme, 1993; *New York Times*, 23 May 1993). Japan's per capita GNP was ranked third after Switzerland and Luxembourg in 1990. The human development index used in the report is a measure of "human happiness" based on life expectancy, educational standards, and individual purchasing power. If Japan's rank in the report is indicative of its advancement, it suggests that the Japanese are now living in a different social and international context. Through the 1970s the nation's development was still guided by what is identified in Japan as the catch-up ideology (Economic Council, 1983). Ever since its modernization began in the nineteenth century, Japan's ideology of national development was to catch up with the West relative to technology, economy, and education. Modernization was likened to Westernization, and national development was synonymous with catching up with the West. To accomplish modernization in a much shorter time than did the West, Japan attained high literacy by developing uniform schooling throughout the nation. In the period following World War II, Japan hardly deviated from uniform schooling with respect to the curriculum, other school programs, and control of education. Until recently, Japan's postwar preoccupation had been to provide society with uniformly well-trained human resources.

Now that Japan has caught up with the West, it is seeking a new paradigm of development to replace the catch-up ideology. In the mid-1980s this undertaking was expressed as an emerging national concern addressed by Japan's Economic Council, Prime Minister Yasuhiro Nakasone's advisory council on culture and education, and by the Kyoto Seminar headed by Konosuke Matsushita, the founder of the Panasonic Corporation. But, short-term, immediate school reform issues were much more directly related to the effects of uniform schooling and the centrifugal social forces generated by economic affluence, social mobility, changing family structures, and information-dominated social life. These social forces represented a far-reaching transformation that had occurred since the late 1960s through the early 1980s. Consequently, deviant adolescent behavior, including bullying, school violence, refusal to attend school, and other forms of juvenile delinquency dramatically increased in the late 1970s and the 1980s. These frequent incidents of deviant behavior, which threatened long-standing social norms in Japan, were extensively reported by the mass media and caused a national obsession. Moreover, the overheated competition in high school and university entrance examinations remained a major concern of students, parents, and society in general. Entrance examinations had a significant polarizing effect on youths, resulting in the considerable disaffection of a large proportion of students with schooling. As Japan became a "mature," affluent society, the social mobility that had characterized the 1960s and 1970s became limited, and youths' aspirations for success had cooled down remarkably (Amano, 1986a). All in all, it became increasingly evident in the early 1980s that Japan's school system, which was effective in meeting the needs of modernization and industrialization for a century, had become dysfunctional in satisfying the diversified values and needs of youth. In other words, the absence of diversity in schooling was seen as a cause of deviant behavior as society became diversified, creating a lack of fit between the school system and social change. This became the principal concern of reformers from the 1980s to the present time.

SCHOOL REFORMS IN THE 1980s

Recognizing this problem, the National Council on Educational Reform (NCER) pointed out that Japanese education was suffering from a "grave state of desolation" caused by pathological conditions in society and the schools (NCER, 1985). The development of such conditions, in its view, led to increasing public criticism and distrust of public education. The Japanese term for desolation is *kohai*, referring to a state of desertedness and deterioration. It was used by NCER to render an emotionally charged indictment of education, an indictment that apparently reflected the Japanese awareness of the emerging crisis in education. In its first report NCER declared:

Most important in the educational reform to come is to do away with the uniformity, rigidity, closedness, and lack of internationalism, all of which are deep-rooted defects of our educational system, and to establish the principles of dignity of individuals, respect for the individual, freedom and self-discipline, and self-responsibility—in other words, the principle of putting emphasis on individuality (NCER, 1985, p. 26).

Although the reformers' rhetoric cited here rejected the schooling of the past, what they actually wanted to accomplish was to introduce diversity and choice in schooling. The most significant feature of the reform movement in the 1980s was epitomized by a shared perception that the orientation and structure of schooling must be altered to meet exigencies of a much more diverse society, where changes in people's lives, including the impact of internationalism and the information industry, became ubiquitous throughout the nation.

In 1982, when the Nakasone Cabinet was first formed, the nation's mood for school reform was growing apace. A perceptive and astute politician, Nakasone wasted no time in appointing an advisory panel on education and culture. The panel was to advise him on reform and to formulate a set of conceptually broad categories of reform issues. The panel prepared a document delineating the scope of work to be considered by the task force on reform (Kuroha, 1985). As anticipated, the panel became a critically important device for Nakasone to enhance his interest in the reform, because not only did it become his key advisory group, on which he relied to develop his views on education, but it also helped generate further impetus for reform (Shimahara, 1986).

Meanwhile, Nakasone was marshalling support for the movement from the heads of other political parties. By the spring of 1984 Nakasone had become thoroughly acquainted with the critical issues of Japanese education and was ready to move ahead. Preparation of the national bill to establish NCER was already under way, and the bill passed in the national legislature in the summer of 1984. The law established the NCER with four divisions responsible for (1) education for the twenty-first century, (2) activating educational functions of society, (3) reforming elementary and secondary education, and (4) reforming higher education.

To illustrate NCER members' interest in loosening up the nation's school system, it is relevant to mention a debate that focused on liberalization of schooling. Of the four divisions of NCER, the one that was considering the educational system for the twenty-first century initially focused on liberalization of the nation's school system as it now exists under control of the Ministry of Education. The division attributed educational desolation to the uniform schooling maintained by the ministry in the interest of providing equal education throughout the nation. At the outset of its deliberation it concentrated on market-oriented strategies to deregulate schooling and debated such radical issues as parental freedom to choose any school (thus eliminating the school district system), the freedom to establish new schools with little governmental interference, the freedom to publish textbooks without the ministry's authorization, the chartering of good *juku*, and eliminating the ministry's control over the curriculum (Duke, 1986b). These were totally unconventional ideas that would have demoted the authority of the ministry to secondary importance (see Schoppa, 1991).

But such radical liberalization of schooling immediately met outright opposition from the ministry and from the conservative chairman of the NCER division on reforms in elementary and secondary education. To avoid public confrontation between the heads of two divisions of the reform task force, the division on education for the twenty-first century went on retreat to produce a considerably compromised position paper more or less acceptable to the other parties (Kuroha, 1985). Both divisions eventually agreed that the rigid uniformity of schooling must give way to greater diversity, especially at the secondary level. Thus diversity rather than liberalization became the dominant theme of reformers' deliberations.

I list here a few relevant items from among NCER's recommendations that addressed the needs for diversity, flexibility, and choice:

1. Replacement of the joint first-stage university entrance examination required for all applicants for national and other public universities by a "Common Test," an improved examination used by both public and private universities as the first entrance examination, prior to the second entrance examination given by individual institutions. It was assumed that the Common Test would alleviate intense exam preparation if used properly.

2. Introduction of choice and diverse programs at the upper secondary level to meet diversified adolescent interests and needs. Proposals included 6-year secondary schools as an alternative to the current 3-year lower and 3-year upper secondary schools to provide continuity in secondary education; an alternative high school education whereby students may complete the required credits at schools of their choice.

3. New provisions that will enable individual schools to gain greater freedom in the use of the course of study; diversification of the curriculum to meet individual needs; greater emphasis on international education, including improvement of instruction in foreign languages and programs for Japanese returnees from abroad.

4. Broadened standards for the establishment of greater diversity in the institutions of higher education; provisions for developing distinctive and diverse institutional structures and programs; improvement of graduate programs and increased access to graduate education; enhancement of research at the university through the creation of flexible research structures and organizations.

SCHOOL REFORMS IN THE 1990s: RESTRUCTURING HIGH SCHOOLS

In the prewar period competition for access to "higher schools," which led to universities, was very intense as early as the 1910s and 1920s (Amano, 1982). In the postwar period, the university entrance examination system has been a centerpiece of high school education. It is a system that drives adolescents to excel. More than thirty years ago Ezra Vogel (1963), author of *Japan's Middle Class*, observed:

No single event, with the possible exception of marriage, determines the course of a young man's life as much as an entrance examination, and nothing, including marriage, requires as many years of planning and hard work. . . . These arduous preparations constitute a kind of *rite de passage* whereby a young man proves that he has the qualities of ability and endurance for becoming a salaried man. [P. 40]

Vogel's depiction of the intensity of entrance examinations represents today's overheated examination pressures no less accurately than it reflected the situation thirty years ago. Moreover, as Amano (1986b) observed,

The tendency toward increased stratification is especially evident in the relationship between secondary and higher education [in the 1980s]. The school hierarchies within both of these educational levels are strengthening, as is the tendency for the position attained in lower high schools to determine students' place in the higher level. The opportunity for admission to the top universities is now virtually monopolized by graduates from the top high schools. [P. 24]

Currently 75 percent of the upper secondary entrants (94 percent of lower secondary graduates enroll in upper secondary schools) attend academic high schools, and the remaining 25 percent attend vocational high schools. The former high schools are ranked by a single criterion in each prefecture or region and sometimes within the nation: the number of students admitted to top universities. Accordingly, the reputation of each academic high school is determined by its competitiveness in preparing students for entrance examinations. Unlike most American high schools, which are comprehensive neighborhood schools where residents of the community attend, Japanese public high schools draw applicants from a number of middle schools within a prefecture, which is usually divided into two or three large districts. Middle school students compete for admission to academic high schools with good reputations through entrance examinations. However, a large percentage of students end up attending vocational schools only because their chances for admission to academic schools were slim.

The Japanese university entrance examination system persists and is a source of perpetual tension in life, especially in adolescent life. The government tried to revamp it a couple of times in the past two decades without much success. For example, identifying the system as a chief source of educational "desolation," NCER proposed a remedy, which was ineffective because it simply replaced one common test with another. The reason is rather evident. There is a covert and persistent belief shared among academics and bureaucrats of the Ministry of Education that the examination system serves well the purpose of objective selection of students, even though it has ill effects on students and their education. In their view, there is no better method of selecting students for admission. Moreover, the entrance examination system drives students to study diligently—a system that generates extraordinary extrinsic motivation to study. Overall, few vicissitudes have been evident with respect to the willingness of Japanese parents to make great sacrifices in the interest of promoting their children's prolonged preparation for entrance examinations.

It is sufficient to suggest that university entrance examinations by and large shape the dominant orientation of high school education in Japan. This is a chief issue as reformers see it. Yet, although 75 percent of all the applicants for high school currently attend academic high schools, 30 to 40 percent of them end up seeking employment when they graduate from high school. Meanwhile, only 10 percent of vocational students seek admission to college. In all, 36.3 percent of high school graduates now advance to college (11.7 percent of them attend two-year colleges). In addition, 16.9 percent attend special training schools and postsecondary vocational schools. In short, despite the fact that only about 36 percent of today's high-school graduates are enrolled in college, the college-bound curriculum is dominant in the nation's academic high schools, leaving little choice for exploring other career interests. Diversity in high school education is thus still severely limited.

Following NCER's reform reports, in 1989 the Minister of Education charged the Central Council of Education, an advisory body, with making recommendations to reform "educational structures" (Central Council of Education, 1991). One important aspect of the charge to the Council was to recommend how to diversify high school education. At the risk of reiteration, let me cite the three major issues the Council pointed out in its 1991 report (pp. 91-92). First, Japan's high school education has failed to reflect the diversity of industry and the economy; second, although the student population has become diversified, high schools have failed to offer programs that reflect student diversity; and third, high school education tends to be focused on preparing students for university entrance examinations.

The Council urged a flexible distribution of credits required for graduation to allow students freedom to choose classes (p. 103). Greater latitude in students' course selection is attainable even within the existing frame of regulations. The Council argued that only 38 of the 80 credits needed for graduation must be taken in the required subjects, while the remaining 42 credits can be earned by taking classes of the students' choice. But the Council pointed out that in reality most academic high schools required that most credits for graduation be in the required subjects, leaving students little choice. Evidently, such a practice in large part stems from entrance examination pressures. To reinforce the Council's recommendation, however, the recently revised high-school course of study also stressed a flexible distribution of credits.

It seems that the current school reform movement, which began in the mid-1980s, is finally giving a new complexion to high school education. Important innovative changes are now being introduced piecemeal. For example, in Osaka in 1992 I observed several academic high schools that somewhat resemble magnet schools in the United States. These schools offer such areas of concentration as English, mathematics, and Japanese to enhance students' interests. High schools with a focus on a comprehensive program or such specialized programs as computer science and international studies are being created. Inagakuen Comprehensive Public High School near Tokyo, which was opened a few years ago, could serve as a model for others to follow (Nishimoto, 1993). It enrolls 3,300 students who may choose from 164 classes in various subject areas. Thirteen programs, ranging from information science to health care, are offered so that students may choose among them. In the first year, students complete the essential requirements, which are reduced to a minimum; in the second and third years, 60 and 80 percent, respectively, of their classes are their own selections.

A COMPREHENSIVE PROGRAM

To implement the Central Council of Education's recommendations, the Ministry of Education set up the Committee for Enhancement of High School Reforms in 1991. It issued four reports in two years to recommend plans to improve high school education (Committee for Enhancement of High School Reforms, 1993). Its central motif was to revamp high school education to empower students to link their personal interests and future aspirations to formal learning in the school. The Committee underscored several points: broad latitude in the selection of courses; a comprehensive program; a credit-system whereby students would choose classes to earn needed credits without structural constraints; interschool collaboration by which students could earn some credits at schools other than their own; and improved procedures for selecting applicants for admission by vigorous consideration of interview results, recommendations, and school reports. (Generally, heavy weight is placed on entrance examinations.)

The Committee's principal recommendation, however, was to implement in each academic high school a comprehensive program the central aim of which would be to promote students' career aspirations by providing opportunity to study both academic and specialized vocational subjects. This comprehensive program would attract students by offering an alternative to the exclusively college-bound program. Students who would choose the comprehensive program would be one of three types: those who are actively interested in linking academic work to career aspirations; those whose primary goal is employment after graduation; and those who have aspirations for college.

The comprehensive program would consist of four parts. The first would include the common requirements for all high school students. The second part would highlight three common areas for students in the comprehensive program, designated as industrial society and human life, basic studies of information technology, and independent study on a selected problem. The third part would consist of rich clusters of elective courses, including information technology, industrial management, international cooperation, regional development, biotechnology, welfare management, environmental science, and art and culture. And additional optional studies would make up the fourth part.

It appears that the comprehensive program just described will provide an attractive and innovative alternative to the hitherto uniform academic program for college-bound students. It will contribute to enriching high school education by diversifying it. The intensity with which high school reforms have been debated since NCER was formed in 1984 seems to suggest that Japan is committed to enhancing high school education by meeting the needs of diverse students and a diverse society. Evidently exciting reforms are about to ensue at the high school level, making the high school a more animated institution.

UNIVERSITY ENTRANCE EXAMINATIONS:
A CRITICAL BARRIER

Educational reforms, however, are not likely to have any significant effect on the university entrance examination system. Major school reform reports in the postwar period invariably characterized the university entrance examinations as a chief, critical problem (see, for example, OECD, 1971; NCER, 1985, 1987; Central Council of Education, 1991). Yet reformers have been unable to make significant structural changes in the entrance examination system or to propose a viable alternative to it. It is no exaggeration to suggest that they have created only cosmetic changes, leaving the basic structure of the system intact.

The report of the Organization of Economic Cooperation and Development (1971) once made a scathing attack on the entrance examination system:

There is a general belief that a student's performance in one crucial examination at about the age of 18 is likely to determine the rest of his life. . . .

The university entrance examination is the primary sorting device for careers in Japanese society. The result is not an aristocracy of birth, but a sort of degree-ocracy. The system is egalitarian and flexible compared to a hereditary class system, but rigid and arbitrary as compared to systems in which individual performance over a much wider span of time helps sort people into appropriate careers and offers an opportunity for the motivated individual to catch up educationally and even change occupational status as he develops in capacities. This pattern will not change greatly as long as the "lifetime employment pattern" lasts. [Pp. 88-89]

In 1985 NCER affirmed the tenor of the OECD report:

In Japan . . . there is a tendency for the value of an individual to be evaluated not from a variety of angles, as it should be, but mainly in terms of the formal school background gained at an early stage of life. This tendency has caused fierce competition among people for a better educational background. [NCER, 1985, p. 34]

In place of "degree-ocracy" NCER advocated lifelong learning to provide individuals with opportunities for evaluating their competence and qualifications throughout their lives. Japanese generally support NCER's characterization of the problem and its emphasis on lifelong learning.

Yet the entrance examination system has changed little in the postwar period. It remains the single most important influence on the orientation of Japan's high school students toward schooling, and it persists because the meritocratic nature of the system is still supported by the majority of the Japanese. But further improvement of high school education will have to entail more meaningful, perhaps drastic, reforms of the system, as well as notable improvement of higher education.

Previous attempts to cut down the overheated competition in university entrance examinations largely failed because they were initiated without regard for the macro context in which the competition is generated. In other words, these reforms attempted to ease the pressures stemming from entrance examinations as independent phenomena. Given the persistent Japanese creed about the entrance examination system, the amelioration of competition for admission to universities can be induced not by trying to change it alone, but by improving the institutions that accept the applicants.

My final comment addresses this issue. The intense competition in university entrance examinations is substantially caused by the fact that too many applicants persistently seek admission to relatively small numbers of universities with fine reputations. Moreover, if applicants fail to gain admission in the first year they are likely to spend another year preparing for the exams for the same universities or equivalent institutions in the following year—a ubiquitous, perpetual phenomenon in

Japan. These students are called *ronin*, or repeaters, and they constitute 35 percent of the university applicants every year (Ministry of Education, 1993).

In 1991, there were 514 four-year universities (of which 378 were private) and 592 two-year colleges (of which 497 were private) in Japan. Differences among the four-year institutions are immense in terms of academic standards, facilities, the quality of programs and faculty, and funding. Diversified institutions of higher education in the prewar period were reorganized as four-year universities (Amano, 1986b). Furthermore, a number of private universities that were established in the postwar period are severely underfunded. These postwar developments by and large account for considerable variation in academic standards among universities. Unlike the United States, where relatively well-funded state universities with high academic standards are spread across the nation alongside excellent private colleges and universities, Japan has only a small number of universities with a national reputation and high academic standards, most of which are concentrated in the metropolitan Tokyo area. Universities are ranked according to reputation and prestige, and the hierarchy of universities is a matter of public knowledge. It is an inordinately challenging task to raise measurably the academic standards of institutions in large cities and local regions across the board, but the challenge must be met if Japan's higher education is to be improved across the nation. That challenge embodies a restructuring of higher education necessitating enhanced funding and considerable improvement of faculty, instruction, and programs. When that reform becomes reality, students need not compete fiercely to seek admission to a relatively few good universities in a few large cities, such as Tokyo, Kyoto, and Osaka.

Such a campaign to enhance institutions of higher education in Japan would pave the way toward normalizing transition from high schools and universities. Meaningful reforms of higher education are Japan's next national agenda. Although NCER recommended a broad range of changes in higher education, reforms in that sector are extremely slow.

REFERENCES

Amano, Ikuo. *Education and Social Selection*. Tokyo: Daiichi Hoki, 1982.
Amano, Ikuo. "The Dilemma of Japanese Education Today," *Japan Foundation Newsletter* 13, no. 5 (1986a): 1-10.

Amano, Ikuo. "Educational Crisis in Japan." In *Educational Policies in Crisis*, edited by William K. Cummins, Edward R. Beauchamp, Shogo Ichikasa, Victor Nubuo Kobayashi, and Morikazu Ushiogi. New York: Praeger, 1986b.

Central Council of Education (Japan). *Educational Reforms for a New Age*. Tokyo: Gyosei, 1991.

Committee for the Enhancement of High School Reform. "Enhancement of High School Education Reforms," *High School Education* 26, no. 8 (1993): 116-154. (Only excerpts included.)

Cummings, William. *Education and Equality in Japan*. Princeton: Princeton University Press, 1980.

Duke, Benjamin C. *The Japanese School: Lessons for Industrial America*. New York: Praeger, 1986a.

Duke, Benjamin C. "The Liberalization of Japanese Education," *Comparative Education* 22 (1986b): 15-26.

Economic Council (Japan). *Japan in the Year 2000*. Tokyo: Japan Times, 1983.

Hirakawa, Sukehiro. *Franklin and Fukuzawa Yukichi*. Tokyo: Shinochosa, 1984.

Husén, Torsten. *International Study of Achievement in Mathematics*. New York: Wiley, 1967.

Kinmonth, Earl H. *The Self-made Man in Meiji Japanese Thought: From Samurai to Salary Man*. Berkeley: University of California Press, 1981.

Kuroha, Ryo-ichi. *The National Council on Educational Reform and Educational Reforms*. Tokyo: Keizai Shimbunsha, 1985.

LaPointe, Archie E.; Mead, Nancy A.; and Phillips, Gary W. *A World of Differences: An International Assessment of Mathematics and Sciences*. Princeton: Educational Testing Service, 1989.

Ministry of Education. *Educational Statistical Abstract*. Tokyo: Okurasho Insatsukyoku, 1993.

National Council on Educational Reform (Japan). *First Report on Educational Reform*. Tokyo: Government of Japan, 1985.

National Council on Educational Reform. *Report on Educational Reforms*. Tokyo: Okurasho Insatsukyoku, 1987.

New York Times, 28 May 1991; 23 May 1993.

Nishimoto, K. "How to Create a Comprehensive Program," *High School Education* 26 (1993): 23-29.

Organization of Economic Cooperation and Development (OECD). *A Review of Education: Japan*. Paris: OECD, 1971.

Rohlen, Thomas P. *Japan's High Schools*. Berkeley: University of California Press, 1983.

Rohlen, Thomas P. "Japanese Education: If They Can Do It, Should We?" *American Scholar* 55 (1986): 29-43.

Schoppa, Leonard. *Educational Reform in Japan: A Case of Immobilist Politics*. New York: Routledge, 1991.

Shimahara, Nobuo K. "Japanese Education Reforms in the 1980s," *Issues in Education* 4 (1986): 85-100.

Shimahara, Nobuo K. "Overview of Japanese Education: Policy, Structure, and Current Issues." In *Japanese Educational Productivity*, edited by Robert Leestma and Herbert J. Walberg. Ann Arbor: Center for Japanese Studies, University of Michigan, 1992.

Stevenson, Harold W., and Stigler, James W. *The Learning Gap*. New York: Summit Books, 1992.

United Nations Development Programme. *Human Development Report 1993*. New York: Oxford Press, 1993.

U.S. Department of Education. *Japanese Education Today*. Washington, D.C.: U.S. Government Printing Office, 1987.

Vogel, Ezra. *Japan's Middle Class*. Berkeley: University of California Press, 1963.

White, Merry. *The Japanese Educational Challenge: A Commitment to Children*. New York: Free Press, 1987.

Chapter 4

RUSSIAN EDUCATION: POLITICS, POLICY, AND PRACTICE

Richard P. Farkas

Russia is in the throes of dramatic system change. It presents special problems for those charting the transition. In spite of this formidable challenge, the value of understanding the pressures for change and the requisites for any system to manage that sort of change is very high. In "transitional" Russia the educational system is intriguing both as an independent and as a dependent variable. It affects most of what happens and does not happen in Russia today. Education is also a phenomenon clearly affected by the socioeconomic and political realities of Russian life and Russian government. When a great deal more settling and crystalizing has taken place, it may be useful to look at the structural mechanics of Russian education. Once it has become institutionalized, it will be useful to look at the dynamic and behavioral features of education. But either effort at this moment would certainly misrepresent reality. Today, the key challenge is to understand education as it takes its new place in the redesigning of Russian society.

To survive over time a social system needs at least three things. We will use this short and simplified list to guide our look at the new Russian state with an eye to the place education has in the developmental process. A system needs:

1. a generic value system (ideas and expectations) shared by the bulk of the masses that enable the leaders to communicate with and anticipate the behavior of the public they are attempting to lead;

2. policymaking machinery (structure or mechanisms) which is institutionalized to the point that it is recognized and can produce outcomes that the leadership have targeted;

3. leadership consisting of a cadre of persons able to pursue goals by making rational policy choices and accounting for costs, payoffs, and consequences.

These themes are woven throughout this chapter. At least in terms of the Russian "transition," there is very serious doubt about whether these minimal requisites are met. In reality, systems must go well beyond this basic list to become healthy and prosperous. The role of education in this future is pivotal.

THE 1990s: POST-COMMUNIST CHALLENGES

To detail the challenges which present themselves to post-Communist Russia would require volumes. The notion that once the limitations and inhibitions of Communism were jettisoned, Russia would be able to duplicate the standard of living, the security, and the political stability common in Western systems, has lingered and has resulted in ever-spiraling frustration. One way to examine this massive inventory of problems is to organize our analysis around the three requisites outlined above: mass value system, systemic architecture, and leadership. Education is central to all of these and each directly affects and is affected by the nature and performance of the educational system in Russia today. The old system in the Soviet Union had two of the three requisites. Over time the USSR did generate a rather amorphous value system which accepted the notion that government had a large role to play in guaranteeing basic needs to its public. The formal and rigidly centralized, controlled, and homogenized Soviet educational system was the key vehicle for this socialization. Socialism also advocated a goal of economic equality or "economic democracy" that in practical terms meant a leveling of the society in economic terms. This "leveling" concept was extended to universal access to basic education.

The Soviet-type Communist system had an elaborate policymaking machinery. It was designed and refined over time to perform its primary function, which was to maintain the Party's power. If the machine's effectiveness were judged only in these terms, it functioned very well until

Gorbachev began tinkering with the machine itself. Setting aside for the moment what one might think of a system designed to keep itself in power, there can be little doubt that both a broad value system and a developed policymaking machine existed in the Soviet Union.

It is far less clear that the system generated even a minimum level of leadership which could direct and manage the society. The recruitment system, the inadequate educational system (in terms of policy-relevant studies), the propensity to quash issue-oriented debate, the minimal relationship between the rulers and the ruled, and the very vertical nature of every feature of the bureaucratic system combined to insure mediocre leadership. The leadership in Russia was generally detached, noninnovative, and passive. It failed to acknowledge that political systems, like all living systems, must adapt to inevitably changing circumstances and environments. The educational system's design reflected this failure by precluding the study of the nature of society itself. All Soviet citizens were exposed to a rigid educational experience through which they became numb to some issues and entirely unaware of others. Without the support and guidance of social analysts, the system ultimately revealed itself to be disciplined and incapable of calculating the costs, payoffs, and consequences of major policy decisions. Simply, the pattern of politics produced leadership that was the functional equivalent of the weakest link in the political system. As described earlier, it was inept and narrow-gauged in its thinking. It committed more energy to illusion making than to problem solving both in schools and in politics.

Gorbachev was the first Soviet leader to wrestle with the breadth and depth of the society's problems. Perhaps this was a function of the fact that he was the first and only "leader" of the Soviet Union with a university education. The seventy-year-long leadership norms were altered by Gorbachev. The political landscape in the Gorbachev era was dominated by uncertainty and unsolidified change. The United States, impassively standing on the sidelines, was "cheerleading" for change—change to "democracy," "freedom," "market economics," and "capitalism." Above all else we should have been sensitized to the partial nature of their (and perhaps our) understanding of these concepts and their transferability. Our efforts contributed significantly to the creation of unreasonable expectations in the minds of both Americans and Russians.

The central reason for the inadequacy of the Soviet leadership can be tied to the design and process of the Soviet educational system. Policy

decisions to reformat education prevailed at all levels but without the
curricular elements which would permit and/or encourage the examination of the society itself. To stifle any political challenge, the system was
designed to eliminate social science and policy-relevant sciences (at various points even including biology, biochemistry, and computer science).
"Economics, sociology, philosophy, and law" were disciplines with no
genuine character at all (Gorbachev, 1987, p. 49). Each of these (and
many others) was compelled to form pictures of reality, analyze behavior
and processes, and reflect on the nature of trends in society only by
employing a single conceptual framework and applying that framework
inflexibly. Whenever social, economic, or political forces juxtaposed one
another, the phenomenon had to be explained in terms of the class struggle. The narrowness of this intellectual path was so extreme that intellectuals and those involved in the higher levels of the educational system
developed an elaborate code (extensive jargon), which had the net effect
of expanding the boundaries slightly. Nonetheless, the Soviet system's
leaders neither learned from their educational experiences about the
nature and complexity of the political system they were trying to manage
nor were they able to find other Soviets who had such experiences to
advise them. Through most of the life of the Soviet Union, two other
voids in the educational system made governing more difficult. The
impact of these areas was much more subtle. First, training for journalists
did not allow for the development of a psychology that emphasized the
role of the journalist as independent critic. The investigative qualities of
journalism along with conceptions of "balance" were simply not a part of
educational experience. In fact, journalism in the classic period of Soviet
education appeared more dedicated to bureaucratic skills than to communication skills. Second, while science was often touted as a key feature
and strength of Soviet education, exclusive emphasis was placed upon
"pure" science or pure research. Basically this rewarded the conceptual
development of new *ideas* without linking to it a concern for *developmental engineering*. The "D" part of the "R & D" (research and development) equation was omitted in the Soviet educational scheme. If one
adds to this reality the fact that the Soviet economy had no industrial pluralism that stimulates and rewards making an idea into a product, the
result is a significant deficiency for the development of the economy.

The comparative analyst must always remain keenly aware of the
rationale for the comparisons he or she makes. The difference between

the optimist and the pessimist examining Russia is, at least in part, a function of the comparison one chooses to make. If one opts to look at Communist vs. post-Communist Russia, a positive sense could emerge from the realization that the old system was nonadaptive, had poor leadership, and had educational, economic, and political structures that stifled initiative and results. Certainly, one could argue (and many do), that off-loading this burdensome and unproductive system was a good thing. At least a greater potential exists for this "new" system (if it develops the qualities of a coherent system) to be better able to solve its problems.

A less common view, and one that is arguably more valuable and productive, is to look at the educational system and the economic and political milieu in which it exists today and compare it to the system that will reasonably be needed to face the future. The debilitating features of the old system will continue to constrain the new system unless Russia seizes the opportunity to design an educational system (and other societal features) that is appropriate and effective in twenty-first century terms.

The comparative dilemma is between comparing the present with the past or the present with the future. The first yields a positive picture; the second, a profoundly negative one. Much of what follows is built from this second kind of comparative focus. In essence, is Russia developing educational systems that will enable it to face and meet the challenges of the decades ahead?

THE "NEW" VALUE SYSTEM

The value system, though imperfectly formed in the old Soviet system, did have some broadly supported and clearly established ideas associated with it. The centrally controlled and politically motivated Soviet educational system played a critical role as it shaped three generations of Soviets. As a value system, its specific detail was not very closely linked to Marxism. The ideas and expectations which have carried over from the earlier socialist society are that government should (1) maintain stable prices for basic commodities, (2) insure everyday security, which means government should make daily life predictable in such areas as education, employment, housing, medical care, and (3) plan society by organizing its future. Objectively speaking, the Soviet system could be understood as a system which prioritized itself around *economic* rather than *political* values. It articulated its goals in terms of the economic and educational leveling of the society rather than political leveling.

In the American system, a commitment is made to political leveling but not to economic leveling. Communism (in the real world) was about explicit political inequality just as much as American society is explicitly about economic inequality. Objectivity in place, Americans can acknowledge that both societies had a rather legitimate though sharply contrasting claim to the term "democracy." Americans give that term a purely political meaning. If the term means doing things for people in response to their needs, the rationale for a narrowly political definition is in jeopardy. The East-West conflict was often characterized as a "battle for the minds and hearts"—an ideological struggle. It may well be that the intellectual debate about whether economic democracy is more important to people in a society than political democracy has *not* been resolved. A protracted debate does rage about whether one goal is intrinsically superior to the other. It can reasonably be argued that the demise of the Communist system was more genuinely a result of its unwillingness to commit itself to "intellectual pluralism" than to any affirmative commitment it did make. The old Soviet system homogenized and severely restricted the educational system and its service to the Soviet public. In one sense, then, the Soviets introduced a kind of educational leveling. Boris Gershunsky (founder of the Russian Academy of Education) in a recently published critique of contemporary Russian education argues that the top priority is to commit to radical policies using all internal resources to "make society richer and end leveling" (Gershunsky, 1993, ch. 8). He is addressing the homogenization that Communism built into education. It prohibited the competition of ideas—diverse ideas debated in an arena of intellectual pluralism. In this sense it did not create the sort of *leveling* in educational and intellectual circles where ideas could compete and the intellectual capabilities of the system could flourish. The old Soviet educational system embraced the goal of raising the level of basic nonsocial scientific education to a standard but stifled the seedlings of original ideas from blossoming in an intellectual sense. Gorbachev wrote, "Scientific, theoretical, and other discussions, which are indispensable for the development of thought and for creative endeavor, were emasculated. . . . [T]he presentation of a "problem-free" reality backfired. . . . The political economy of socialism is stuck with outdated concepts and is no longer in tune with the dialectics of life." (Gorbachev, 1987, p. 21)

The so-called VNIK-shkola team ("experts and reformers" charged with creating a report in the style of a "white paper" on Soviet education for the Gorbachev leadership) assessed the situation with these words: "In short, overworked teachers, whose status in society is rapidly declining, are being required to teach an overloaded curriculum to an increasingly unmotivated student body in crowded classrooms, with inadequate facilities and few amenities, and using antiquated methods" (Eklof and Dneprov, 1993, p. 5).

Equality, competition, and leveling are all related concepts which can provide insight into Russian society in terms of its politics (parties, candidates, etc.), its economics (material well-being, jobs, incomes) or its ideas (the educational milieu). In the East-West competition, the West ultimately prevailed because it was committed to the open competition of ideas and to the educational environment which that competition requires.

With the collapse of Communism, a euphoria took hold that was articulated as confidence that "genuine democracy" would naturally evolve and bring with it prosperity, other economic achievements, and educational reform. It became clear instantly that many in Russia, encouraged by many others in the West, were prepared to *assume* the therapeutic effects of capitalism and participatory democracy. This naiveté is at least in part attributable to the absence of social science in the educational experiences of generations of Soviets now living in a post-Soviet society. A harsh reality penetrated this new system and dramatically unsettled its public. The newly forming value systems are being met with apprehension and confusion. The people in these systems discovered that their old values, which were directed at order and economic security, were not a part of a capitalist market economy nor was order a quality of the new political system they saw forming. In fact, the market system was no "system" at all. It had no rules, no protections, no established behaviors. It advocated the complete decentralization of authority in the economy without regard for whether key items would be produced or be affordable. It should not be surprising that Russian people had little opportunity to inform themselves about Western style systems (because of the voids in the educational system) and would manage only fuzzy ideas about the consequences of the changes taking place. The sum of this uncertainty resulted in a kind of "value shock" which reintroduced a pessimism into contemporary Russia and may well make effective governing exponentially more difficult. A Gallup poll (Bercsi, 1993, p. 12) revealed that 44 percent of the Russians believed that "the free market system is not right for Russia." The higher levels of the educational system needed to buffer presumptions about magical change and hope for a "ripple" effect that would reach the common man. But that did not happen.

What key idea is basic and essential for the construction of a new value system that can support the kind of polity and economy which Russians seek? The answer is at the same time simple and perplexing. Values supporting *tolerance* are the key ingredients. On reflection, it may be that historians will write that the characteristic which set the American political system apart from others in the late twentieth century was its commitment to tolerance. From a political perspective it can be argued that tolerance is essential for debate and dialogue about issues, for party and candidate competition, for dealing with defeats in politics, and in casting a constructive relationship between the ruling group and the opposition. From an economic perspective, it can be argued that tolerance is basic to the competitive market system and without it American style capitalism would be impossible. Corporations may wince at the notion that they think tolerating the competition is a good thing but in broad terms would concede that having and living with competition is a positive thing for the system-at-large and even for themselves in the long run. Most obviously, tolerance is critical to any intellectual or educational system which hopes to understand challengingly complex subjects. Only in this way can such an intellectual system nurture and harvest the ideas and energies of its citizenry.

Two central questions arise: Do values supporting tolerance exist in the minds of Russians? Are their institutions nurturing these values? Tragically, the answer to both is "No." The pre-Communist history was devoid of this element. Communism itself shrunk from making a commitment to tolerance. Much of the West's public perception of Soviet Communism focuses on that system's intolerance.

But are there social institutions that are working to develop the necessary values of tolerance? In other societies that have pursued this goal, the classic "agents of socialization"—elements of society that help shape the public's thinking and attitudes—work toward establishing or reinforcing this goal. Russian institutions today do not seem to be so committed. The family structure in Russia is either very traditional and hierarchical or disintegrating. It does not seem to be stable enough or inclined to establish tolerance as a core idea and behavior. The schools are still hierarchical, rigid, and authoritarian, stifling or at least not exemplifying tolerance. Religious organizations which can be heard resoundingly to promote tolerance of their religion are nonetheless not prepared to advocate the tolerance of all religions. Russian economic managers advocate the dismantling of state monopolies but maneuver constantly to establish private monopolies. In politics, new competitive party systems have been established. But they have revealed themselves to be prone to intolerantly advocate the elimination of their most radical opposition groups. The Yeltsin government has declared two such groups illegal and closed a significant number of newspapers. The record then reveals that grass-roots ideas of tolerance are not forming because they have no fertile soil to grow in. Still worse, the Establishment (political, economic, social, educational, and religious) is sending clear signals that are intolerant in substance and style.

It is fair to say that Russia is searching for a path to the future, searching for an ideological map which can lead to a better future. However, the overriding perspective that guides this effort is tied to the past. The search for new values and ideas has not turned to the future nor even other political systems in the present but has instinctively turned to Russia's past as if it were an untapped resource. The trend has been reinforced by the strong habit of the pedagogical elites to dwell on rewriting Russia's history with the promise that this will "unlock" centuries of "knowledge and solutions." Because Communism in many ways turned away from the past (at least rhetorically) and Communism is gone, many concluded that turning to the past is the right thing to do. Reinforcing this notion is nationalism. In the effort to find a new non-Communist identity, Russia has resurrected the handiest old identity without concern for how constructive or destructive a force it might be. Nationalism solidifies people who are a part of the dominant group. It gives them identity and at the same time invites them to feel superior to or to fear those of other national identities (inside or outside Russia). Given Russian history, such fears and arrogance are powerful feelings. *Every* national group in and around Russia has had episodes in its history when it was abused at the hands of a rival nationality or when it did the abusing. These latter epochs are often touted as "moments in the sun" for the nation, when "justice and reason" prevailed and the "good guys" were on top.

To the extent that any one value dominates the attitudinal landscape of Russia, it is clearly nationalism. It is a persistent and recurring theme in the new Russian classroom. Nationalism asks students and others to think with their hearts rather than with their heads. It encourages them to "feel" about politics rather than "think" about politics. Tragically, this means that it can be and is used by politicians in Russia to (a) explain away failure, (b) easily find scapegoats, (c) create artificial confidence and arrogance, and (d) shatter tolerance. Armed with nationalism, Russian political "leaders" can shield themselves from the hard-nosed scrutiny of pragmatists who ask about policy effectiveness and real political performance. In contrast, nationalists can guarantee that they can trigger spiraling intensity of feeling which in Russia frequently erupts in violence and inhumanity.

Nationalism as a value set is devoid of tolerance and cooperative behavior. As a concept planted in youthful minds it is an intellectual sedative. It compels persons to "face backwards." It demands a highly selective historical analysis which not only describes where the nation has been but also prescribes where the nation should be going, that is, to recapture the epoch when Russians prevailed. The spasmodic and twisted histories of Russia give this a perverse significance. The most ethnically diverse political systems from the Communist era (USSR, Yugoslavia) have been the first and most violent cases. Nationalism functions like a cancer in Russia. It was a threat to Soviet Communism but is no less a threat to post-Communist Russia.

Critically, nationalism and intolerance prevent these political systems from facing forward. In most of the Western world, young people in school are keenly focused on the future. Their lives are ahead of them and school is perceived as a vehicle which they can use to drive into that future. The educational system in Russia could emulate this role but is not doing so. Evidently, Russia needs to attempt to focus on the *problems* of today and tomorrow. Russia needs to marshal all its human capability to identify the range of policy *alternatives* available to it. The political system then needs to be able to select a course with enough confidence to stay with the selected policy to give it a chance to succeed. These leadership challenges will be examined later in this chapter. The challenge Russia faces is worse because other political and economic systems are "sprinting into the future" while Russia is "backing into the future."

At the very heart of the changes is a trend in which the political masses in Russia are reorienting their thinking increasingly toward seeing themselves as the *shapers* of politics rather than the *consequences* of politics, as those who can do in politics rather than those who have it done to them. While this parallels our thinking about politics, it is both idealistic and fraught with practical problems for politics in Russia's transitional era. The profound and explicit challenge to the educational system is clear: Can the schools provide young, soon-to-be-adults with the tools and concepts to engage themselves in the management of society? A further complication to this challenge is the commitment of the new system to use the potential of all students. Buried beneath the statistic that 60 percent of all applicants to higher education are women and 52 percent of all enrollees are women is a reality that is less neutral. The VNIK-shkola Report suggests that "gender and sex-role stereotyping are, lamentably, not issues adequately dealt with by the reform movement in Russia today" (Eklof and Dneprov, 1993, p. 13).

The people of Russia will certainly suffer from postreform trauma as they discover that participatory democracy and market-based capitalism in fact provide no guarantees and few short-term results. These new systemic models provide just one promise: that the pursuit of genuine solutions is possible in a system constructed around tolerance. Unfortunately, this will provide little solace for many Russians.

THE "NEW" POLITICAL MACHINERY

The institutional arrangement in the old Soviet Union was both unique and not true to the constitutional designs upon which it claimed authority. The actual political structure of the classic Soviet system was designed to (1) keep the Communist Party in power, (2) quell change, and (3) prevent the public from approaching the establishment. The old machinery was constructed to maintain power in the hands of a specific elite. As instruments of power, the institutions of the old system functioned effectively or effectively enough to resist change for many decades. In retrospect, we know that the beginning of the end was Gorbachev's effort to tinker with the political machinery in the hope of making it capable of producing what he hoped would be measured change. Once tinkered with, it proved unable to perform either its original *system maintenance* function or its new *system adaptation* function. Basically, it was "neither fish nor fowl" and frustration with it was apparent from both old "apparatchiki" and reformers. The old machine had been more delicately tuned to its old task than we had realized. Its performance diminished as new elements entered politics and its anachronistic features became more apparent as old elements behaved as if they still held exclusive power.

A strategy for post-Communist institutional redesign emerged. The new Russian leadership placed no faith in even the enlightened features of the conceptual design of the old Soviet constitutional system and chose instead to "start from scratch" in politics. This strategy argues that a uniquely Russian system must be designed to meet the unique and specific needs of the Russian nation. Such a strategy is fed by thrusts of nationalism that reject the adaptation of models from any other political venue. In education, though, the old pattern held. The entrenched patterns and personnel were able to maintain the Soviet paradigm. The pedagogical foundations of the Soviet educational system were clearly drawn from the classic Prussian model, with elements of the thinking of Tolstoy and Dewey added. A rigid pattern became clear in the Stalin era when the intensely vertical hierarchy took shape. The system was characterized over time by an authoritarian quality, uniforms, homework, rote learning in large classrooms, and a uniform and tightly controlled curriculum. The system embraced virtually no teacher autonomy and the main objective was to serve as the central "transmission belt" for establishment values and behaviors. In Russian education this was referred to as "ZUNY"—an abbreviation for the "knowledge, habits, and skills" that were to be routinized.

For the system-at-large, the issues were as fundamental as any could be in a political system: What will be the relationship between the executive and the legislature? How centralized or decentralized will the distribution of power be? The relationship between the President and the parliamentary style legislature is contentious to the point of systemic paralysis. The "architecture" which is absent here is critical for many reasons. Without it, authority is not clearly placed nor balanced in Russia. Without it, leaders have neither clearly delineated responsibilities nor clearly defined constraints. Without it, the working relationship among parts of the government cannot be predicted. And without it, the public has little chance to interact with government bureaucracies because there is no map of the paths (processes) or obstacles (bureaucracies) for them to follow. In practical terms, this means that Russia has not yet turned to the task of making educational policy which could shake the system out of its lethargy. No one is even debating whether "shock therapy" for Russian education is needed.

The malaise is evident. At the very top of the policymaking system there is confusion and a poignant lack of focus. In a meeting with officials at the State Committee on Education in Moscow (June, 1993) in which I participated, a discussion was held on the nature of the relationship among the key players in the educational policy process. The Chair of the State Committee on Education is one key element in the puzzle. The President's Counselor for Education is another. The Education Minister in the Cabinet is a third and the Chairman of the Legislative Committee on Education is a fourth. The central question was put: What is the nature of the relationship among these similarly focused parts of government? The resounding answer from each was, "We don't know." Next question: Do you differ with one another philosophically or politically? Answer: "We don't communicate with one another enough to know." They did agree with one another that the two key problems in curricular reform of the schools are to develop the social sciences and "de-ideologize" the whole curriculum. The fundamental experience of Russian students today has not changed. The pattern is represented in figure 1. It mirrors the Soviet experience. Further, direct reports from the Ministry of Education indicate that the curriculum "has the same content" as before and that new curricular materials, while planned, are neither available nor currently funded.

One overarching transition in structural terms is the change from a vertical management structure (old system) to a new horizontal structure. It may be that some of the confusion stems from this very basic change, which represents a major innovation in thinking and behavior in politics and education. Elaborate schematic diagrams notwithstanding, the channels of responsibility and power have simply not been delineated. Horizontal structures provide for (a) more functional differentiation—specific tasks assigned to specific bureaucracies, (b) more communication between elements with comparable responsibilities and power, and (c) more points of access for those outside the government. These institutional advantages may be offset in Russia by the short-term (and perhaps long-term) reality that government and education and the costs of government and education are perceived by the public to be growing. The promise of the new system is that government would shrink and "get out of the lives of its citizens." It is unlikely that however the issues

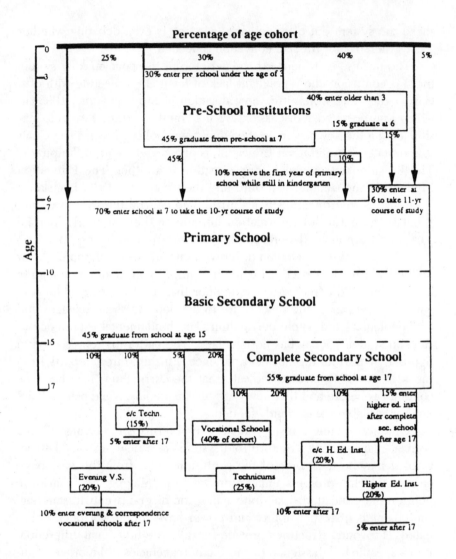

Figure 1

**The State System of Education in the Russian Federation.
Reprinted from *Democracy and the Russian School*, Eklov and
Dneprov, eds., 1993, by permission of Westview Press, Boulder, CO.**

of centralization or decentralization are resolved, the redesign of an
essentially horizontal framework for government and education (on
some variant of the Western model) *will* violate that promise. The size of

these systems and the attendant costs will rise. Public reaction is and will continue to be negative.

A prominent article on education in *Pravda* concluded, "The root evil of the existing system of educational governance is its bureaucratic nature which precludes any chance for the population to play any role in running the schools" (*Pravda*, Feb. 13, 1988, p. 1). Considering the source, such a conclusion should be understood in dramatic terms. The same article observed,

The present structure of governance is a highly articulated hierarchical system of bureaucratic institutions which functions more to serve its own needs than those of the schools or of society. . . . It stands for the absolute tyranny of the educational bureaucracy. . . . It is difficult to think of any other branch of the bureaucracy wielding such untrammeled and unchallenged power over such a large number of hapless subjects.

Two important structural features of the Russian policymaking system (the *extractive* and *distributive* mechanisms) are selected here to underline the difficulties of the transitional period in Russian policymaking. It is easy to see how extracting resources from people (taxes, ideas, labor) and distributing goods and services to people are essential mechanisms for the process of governing. Both are critical problems in the new Russian system. In the Soviet system, the extractive function was performed in largely invisible ways by the supracentralized management of the economy. Though a taxation system existed, it performed a secondary role in the process of financing government. The primary vehicle for financially lubricating government was the manipulation of prices and wages in the old system. By monopolistically controlling these things as well as the banking function, the system was always able to marshal the necessary funds to operate. The nature of this system generated a general discontent but it had the advantage of reaching into people's pockets for revenue without their noticing it. It was a relatively invisible method of *extracting* resources from the public. The Soviet educational system was massive, accessible, and apparently free. The Russian public seldom reflected upon where the money came from to run the system.

With the post-Communist system in Russia and, in principle, its rejection of price and wage controls, and the pluralization of business and banking, the government can no longer use the old technique. Instead, the leadership have turned, with only modest awareness of the fallout, to more conventional taxing schemes. Such taxes are visible, painful in a struggling economy. Perhaps most dramatically, the cost of governing is coming into alarming focus for Russians. The numbers take shape well beyond what any of them had imagined. Politically timid leaders operating in institutionally unclear systems are unable to make the policy decisions to impose taxes and firmly stand by those decisions. They do not know whom to tax, what to tax, or at what level to tax. It is fair to say that the Russian public perceives such efforts by the new government to be obtrusive and unreasonable, resulting in immense pressure. This happens as the Russian government claims to be popular, elected, and democratic.

The *distributive* mechanisms leave the new Russian government in a similarly unworkable dilemma. The old system distributed some goods and services to everyone (everyone not singled out as a dissident) and distributed the rest by way of the vertical organizations known as "mass organizations." To benefit, one had to join, pay very modest dues, and get the benefits which were associated with whatever that organization was designed to do—learn to fly, meet famous writers and poets, take camping trips, engage in youth activities. Many "extra-curricular" activities were provided outside the school by youth-focused state- or Party-supported mass organizations. This appeared to place the onus on the individual and connected the public to the system's distribution network. It was not a perfect system and it did frustrate some; but for the overwhelming bulk of people, it made the system understandable and accessible. With the dismantling of these quasi-official organizations and their special privileges, the government has gotten out of the business of providing many of the goods and services it previously distributed. In theory, such opportunities are now available to everyone by way of the private sector. In reality, the private sector has not responded and, where it has, the costs prevent most from participating or benefiting. Theater tickets, skiing lessons, vacations, and many other services are not affordable. With budget constraints tightening rather than loosening, the ability of government to provide benefits of either the essential variety, let alone the more life-enhancing variety has virtually vanished. Soviet higher education *was* free. Subsidies of various sorts encouraged and induced students to commit themselves to it. Today, Russian universities are charging tuition (variable but significant amounts). Educational policy now requires that Russians pay in rubles while non-Russians pay in a "hard currency." This has driven large numbers of students from the universities.

It has forced many former "Soviets" to leave Russia and return to the other successor countries of their origin. As enrollments decline (in some cases by one third), government subsidies (calculated by head count) have been reduced proportionately. In a number of prominent universities this then manifests itself in the cutting of professors' salaries proportionately. In some reported cases, professors are now making between $14 and $15 monthly. Universities have responded by taking to crude entrepreneurial ventures (often soliciting Western tourists) which prostitute and in some cases abandon their serious scholarly roles.

Is life better today than it was yesterday? If that commonplace question is raised in Russia, the predictable answer in these transitional times is "No"—at least in the minds of most people. A Gallup survey in the spring of 1993 indicated that 59 percent of Russians responded that "life was better under Communism" (Bercsi, 1993, p. 12). They are certainly saying that life was more predictable. One important reason is that the system has not designed the new architecture for the political and economic lives of its citizens in ways that can be understood and appreciated by them. In social systems where guarantees of basic lifestyle were characteristic, the new system *seems* to be taking more and giving less. This is a pressure which the new government must address proactively or face mounting alienation. As challenging as this is, most analysts would find hope *if* the educational system were meaningfully restructuring itself. If this were the case, perhaps the new Russian system could weather a generation-long storm of frustration and confusion to be saved by a new elite educated, attuned, and prepared for leadership. Little evidence exists beyond the rhetoric of reform.

The lack of systemic architecture is also reflected in the absence of features in the social system which could work toward developing the public's awareness of and confidence in political institutions. Materials for schools, media campaigns, public forums, and public interest or "watch-dog" organizations are just a few illustrations of mechanisms that could have been designed into the system but to date are not. The design of any political system must include both the structure of authority and mechanisms that will enable the system to establish public confidence in it, that is, to build legitimacy. There are many perspectives in political science on how this is most effectively done. In the special context of the transitional Russian system, one obvious answer is to insure that an infrastructure is created for education which can actively support policymaking at all levels of the society. The Soviet system by design neglected the social sciences, journalism, and "developmental" engineering (technology). It restricted the comparative study of politics, economics, sociology, and management. In this way, it left its successor system with a shortfall in expertise that makes "solving" problems (especially when nationalistic impulses insist on indigenous "solutions") next to impossible. If there was evidence that the educational system in Russia was renovating itself to position education on the cutting edge of the transition, one could be more sanguine. No such evidence exists in the policy sciences, and only formal, structural changes have emerged involving the "management sciences" curriculum. A brief look at the data in table 1 indicates that in terms of training new teachers there is little hope that anything will change. Notice the remarkable omission of most of the social sciences.

Table 1
Targets for Admissions to Pedagogical Institutes by Specialty
Percent Increase, 1985 to 1990

Mathematics	.3	Physical Culture	34.9
Physics	4.0	Military Drill	83.6
Chemistry	49.5	Music	-5.1
Biology	9.4	Fine Arts	10.7
Geography	36.7	Pedagogy & Psychology	124.3
History	19.5	Pedagogy & Methods	9.3
Russian Language/Lit	7.3	Defectology	31.8
Foreign Language/Lit	8.5	Labor	19.2

Source: Eklof and Dneprov, eds., *Democracy in the Russian School,* 1993, p. 211.

In the course of thinking or rethinking the shape of new political, economic, and educational systems for Russia, a number of critical considerations have been overlooked. As suggested, the trend is to look to the past for a remedy for the future. Bolstered by nationalism, a distasteful experience with Communism, and a soft foundation of expertise upon which to base decisions, the design function has been seriously corrupted to the point that Russian leaders can be indicted for trying to "reinvent the wheel." They neglect to use cross-national studies and experience to accelerate constructive change in Russia. They are neglecting the important signals emanating from Western Europe. The political/economic/educational systems in Western Europe, most of which are the envy of their Russian counterparts, have dedicated their leadership, education, and intellectual resources to the task of assessing the challenges of the twenty-first century. What they "see" is an economic world with hyperchallenging markets, global interdependence, exotic complexities, and a breakneck pace of technological change. In order to meet these challenges and to play a meaningful role, the relatively strong West European countries have set about the arduous task of redesigning their political, economic, and educational structures (and their collective identity) to enable them to cope with the future. The European Union is the result.

At the same time, countries are disintegrating in Eastern Europe. Even the Russian Federation is threatened with defections of some of its major parts. The "independence" spurred by nationalism has created and seems bound to continue to create ever smaller political and economic states. In these new smaller states, education will be exceptionally vulnerable.

If political machinery is a requisite for a system to survive (and prosper), the unsettling reality seems to be that the old Communist system had machinery; the new Russia does not. The pressure to form the machinery for policymaking and education is acute, yet little has developed. The short-run remedy is obvious: borrow structures—political, economic, legal, educational—from functioning systems that are in some meaningful way comparable, and use their routines and credibility to develop a relatively stable pattern of politics. With this strategy, legislatures and national leaderships could then go about the task of tinkering, fine-tuning, or making adjustments to idiosyncratic sensitivities or priorities. The alternative driven by arrogance or naiveté (the notion that each nation is altogether politically unique) is for inexperienced legislatures and executive branch officials to incrementally build a unique and untested social system. If that sounds a bit reminiscent of the Communist experiment, it should.

THE "NEW" LEADERSHIP

The Soviet system failed to produce leaders who could assess and guide the system through its problems and toward its goals. Leadership has been characterized as the weakest link in the old Soviet political system. It is broadly assumed that with the transitional political climate established, new, talented, and sophisticated persons will come forward to lead from a platform of popular legitimacy. Upon closer scrutiny, it is an unfounded assumption and an unreal expectation.

Those who did step forward in the years and months before the collapse of Soviet Communism were of two types. They were politicians who had been convinced that change was essential. They enjoyed modest popular support and prevailed in their political hierarchies because the leadership was split. These had all been professional politicians in the Communist system. Examples include Gorbachev, Yeltsin, Kravchuk, and Shevardnadze. It is reasonable to label them "born again democrats." The second variety were those who were not insiders pressing for change but instead were voices for the "politics of principle"—outsiders, "rookies." They carried no political "baggage." Both types of leaders shared a common critique of the classic Communist system—mismanagement of the economy, arbitrary politics, and the subjugation of productive cultures.

The "rookies" were without responsibility for what the system had done in the past. In fact, they were among the masses who had been the subjects and targets of politics. They were not distinguishable by their knowledge of politics or of the non-Communist world. They were credible by default and untainted by the narrow Party politics of the past. They were also not experienced in politics nor were they versed in the study of policymaking or conceptually sophisticated about how political systems are structured or behave. They *were* courageous in a very special sense of that term.

When a man stands on the edge of a pit and has no idea of how deep it is, what the bottom is made of, or what will happen to him if he jumps in, and he still jumps in, he has *courage*. If he knows how deep it is, what the bottom is made of, what bones he will break when he jumps, how long it will take to heal, and he jumps in, he has *wisdom*. In Russian politics, this distinction is meaningful. In the first case, no calculation is possible and yet leaders have "taken the leap." They displayed raw political courage. Alternatively, political systems might hope for a leadership which could make calculations about the consequences of their actions and act accordingly—that is, act wisely. The point here is not that timidity is best, nor that leadership can always act wisely based upon information and experience, but rather that raw political courage must be recognized for what it is and acknowledged to have serious shortcomings.

Most everyone (save for the old Communist establishments) applauded the political courage of leaders like Yeltsin and Gorbachev but it is important not to attribute political wisdom to their actions. They did not know what would happen to themselves or the masses they were leading when they did what they did.

The absence of political wisdom as described here is not the fault of the leaders themselves. It is a direct reflection of the shortcomings of the educational and political systems which prevailed in the Soviet Union for generations. From the pressurized position of leadership he held Gorbachev (1987) observed, "Philosophy and sociology, too, are lagging behind the requirements of practice." The expertise, experience, and perspective are absent to the point that there is no foundation upon which leaders can assess policies, predict consequences or remain confident.

The challenges of effective governing given Russia's situation are so formidable that leadership and masses alike need a genuine sophistication and patience. Both commodities are in short supply. The political results are (a) unstable and profoundly frustrated leaders, (b) policy which, at best, appears in fits and starts, (c) naive and manipulable masses, and (d) a mutual and poignant frustration between rulers and the ruled.

When history judges this transitional period, it will observe that the leadership which followed the Communist period was weak, directionless, and without the fundamental skills to be effective. The overwhelming number of leaders of universities, institutes, and prominent schools in Russia today are led by "born again" intellectuals, recycled from the old regime. Any system can survive (perhaps marginally) if the society has a broad value system and policymaking machinery with institutions and routines that the masses and the elites understand. However, without these and without strong leadership, a negative prognosis for these systems is inescapable. They cannot be healthy today and they will certainly struggle to stay alive tomorrow.

MORE CHALLENGES FOR RUSSIAN EDUCATION

The economic infrastructure was neglected in many ways under Communism resulting in fundamental problems in transportation, communication, energy, pollution control, financial accounting, and banking.

Education is a primary example of a profoundly damaged sector of society. A penetrating study completed in 1988 by the Gorbachev leadership revealed that of the 130,000 schools (primary and secondary) in the USSR 65,000 had no central heating, running water, or sewage facilities (*Moscow News*, 20 February 1988, p. 1). Estimates accounting for the now smaller Russian Federation place the numbers at 21 percent with no central heating, 30 percent no indoor plumbing, and 40 percent with no sewage system. Forty percent have no recreational facilities and more than one quarter of all schools operate on two or three full shifts (Eklof and Dneprov, 1993, pp. 4, 195). In 1988, 127,400 of the 130,000 schools taught "computer usage." Of these only 2,080 schools have even a single personal computer (*Moscow News*, 20 February 1988, p. 2). To respond to these shortcomings in post-Soviet Russia requires time, expertise, and finances that are simply not there.

More subtle, experience with the Soviet system (four generations) has left people without one other key ingredient for their participation in the new capitalist systems. The public's aversion to risk has thwarted a number of the reform programs. The school environment, while not primarily responsible for this problem, has reinforced it. Russia has underestimated the degree to which people have become risk-averse. This is not so surprising if you remember that one of the carry-over value sets is security—the desire to be able to anticipate and rely on tomorrow. This reflects itself in a dampening of the entrepreneurial spirit and has meant that the overwhelming majority of new businesses are small, labor-minimal, productionless, and mobile so that little or no investment is required. Such efforts in the service sector or in retail do little to bolster the system's overall economic strength.

Perhaps because political and university-level dialogue was absent for generations, Russia has not found itself able to focus on the challenges which lie ahead. Facing backwards, it compartmentalizes its problems looking for uniquely nationalistic solutions and frequently balking at radical policymaking. Nationalism and failed leadership have driven parts of countries to believe that their problems would go away if they could organize themselves into a homogeneous nation. The absence of a social science based dialogue in society has prevented a central question from being raised: If the society were ethnically homogeneous, would economic and political problems be more solvable and success more assured? Edward Dneprov, Minister of Education under Yeltsin observes, "Today schools seem mired in the woes of society, incapable of holding up against powerful currents increasingly marginalizing formal education, or subverted by . . . the seeming irrelevance of the curriculum" (Eklof and Dneprov, 1993, p. 1).

SYNTHESIS: PAST, PRESENT, FUTURE

This moment in Russian national development is an especially troublesome one. It is made more unsettling because so many Americans and Russians want desperately to believe in the future of Russia. The claim is made here that Russia is facing backwards and is backing into the future. This is a poor strategy which severely limits its ability to compete and survive in the next century. The past is a bedeviling guide to a bright future. The present is barely manageable because Russia is saddled with problems carried over from the past and has little way of marshaling human resources and experience to design political, economic, and educational structures. Without a master societal architecture in which people can believe and to which leaders can turn for guidance, coping and muddling become the order of the day.

A 1993 study on the state of Russian education today, completed in Russia by Russians, warns:

Our society has entered a period of fundamental change in its socioeconomic and political relations. Nobody any longer challenges the need for such change and for the transition to qualitatively different types of relationships, but it is much less clear where we are going and how to get there. The search for answers is made more complicated in the sphere of education by the profound internal crisis it is now undergoing. Finding a way out of the educational crisis, given the significant uncertainties surrounding the socioeconomic changes taking place in the country, is possible only if we have a detailed, well-worked out strategy which takes into account not only the present situation in education, the tendencies and relations now prevailing therein, but also the various scenarios for the future direction society might take. (Cited in Eklof and Dneprov, 1993, p. 148.)

Concerned persons with comparative interests will watch carefully to see if values, political machinery, and leadership emerge from this societal drift. If that is to happen, education will have to be the catalyst. The educational bureaucracy in Russia shows no signs of interest in or capacity to step up to this critical role. In the interest of the survival of the new Russia, the questions raised here must be answered in the next few years. Russia brings to mind a classic lament: "If you don't know where you're going, any road will get you there."

REFERENCES

Bercsi, Janos. "Eurobarometer," *Hungarian Observer* 6, no. 4 (April, 1993).

"Bureaucratic Tyranny," *Pravda*, 13 February 1988.

Eklof, Ben and Dneprov, Edward, eds. *Democracy in the Russian School: The Reform Movement in Education Since 1984*. Boulder: Westview Press, 1993.

"Failure and Falling," *Moscow News*, 20 February 1988.

Gershunsky, Boris S. *Russia in Darkness: On Education and the Future*. San Francisco: Caddo Gap Press, 1993.

Gorbachev, Mikhail. *Perestroika*. New York: Harper Collins, 1987.

Chapter 5

CIVIC EDUCATION IN THE ROMANIAN EDUCATIONAL SYSTEM

Elena Nedelcu

While urgently needed during Romania's current period of transformation, civic education confronts deep-seated problems. To explain both the special importance of, and the obstacles to, a modern democratic program of civic education I will first survey the teaching of civics in the Romanian educational system in the twentieth century, with emphasis on the last five years. I then discuss the special problems of teaching civics under prevailing conditions.

Romania's population is 23.2 million. The nation has an area of nearly 92 million square miles, slightly smaller than the state of Oregon. Former communists lead the nation. The next elections will be held in 1996. Inflation is over 260 percent; the average wage is $70 per month. There are currently 3.6 million students attending school. The educational system includes preschool programs, primary and gymnasium education, secondary schools (vocational and specialty schools), and higher education.

Development of the education system in Romania in this century falls into three main periods: 1930 to 1944; 1944 to 1989; and 1989 to the present. Each period is defined by a distinct educational system and each of these has its own type of civic education, with its characteristic content and objectives.

DEVELOPMENT AND DECENTRALIZATION
(1930-1944)

This period is marked by both quantitative and qualitative progress throughout the public educational system. The number of buildings assigned to education increased, especially for secondary schools. The teaching staff increased, and public education was extended to all. By the end of the 1920s, the economic development of the country was contributing to this process. Private education also showed some progress during these decades.

The educational system of this period was moderately decentralized. Thus, in 1938, a uniform base curriculum for elementary schools was combined with an additional one adapted for regional variations. Disciplines of instruction were grouped by "centers of interest." Thus within a common framework, room was made for various themes specific to different regions and types of secondary schools. More than one textbook was available for a given subject and level, and there were even separate civic education textbooks for girls and boys.

During these years the Romanian educational policy emphasized a practical, realistic, and formative approach. It conformed with the developmental requirements of the country at the time. The Education Act of 1924, drawn up by Constantin Angelescu, implemented the practical orientation of the secondary educational system by establishing vocational workshops or agricultural fieldwork programs according to region. The Education Act also extended the period of compulsory elementary education. This additional "super-elementary" cycle was intended for those categories of pupils who lacked the material means to attend secondary education. The emphasis was on vocational education. In 1932, the system introduced four-year agricultural and secondary schools, and in 1936, industrial and commercial secondary schools.

The great Romanian educators drew up laws that invested Romanian education with its active-formative character. The laws and directives elaborated by Spiro Haret, Simion Mehedinti, Constantin Dimitrescu Iasi, Constantin Angelescu, Petre Petre Negulescu, and others recommended the use of active methods in teaching and learning and accorded more importance to individuality and originality in the work of the pupils. Memorization was to be resorted to only where judgment could not be applied. These educators believed it essential to give up the abstract and theoretical approach to education and urged teachers to emphasize what would now be called hands-on learning, judgment, estimation, experience, and knowledge.

During this period, civic education played an important part in the educational system. Legislation for elementary education attached the same importance to the teaching of civics as to the teaching of writing, reading, and arithmetic. At the secondary level, civics was one of the disciplines common to all types of schools. But whereas elementary schools taught a fairly uniform course of moral-civic education, secondary schools used a multitude of textbooks and curricula, depending on their vocational or academic orientation. However, almost all curricula covered these themes: the nature and fundamental rules of human society; the Romanian government, the constitution, and history; patriotism and one's duty to one's country; citizenship, civic and political rights, and civic, military, and fiscal duties; sovereignty, separation of powers, and the nature of judicial powers; criminal law; administrative organization; civil and commercial law, the right to property; the nature and effects of commerce and corporations; the organization of labor, laws of labor contracts and conflicts.

Thus, the moderately decentralized educational system made possible variation in the themes of civic education according to region and school type. At the same time, the practical-active and democratic emphases of educational policy allowed for an understanding of the part played by civic education in the development of citizens and it was thus accorded high importance within the curriculum. That situation changed entirely in the following period.

TOTALITARIAN COMMUNISM (1944-1989)

Essential features of the next phase of Romanian education were extreme centralization, with a single text and curriculum in each discipline for the whole country; excessive politicizing, especially in the subordination of socio-humanistic disciplines and the promulgating of communist ideology; and an emphasis on the abstract and theoretical in method and objectives. This emphasis on the abstract aimed at informing pupils rather than training them and perhaps made it possible for Romanian pupils to achieve excellent results in international school competitions.

As the educational system was centralized and politicized, the multitude of civic education curricula and textbooks of the previous period were replaced by a single curriculum and textbook with an obviously political character. The curriculum for the 1970s and 1980s stipulated the teaching of "the constitution of the Socialist Republic of Romania" at the elementary stage and of "social-political knowledge" at the secondary stage. The elementary curriculum comprised all the articles of the fundamental law of the Romanian socialist state and declared as its objectives (1) knowing and observing the provisions of the constitution and (2) affirming the conviction that Romania was a democratic state—in spite of the fact that it was in reality a communist dictatorship.

Similarly, at the secondary level the objectives of "social-political knowledge" were declared to be: (1) knowing the policy of the Romanian Communist Party and its foundational texts; (2) understanding that a socialist society was superior to that of a capitalist society; and (3) adhering to and putting into practice the principles and policies of the Romanian Communist Party. Civic education under communism had in view not the training of citizens who could take an active part in the life of the democratic society (for in fact such a society did not exist), but the training of citizens who would submit to this form of government and remain devoted to the policies of the Romanian Communist Party. To this end, the required curriculum purported to prove the superiority of the so-called socialist democracy. To do this it misinterpreted reality and made contradictory arguments, some of them downright ridiculous. For example, it claimed that Romania had one of the highest rates of labor productivity in Eastern Europe when, of course, the opposite was true.

The party referred to this stage as "the period of the many-sided development [of a] socialist society," cynically denying prevailing economic reality, including the acute scarcity of food products in the market. The chapter on "Civic Rights and Liberties" in the secondary textbook asserted that freedom of thought and expression are a right of all citizens, but at the same time stated that it is necessary to fight vehemently against mystico-religious and opportunist conceptions—that is, those that did not agree with the ideological policy of the Party as "conceived" by its General Secretary. Elsewhere, the standard textbook claimed on the one hand that in socialism the human being is of supreme value and, on the other hand, that society is a decisive and primary factor in the existence of the individual.

Civic education under the communists, then, consisted of indoctrinating pupils with the policy and writings of the Party, and the contents of the textbooks were essentially slogans and information. Appeals to daily reality and analysis of social and economic phenomena were impossible. There were exceptions, however, like courses entitled "Contradictions in Socialism"; in these the teacher could freely use examples from everyday life. But the conclusion had to be always the same: the superiority of socialism. Such lessons always turned out to be demonstrations that the antagonistic contradictions of capitalism must be distinguished from the nonantagonistic contradictions of socialism.

TRANSFORMATION (1989-1995)

The sociopolitical and economic transformations in Romania since 1989 have eventuated in reform of the educational system. Romania's development toward a market economy and democracy requires a decentralized and depoliticized educational system which can train students both for greater professional and geographical mobility in response to rapid economic change and for active participation in the democratization of the society. But reform of education must not be limited to changes that accord with social and economic change. The educational system must not wait to react to the evolution of other social subsystems. It must be a force that accelerates and stimulates the democratic development of the society, and for that reason its rapid reform is critically important.

It is now expected that nationwide reform will be completed between 1995 and 2000. A big first step toward reform has already been taken by depoliticizing the educational system and eliminating the ideological substance from the socio-humanistic disciplines. Reform began with these subject areas. The curriculum no longer covers "the constitution of the Socialist Republic of Romania," "social-political knowledge," or the history of the Romanian Communist Party and of the working-class movement. Several new subject areas have been introduced: "Civic Culture" in seventh and eighth grades and the third year of professional school, logic in the ninth grade, and psychology in tenth grade.

The contents of economics and philosophy have been radically changed. Economics now covers the mechanism and laws of the market economy and philosophy introduces major philosophers of the world and analyzes different ideologies rather than being restricted to Marxist-Leninist philosophy.

An element of absolute novelty is the introduction of "Civic Culture" into the curriculum in 1992. The goal of this discipline is to assure the understanding of democratic values and the principles of their application that lead to active and responsible participation of citizens in the life of the democratic society.

During this period of transition toward a market economy, civic education must emphasize the general values of democracy. Study of existing sociopolitical institutions is difficult and even irrelevant under conditions of constant institutional and legislative change. Elaboration of these developments in civic education has been facilitated by examination of western and especially American experience in this field. Direct contact with the pedagogical experience of other countries has unquestionably had a salutary effect on the Romanian educational system.

Present civics curricula and textbooks are radically different from those of the preceding period. Stress is now laid not only upon the cognitive objectives of the discipline, but also on skills important in a democratic society. With each lesson, different points of view must be debated and a clear analysis made of everyday reality. Slogans and dogmatism are now obsolete. Constrained acceptance of an idea or theory must be replaced by a free conversation that makes it possible to develop the aptitude of young people for identifying problems and their ability to reach acceptable solutions.

The Course in Civic Culture

I outline here the objectives and course content of the course in civic culture as it is now taught to thirteen to fifteen year olds in Romania. The curriculum guide for this course is at present uniform throughout the country since the educational system remains centralized. The guide distinguishes among "general," "cognitive," and "educational" objectives as follows.

General objectives. The primary goal is to equip students with basic knowledge, skills, and attitudes that allow them to (1) take an active and responsible part in the economic, political, and social dimensions of a democratic society; (2) be aware of basic values and be able to choose among them; and (3) be aware of old and wrong mentalities and be able to transcend them.

Cognitive objectives. Students must acquire basic knowledge about surrounding reality and themselves. Therefore they should (1) have information on social relations; (2) know and understand similarities and differences among human beings and their implications (for example, the need for tolerance); (3) know civic rights and responsibilities based on source documents (declarations, conventions, constitution, students' code); (4) be aware of the functioning of the local community; and (5) understand major problems of the world.

Educational objectives. Students should acquire the following skills: (1) acting in a group (expressing one's own opinions and respecting opinions of others; (2) applying democratic procedures (negotiation, organized protests); (3) critical evaluation of information, social activities, and mentalities; (4) making decisions and understanding their impact on oneself and others; (5) exercising the individual's rights and defending the rights of others; (6) showing tolerance toward others—their features and attitudes.

The textbook content for the course includes such issues as human identity, social group dynamics, and patriotism. Eighth grade texts treat such topics as state constitution functions, human rights, democracy, and current social justice issues.

PROBLEMS IN THE TEACHING OF CIVICS

In Romanian society today, the need for civic education is urgent because the development of civic spirit is a condition of the democratic evolution of society. Democracy entails the responsible participation of citizens in the economic, political, and cultural life of the society, and such participation is impossible without civic education.

To understand the role that civic education must fill, we must first examine the needs and dysfunctions of Romanian society. Since 1989, the main preconditions for democratization have been met—separation of powers, institution of political pluralism, establishment of the legislative framework of fundamental rights and liberties. Still, democratization advances slowly. The society is confronted with a great number of problems that are at the same time consequences and causes of dysfunctions of the democratic government.

One of the most important of these is the insufficient participation of citizens in the life of the society, caused in part by the general confusion induced by the overturning of values, and by the clash between new and old mentalities. For example, old bad habits persist. One is the ideological approach that sees an undifferentiated whole where an individualized, ad hoc approach sees distinctions. Another is the ambiguity of conception that still afflicts the government platform. Another is the habitual lack of interest in political life.

A second major problem is the continuing lack of social cohesion and the tendency to disregard law and discipline. Closely related is the exponential growth of corruption. To some extent these problems are due to legislative deficiencies, to errors and dysfunctions in the government. But in great measure they are caused by the absence of a civic spirit and of prodemocratic behavior in Romanian society.

The main role of civic education must be to develop the sense of civic responsibility, of personal independence, cooperation, and tolerance. This must lead to willingness to observe the law and so reduce corruption and, finally, to social cohesion. Civic education must make civil rights and liberties not just a creed but an effective reality.

Democratic freedom of expression can be turned into its contrary in the absence of willing civic responsibility. No one would deny that freedom of speech should be a right in our society. But the exercise of this right in the absence of tolerance and responsibility can boomerang, and undermine the democracy. Thus, the confrontation of different political views in the mass media can take the form of false information, vituperation, and threats that create confusion and diminish the motivation of citizens' participation in political life instead of shaping enlightened opinions.

Unfortunately, the Ministry of Education, the present government, and the media are all too little concerned with these priorities. Nevertheless there are some prodemocratic organizations whose direct or indirect goal is civic education. In comparison with the huge need for civic education in Romanian society, the activity of these organizations is entirely insufficient. To deal with this problem it would seem imperative to organize a National Center for Civic Education which would join the prodemocratic forces interested in this field. Such a Center would be a governmental, nonprofit, nonpartisan organization with the major objective of analyzing, developing, and implementing civic education programs for youth that promote (1) better understanding of the principles and basic values of democracy; (2) better understanding of the functioning of democratic institutions; (3) codes of behavior necessary for effective and responsible participation as citizens, and (4) the ability to use democratic procedures to make decisions and resolve conflicts.

The activities of the Center would include (1) analysis of the values, norms, and institutions of democracy as well as nondemocratic practices and mentalities; (2) publication of reviews, booklets, and textbooks for civic education; (3) organization of symposia, competitions, conferences, camps for civic education (meetings between youth and members of Parliament jurists, government representatives); and (4) collaboration with the Ministry of Justice, Ministry of Education, media, civics educators of other countries, and with all persons concerned with these problems in the development and implementation of programs of civic education.

In addition to institutional limitations impeding the development of effective civic education, the prevailing political climate of Romania creates profound problems. The political community has its left and right, and each of these has its own agenda for civic education. Conservative groups stress the need for order and discipline, and observance of existing laws. Progressive groups support expansion of the role of civic education by teaching prodemocratic behavior, encouraging active participation in society, and in surmounting old mentalities. The former believe the basic objectives of civic education should be to teach obedience and conformity, while the latter would have civics teach critical understanding of laws, including the ability to see that some of them are obsolete, and encouraging active participation in the making of new legislation.

In the first months after the introduction of civics to the reformed educational system, some teachers were promoting political propaganda in the guise of civics lessons, supporting their party's platform by denigrating others. Some believed a legal institutional framework for political propagandizing had been created. The consequences were immediately visible: general confusion and increased conflicts among pupils, between pupils and teachers, and among teachers. Teachers had difficulty accepting the idea that the teaching of civic education requires methodological and scientific training. There was a period when everybody considered himself or herself capable of teaching civic education simply because everybody had a political platform that was infallible. The result was indoctrination and a repetition of history. The difference consisted in the fact that while under communism the pupils were all indoctrinated with the same communist ideology, they were now being indoctrinated with a range of left-wing and right-wing dogmas.

These teachers were not ill-intentioned. They reasoned that, to avoid the errors of the past, we must each indoctrinate our pupils with our own ideology. Since we all have different positions, we will remove the risk of all becoming partisans of the same ideology. Their reasoning was of course faulty, because its basis, in concealed form, was the same mechanism of indoctrination—the same demand that a given ideology be accepted as complete and perfect.

Civic education must, then, be based on political science and political philosophy and on no account on political propaganda. It must teach the art of identifying problems and questions to which pupils must freely give critical answers. It must not impose ideas, give unique and rigid answers, or "mold" pupils in an ideology. The teacher has a right to inform students about different ideologies but not to convert them to a single ideology, whatever its nature. Unfortunately, the identification of civic education with political propaganda has created problems in understanding that giving civic education a place in the Romanian educational system does not undermine or counteract the depoliticizing of that system.

A further problem is the insufficient methodological and scientific training of teaching staff. Some teachers are still caught up in the old mentalities, unable and in some cases unwilling to give up old stereotypes, patterns, and slogans with which they have been indoctrinated. Traditional methods—examination, writing about rather than experiencing or doing, and repetition have proven ineffective in conveying civic spirit. These methods need to be replaced by learning through exploration, role playing, case analysis, exercises, and brainstorming. But there are still many impediments to implementing these methods, among them undertrained teachers, huge classes (35-40 pupils), seriously inadequate space.

One partial solution for teacher training is to establish permanent contacts with teachers of civic education from the West. To this end, the chair of humanities and social sciences of the School Inspectorate of Bucharest organized an International Seminar on Civic Education in September 1993 at which American and French teachers were present as honored guests. The Civic Alliance, the Romanian Institute for Human Rights (IRDO), the Romanian Independent Society for Human Rights (SIRDO), and the organization Prodemocracy have held similar events especially emphasizing human rights. The national television channel has broadcast a series of lessons on civic education for teachers and pupils.

While all of these events were beneficial, such efforts must be increased, because the foothold of democratic enlightenment is precarious in Romania, where ideological fluctuation has a long history.

Chapter 6

EDUCATION IN THE CZECH REPUBLIC

John J. Lane

Education in the Czech Republic is in transition. Before 1989, the profile of the Czech educational system essentially matched those in other Central and Eastern European nations whose chief characteristics were: extreme centralization, a dominant Marxist ideology, underfunding, limited access to secondary and higher learning, huge inequities between urban and rural areas, and greater or lesser isolation from the international educational community. But, as I learned in a recent study visit to the Czech Republic, neither the government nor the educational community is eager to trade one rigid system for another in the name of reform. Thus, the transition is incremental yet noteworthy for its entrepreneurial spirit manifested in numerous educational experiments at the local school level.

There are other reasons to explain why educational reforms are not moving faster. Many Czech educators correctly point out that, for all its shortcomings, the old system did produce some good results, people with "a capacity of analysis, sound knowledge of the latest developments in their fields, and fluent command of at least two foreign languages" (Sandi, 1992, p. 630). They admit, however, that relatively few students received the full benefits of the educational system and that the values underlying the system may have been flawed. Further, while there may not be much regard for teachers and professors who for years were regarded as political appointees and puppets of the state, there is great respect for education. Traditionally, competition for access to college preparatory programs and higher education has been keen. No one wants precipitous change to jeopardize these values. Also, as the Czech Republic moves to a market economy, manpower studies are underway.

But both the government and educators seem to believe that it would be premature to predict what knowledge and skills will be needed in the future. Then too, the Czechs are increasingly aware that the United States and many other Western nations have their own educational crises and consequently are reluctant to look to them for solutions. They are content to wait to see what educational changes work.

As recent government documents attest, the Czechs hope to become a member of the European Union. The Czech Ministry of Education stipulates that one of its major goals is to develop an educational system that would qualify the nation for membership in the European Union. Yet, there is no rush to achieve this goal. Various news reports indicate that the Czech prime minister, Vaclav Klaus, has said that while his country seeks integration with Western Europe, it does not at this time want formal ties with the European Union. National pride may also be a factor contributing to the Czech Republic's reluctance to change too quickly. There is no denying that the Czech Republic is experiencing a mild wave of nationalism recalling and, perhaps romanticizing, its medieval past. The local and international press indicate that the Czechs relish being rediscovered as the cultural heart of Central Europe. It is no wonder that, for a time at least, this ancient but new nation will take a wait-and-see stance on educational reform.

The Czech Republic, a nation of about 10.5 million people, was created on January 1, 1993 following the dissolution of the near seventy-five year marriage with Slovakia. But the separation of the two territories pales by comparison with the unprecedented series of political events that led to the so-called Velvet Revolution in the fall of 1989. On November 17, 1989, within a few days of the fall of the Berlin Wall, mass demonstrations were held in Prague. A week later the Czechoslovakian Communist government collapsed. On December 29, 1989, Vaclav Havel, dissident playwright and recently freed political prisoner, was elected president of Czechoslovakia. Three years later he was elected president of the Czech Republic.

Between 1991 and 1992, numerous economic and social reforms were enacted. At that time, Vaclav Klaus, then serving as Finance Minister, privatized numerous state services, restored nationalized properties to their original owners, and abolished price and currency controls. But with the notable exception of two key education acts that restored traditional academic authority to universities and made precollegiate programs available to larger numbers of students, there has been little direct government involvement with the schools. While there have been a considerable number of educational reforms and innovative practices initiated throughout the Czech Republic, the government has not been the sole or even the major impetus for change.

The educational system of the 1980s in the lands now known as the Czech Republic was, as indicated, not unlike those in other Central and Eastern European nations, producing some well qualified individuals. Moreover, despite extreme centralization and underfunding, children and adults were motivated to attend school because they attached high value to education. But under Communist rule, what kinds of individuals was the system designed to produce? What was the place of critical thinking in a curriculum dedicated to forming personalities that conformed with communist morality? How did the educational system meet the needs of children with special needs and of women and minorities? And how accessible was the system to all its people? The Czechs acknowledge the need for change.

Before discussing what changes are on the horizon for Czech education, however, it may be useful to consider briefly some of the major accomplishments of the long and distinguished Czech educational history. While acknowledging the dangers of lapsing into reductionism and distorting history, I believe it is necessary to indicate that the educational system that will help to carry the Czech people into the twenty-first century is, in part, a product of a centuries-old interaction of national, cultural, political, and economic factors.

OVERVIEW OF THE CZECH EDUCATIONAL SYSTEM

Czech education began with the church schools of the ninth and tenth century monasteries. Lay schools were established in the thirteenth century. Charles University, the oldest university in Central Europe was founded in 1348. In 1556, a prototypical, Jesuit-run Latin gymnasium was founded. The modern Czech Technical University succeeds the Engineering Academy of the Estates which was founded in 1707, making it one of the oldest technical universities in Europe.

Compulsory six-year education was decreed as early as 1774. The law provided for two kinds of schools: "trivial schools" located largely in rural areas and "main schools" established in every governmental district. The trivial schools, founded as much for economic as for humanitarian reasons, combined mainstay subjects like reading, writing, mathematics, and religion with practical subjects like agricultural economy, sewing, and knitting. The main schools followed a curriculum of history, geography, Latin composition, drawing, and industry for the benefit of students who would later join the military or enter a trade. By 1869 a compulsory eight-year program for children aged six to fourteen was mandated. Then, with the creation of an independent Czechoslovak state in 1918, a common school system was completed and additional secondary schools and universities were established.

World War II created havoc for the schools. Basic school programs were curtailed or discontinued; many secondary schools and universities were summarily closed in 1939. Following the war, education under communist rule (1948-1989) was characterized by a series of reforms designed to mold education to the Soviet model. In the 1950s and 1960s, course content, instructional methods, the length of compulsory education, and even the names of schools were changed.

Throughout the Communist era, political and educational leaders made every effort to maintain ideologically pure socialism. Understandably, respect for teachers declined as they together with professors were increasingly perceived as mindless pawns of the state paid, albeit poorly, to parrot socialist maxims. Access to university education became a highly politicized process. For example, in 1971, the regime declared that "the selection of applicants must be clearly political in character. . . . We make no secret of the fact that we want to do this at the schools in a manner that will guarantee that future graduates will be supporters of socialism and that they will place their knowledge at the service of socialist society" (Nyrop, 1982, p. 110).

As the System became increasingly centralized, the power of the Ministry of Education extended beyond the basic and secondary schools even to the universities. Curricular uniformity was the order of the day. Few teachers or professors developed new courses, the Russian language was mandatory, critical thinking and innovation were discouraged. Yet, one should not conclude from these statements that the educational system produced poor results. On the contrary, literacy rates continued to improve. Students' achievement in mathematics and science education compared favorably with that in Western nations.

There are five levels in the Czech educational system: (1) nursery school, (2) kindergarten, (3) grammar school, (4) secondary schools, and (5) university.

Nursery schools and kindergartens. Established early in the nineteenth century, preschools are now administered by the health care sector of the government. Nursery school children may be as young as six months at entry and continue until they are three or four. The schools engage children in simple activities, often game-based or meal-related and designed to increase basic thinking and social skills. In 1948, preschool education was integrated into the educational system with the added objective to permit women to work outside the home. In the mid-1970s it was estimated that less than 10 percent of children under age three participated in the programs. At present, though this level of schooling is optional, if both parents work, as is increasingly the case, nursery school enrollment is expected to increase dramatically. For many years nursery schools were completely state supported, but the level of state support is predicted to decrease and parents expect soon to be charged tuition to underwrite some of the costs.

Like nursery school, kindergarten education is optional and, for now, largely state-supported. In the mid-1970s, nearly 70 percent of children aged three to six attended kindergarten. Some kindergartens, until recently supported by individual enterprises and cooperatives, have closed. It is now estimated that 84 percent of children of this age-group are in school (Kalous, 1993).

Ordinarily, children begin kindergarten at ages three or four and remain until they turn six. Czech kindergarten programs, consisting largely of activities to develop language, thinking, social and motor skills, closely resemble their counterparts in the United States. Many kindergartens provide all-day care with hours scheduled to coincide with the typical work day. Since 1992, a growing number of private and church-related nursery schools have been established to meet the increasing demand from working parents and to replace closed kindergartens.

Grammar schools. The third level of the Czech system is the equivalent of U.S. elementary education and is known variously as grammar school or basic school. It consists of two cycles or levels, grades 1 through 4 and grades 5 through 8. As in the United States, the primary grades are taught by one generalist teacher who instructs about four hours a day. First cycle students are expected to acquire fundamental knowledge of the Czech language, basic scientific principles, mathematics, civic and moral education, art and aesthetics, physical and health education. Work habits are taught; and, in the second cycle, students are prepared for advanced vocational education.

The second cycle continues many of the subjects taught in the first but adds courses such as chemistry, physics, history, and civics. Foreign language study begins at the second cycle with English being the language of choice of the majority of students. Each subject is taught by a specialist. Some basic schools have enriched or extended programs for talented students in language, mathematics, sports, dance, and fine arts.

Secondary schools. Three tracks are available to secondary students: (1) vocational schools that continue for two to four years depending on the level of knowledge and ability required by the profession; (2) secondary technical schools that prepare students for highly specialized professions like engineering, architecture, electronics as well as higher education, and (3) the gymnasium, which ordinarily lasts four years and is designed to prepare students for university education. The gymnasium has perhaps undergone more changes than any of the other levels of education. The first changes occurred in 1948 as a consequence of the Soviet occupation. Between 1968 and 1990, the grammar school became increasingly vocational and technical, a blend of Soviet-style education with a dash of liberal studies. Since 1990, the gymnasium curriculum has returned to its original design with an emphasis on the humanities, science, and general education including civic education. A matriculation examination is required for entry into Czech higher education.

In the recent past, quotas for entry into secondary schools were determined by the Ministry of Education or some other central agency. As indicated, access to precollegiate and collegiate education was a highly politicized process with preference given to children of members of the Communist Party. Children who professed any religious affiliation were dismissed from the gymnasium and excluded from certain professions like teaching. In 1990, approximately 6 percent of the basic school leavers entered the ninth grade. By 1993 over 30,000 or nearly 32 percent of eighth-graders entered ninth grade. Today the number entering ninth grade continues to grow. Interestingly, by contrast with some other

Central and Eastern European nations, over 50 percent of the students
in the college preparatory programs are female.

Higher education. Higher education in the Czech Republic consists
of a complex of faculties akin to colleges in a university in the United
States. Each faculty has its own curriculum requirements and professors.
Courses of study are organized on two levels, basic and specialist. Basic
programs provide core programs of study and exposure to the requirements of specialized areas of study. Ordinarily specialization in what in
the United States would be called one's "major" begins in the fourth
year. Higher education programs in the Czech Republic last between
four and six years. But as the cost of higher education escalates and as
the likelihood that students will be expected to share the financial burden of their education increases, college completion may take longer.

Typical university faculties include: the arts (languages, philosophy,
sociology, and, since 1989, history, political science, and aesthetics); med-
icine; law; science (biology, chemistry, and physics); education with
departments dedicated to each level of the Czech educational system;
and world economics (another curricular innovation since 1989). Courses
of study for teachers vary with their desired level of teaching. Teachers
preparing for the lower level basic schools study four years and, if successful, are awarded a master's degree. Secondary school teachers are
generally required to take a five-year program that also culminates with a
master's degree with specialization in two fields of study.

Founded in the early fourteenth century, Charles University remains
arguably the premiere university in Central Europe. In 1945, the former
Czechoslovakia had eleven higher education institutions with forty-four faculties and nearly 55,000 students. Eight of these institutions were located in
what is now the Czech Republic. After 1948, under communist rule, Czech
and Slovakian schools at every level lost their autonomy and were reorganized and staffed by personnel sympathetic with communist ideology. Also,
curricula at every level including the university were changed dramatically.
Today, according to Kalous (1993, p. 11) there are twenty-three institutions
of higher education with 100 faculties and over 100,000 students represent-
ing 15 percent of the nineteen-to-twenty-four-year-old population. Forty-
five percent of those enrolled in higher education are female.

Among the major challenges facing Czech education today, one of
the most acute concerns how to make secondary education, especially

college-preparatory programs, available to more students. With the same entrepreneurial spirit noted at the outset of this chapter, the Czechs are meeting the challenge. Alternative schools, including church-related private schools approved by the Czech Ministry of Education, are cropping up everywhere and especially in Prague and other urban areas. In sharp contrast to government schools, alternative schools make special efforts to meet the needs of individual students and, as a result, are becoming centers for curricular reform. Since there were only seven alternative schools by the end of 1991, it is too soon to predict what lasting effects these schools will have on the Czech system, teachers, curriculum, and administration.

PRVNI OBNOVEN REALNE GYMNASIUM (PORG)

By arrangements made through the courtesy of the American consulate in Prague, I was able to visit PORG, the first and best known independent school in the Czech Republic. Housed in rented space, a 1896 former public school building, the PORG project, Prvni Obnovene Realne Gymnasium, or Real Gymnasium for short, began in January 1990 immediately following the Velvet Revolution. Lending tacit approval to its existence, the Czech Minister of Education attended the school's dedication. According to its first headmaster, Ondrej Steffl, PORG is a highly selective eight-year high school, modeled after "Reform Secondary Schools" common in Czechoslovakia between the two World Wars. The program reflects a strong nineteenth-century German influence. The school is designed to allow students access to educational programs that balance classical studies with scientific studies. The Real Gymnasium programs are touted as a cure for the restrictive "unimaginative State regulated curriculum," according to Steffl. Class size is limited to twenty-two students. State schools have about forty in each class. There is a conscious effort among faculty and administrators to create a school atmosphere which is at once informal and highly charged. That is, students, ten to eighteen years old, are encouraged not so much to compete with one another as to challenge themselves to higher levels of achievement. Entry to the school is highly competitive with seven hundred students applying for about a hundred and sixty places.

Teachers in this school are a breed apart. Most of them are in their late twenties and early thirties; half of them hold the Ph.D. Teaching positions at this and other independent schools are competitive. Higher pay, smaller classes, and greater autonomy make these schools very desirable to teachers long disenchanted with state schools. When the school started, there were thirty applicants for each grade level. Because books and curricular materials are scarce, teachers resort to developing their own curriculum guides and supportive materials. Providing scope and sequence in the curriculum is an informal matter. Teachers gather at hastily called meetings to debate what students' educational requirements for a particular class might be, a process that I witnessed in a makeshift common room for teachers.

The curriculum is indeed broad and rich. For example, in addition to the Czech language, English, Latin, French, Spanish, German, Japanese and a variety of foreign literature courses are taught. Interestingly, while Russian is no longer required, English is required because it is viewed as a key to future employment. Science includes biology, chemistry, physics, geology, paleontology, and gynecology. The history of religions, forbidden under communist rule, now enjoys a special place in the curriculum. However, in reaction to the years when "civics" meant lessons in communist propaganda, it is not included in the curriculum. Music also figures prominently in the educational program. Numerous educational and cultural exchange programs are also offered. Memorization, a staple of Soviet-style classroom technique, has been abandoned in favor of creativity and critical thinking.

Tuition is expensive, about 10,000 korunas or the equivalent of two months' income for the average Czech worker. But parents invest their time as well as their money in the school. They are expected to attend monthly "Open Saturdays" where they can meet with teachers and participate in a variety of educational conferences. Headmaster Steffl encourages parents to find and donate pre-World War II textbooks, "At least they are not full of lies," he says. The school relies on parents to make key decisions affecting the budget, raise funds for scholarships, and elect the headmaster—the duties of local school boards in decentralized school systems in the United States.

Currently no laws exist to govern the establishment of independent schools. Neither are there not-for-profit guidelines for corporate donors and others interested in supporting the independent school movement. About one third of the Real Gymnasium's budget comes from the Czech government's Ministry of Education. For now, the independent schools have freedoms that far exceed, say, the powers of local school councils that resulted from U.S. school reform efforts. However, the Ministry of Education is considering some sort of approval process for independent schools. At the same time, the Ministry seeks to develop some sort of regional or statewide accreditation process for all schools similar to the Mid-Atlantic and North Central Accrediting Associations in the United States.

CHANGE AND EDUCATIONAL PROSPECTS

The independent school movement is a major reason to hope for systemic reform of the Czech educational system. Yet no one knows for certain that the movement that began only recently with one school and since has grown to a loose network of over four hundred schools will attain its goals to prepare more students for higher education, help them to enter productive careers, and instill in them a desire for lifelong learning. Systematic study of the alternative and independent schools is a long way off.

There are other important, though less-publicized, signs of change that should be noted. For example, salaries and working conditions for teachers have improved as a result of the combined efforts of the Ministry of Education, the pedagogical faculties of universities and parents. Professional improvement in the form of postgraduate study, institutes, and short-term study opportunities are also more available to teachers now than in the past.

Principals, whose appointments under Communist rule were based more on their loyalty to the Party than their competence, now compete for their jobs. Many of the new principals enjoy good reputations as teachers, but few have had formal administrative training which creates special problems for them as increasingly authority and responsibility devolves to them from regional and central education offices.

Teachers and administrators have considerably more freedom to design courses and select books and curricular materials than they did five years ago. However, without a significant increase in resources, these and other new freedoms cannot be exercised to their fullest.

Other curricular changes may be identified in both lower and higher education. The special status ascribed to the Russian language and culture in the secondary schools and universities has been greatly diminished.

Students may now select from a wide variety of language and literature courses. If any foreign language study dominates the schools, it is English and that for business reasons. Similarly, the almost exclusive emphasis on Marxism and socialism has been replaced by a balanced study of world politics and comparative economic theories.

Greater attention is being paid to the needs of students with educational and physical handicaps. In the past, the educational system segregated special students from the others. Since 1990, efforts are underway to "mainstream" special students into the regular schools wherever possible. My interviews with key administrators in the Ministry of Education and at the Institute for the Development of Education at Charles University revealed keen interest in U.S. Public Law 94-142 on the free and appropriate education of handicapped children.

The role of parents in the school is being redefined. In the recent past, parents were almost systematically excluded from the schools except to perform menial tasks. Today there is greater recognition of the fact that the quality of a child's education is a function of close collaboration among the home, school, and community. Parents will soon have a greater voice in the governance of the state schools as well. Parents in the alternative and independent schools already play a decisive role in school management, including hiring the principal and overseeing the budget.

As indicated earlier, more students who leave eighth grade enter ninth grade than was the case in former years. Several recent government reports show that access to college preparatory programs and higher education has improved dramatically over the last five years.

Officially, education in the Czech Republic is free. Students enjoy special rates for transportation between home and school. Free medical care and some scholarship money is available for indigent students. This situation will soon change. Government officials predict that even with massive aid from the West, the Czech peoples will shortly have to assume some, as yet undetermined, share of the cost of their education. Capital improvements will be a major drain on the public purse. Schools will have to compete with other government agencies for scarce korunas to replace dilapidated buildings and a crumbling infrastructure left largely untended for the last five decades.

Educational opportunities for women have improved in terms of access to higher education, but the place of women in Czech society is as problematic as it is in the Western world. Treatment of minorities like Gypsies (or Roma, as they prefer to be called) presents still another challenge to the educational and economic system of the new democracy. Many of the Roma were brought to the Czech Republic (Bohemia) from their native Slovakia as unskilled laborers. As factories have closed in some of the smaller towns, unemployment has risen dramatically among the Roma. Unemployment estimates in some towns run as high as 60 percent for the Roma in a nation with a general unemployment rate of about 4 percent. As of January 1, 1993, following the breakup of Czechoslovakia, the Roma have to apply for citizenship in order to qualify for social benefits like unemployment compensation and education. The current application procedures make it very difficult for Roma to qualify.

There is now no unifying vision for a national educational system in the Czech Republic. One sign that the Czech Republic is in no rush to develop such a vision is that in the last five years it has had three ministers of education each of whom represented quite different philosophies of education. At this writing, however, new education law is being developed especially in the areas of school finance and educational policies in an effort to make education more accessible to a greater number of students and to give greater autonomy to local schools. These legislative efforts in combination with the cumulative innovative effects of the growing number of alternative and independent schools may well produce an educational system worthy of the high moral, political, and economic aspirations of a dynamic new democracy.

REFERENCES

Kalous, Jaroslav. "The Educational System of the Czech Republic." Unpublished paper. Prague: Institute for the Development of Education, 1993.

Nyrop, Richard F., ed. *Czechoslovakia: A Country Study*. Washington, D.C.: Headquarters, Department of the Army, 1982.

Sandi, Ana M. "Why Is It So Difficult? Misconceptions about Eastern European Education in Transition," *International Review of Education* 38, no. 6 (1992): 620-639.

Chapter 7

REFORM AND DEVELOPMENT IN TEACHER EDUCATION IN ISRAEL

Tamar Ariav and Aaron Seidenberg

This chapter deals with the current state of teacher education in Israel in a sociopolitical context. We begin by providing a general background of the complexity of Israeli society and a portrait of the educational system. We then describe the present situation of the teacher education system as an outgrowth of historical developments in response to social changes and educational reforms. In the third part of the chapter, we present Beit Berl College as a case study illustrative of the issues discussed earlier. We conclude with a critical analysis of the present situation and a consideration of possible future developments.

THE COMPLEXITY OF ISRAELI SOCIETY

Israel is a small and young country beset with security and economic problems. Established in 1948 as a home for the Jewish people, it has continuously attracted Jews from countries where they were persecuted and harassed. Survivors of the Holocaust, refugees from Asian and African countries, and immigrants from all over the world have contributed to the cultural mosaic that makes up Israeli society. Tensions have always existed between ethnic groups whose religious customs, social traditions, languages, and political cultures differ greatly from one another. Ideological conflicts in the interpretation of the meaning of a welfare state and disagreements about religious orientations have manifested themselves in rival political parties, in types of settlements such as kibbutz and moshav, and in multiple educational systems. Moslem and Christian Arabs, Druze, and Bedouins, who are all citizens of Israel, compose about 18 percent of the population and contribute to the multidimensional patchwork of the society.

The ongoing Arab-Israeli conflict is a major aspect of life in Israel. Serving in the army is compulsory for men and women (with some limited exceptions). Military service comes before the start of higher education and continues with reserve duty through college or university and beyond for many years. Security expenses amount to 17 percent of the GNP and security-related issues occupy the news constantly. The peace agreement with Egypt in 1978, the Declaration of Principles recently signed between Israel and the PLO, and the accord with Jordan in 1994 are examples of Israel's desire to reach peace in the region and of the changing political scene in the Middle East.

Israel is a democratic society that has experienced a number of significant political changes in its relatively short history. These all occurred during a period of major social change. The first occurred in 1977 when the Labor party lost to the right-wing Likud party, reflecting social dissatisfaction of the Sephardi Jews (mostly of North African and Middle Eastern origin) with the dominant Ashkenazi establishment (mostly of European and Anglo-Saxon origin). The second occurred in 1992 when the Labor party once again took office, replacing the Likud party as the head of the government at a time when the crucial issue at stake was that of the peace process.

In many ways, Israeli lifestyle is western and strongly reflects the influence of American and European cultures. This is expressed in consumption and marketing of goods, research, technology, agriculture, and industry. Educational fads are imported from abroad and reforms in the United Kingdom and the United States, in particular, have left their mark on the Israeli educational system.

Education has always been held in high esteem in Israeli society and in Jewish tradition, and the value placed on education and educational issues is consequently at the heart of social and political discourse. In the last thirteen years, the educational system from nursery school to college has gone through major transformations that have also had an impact on teacher education. These changes are described below with the focus on the system of teacher education.

THE EDUCATIONAL SYSTEM

In 1953, the State restructured the educational system, doing away
with the separate ideological school boards that existed in the pre-state
Jewish community. Public schooling was divided into three sectors: Jewish secular, Jewish religious, and Arab. In addition, some ultraorthodox
Jewish streams have kept their own independent educational system.
These formal divisions still exist today, with the Jewish secular sector the
largest. By 1986, the Ministry of Education controlled the education of
93.5 percent of all kindergarten and elementary students and 96.5 percent of all high school students (Gotlieb, 1991).

Compulsory education has been slowly extended from grades 1
through 8 in 1953 to pre-kindergarten through 10th grade today, but
public education is free until the end of 12th grade. The K-8 and 9-12
system was redivided in the late 1960s into preschool programs for four
and five year olds, elementary school for grades 1-6, junior high school
for grades 7-9, and senior high school for grades 10-12. The main reason
for this reform was twofold: (a) the recognition that as massive waves of
immigration ceased, primary schooling no longer seemed sufficient; and
(b) the realization that the educational system had perpetuated rather
than closed the socioeconomic gap between Ashkenazi and Sephardi
populations (Gotlieb, 1991). This structural reform, which focused on
the new junior high school and its differential and compensatory curriculum, had a significant impact on teacher education, as we shall
explain. In 1992, the Ministry of Education extended its control over the
education of children by including programs for two- and three-year-
olds under its supervision.

The school curriculum is centrally controlled by the Ministry of Education in a variety of programs and policies. These include curriculum
frameworks, approved curriculum materials, curriculum development
projects, curriculum initiatives, national testing and assessment, and the
high school matriculation examination (which is the prerequisite for
applying to institutions of higher education). During the last decade the
Ministry has relinquished some of its centralized power by delegating
more autonomy to local school districts and allowing individual schools to
design their own curriculum as long as 75 percent of the curriculum
adheres to the State's framework. This was accompanied by expressions
of parental choice of schools and opportunities for individual and local

control. In fact, this transfer reflects two phenomena: (a) the decreasing ability of the Ministry to continue its centralized control because of diminishing resources while the educational system continued to grow, and (b) the changing political climate when the Labor party lost its long influence over the educational agenda. This last point is a common experience in societies when a more conservative and right-wing government takes over from a more social-democratic one (Holt, 1993).

The teaching force has suffered from a continuous decline in the socioeconomic status of the teaching profession over the last two decades (Eddy, 1992). Teachers' prestige scores relatively low among the professions, especially for elementary and junior high school teachers. Teaching is still perceived as a feminized profession with convenient working hours for the family's "second wage earner."

Higher education in Israel takes place in public institutions for higher learning: universities, technological and agricultural schools, scientific and art institutes, and undergraduate colleges for education and management. Generally, undergraduate studies include three- or four-year programs focusing extensively on one or two subjects. Universities offer graduate studies at the master's and doctorate levels. All institutions are accredited by the Council for Higher Education (CHE), which is the supreme authority for higher education issues and policies. The members of the CHE, headed by the Minister of Education, are representatives of the more established institutions, primarily universities. The power of the Ministry of Education is exerted through the budgeting process of higher education and the role of the Education Minister in the CHE's work.

Until very recently, the CHE acted much as a "gate keeper" to higher education, making it hard for tertiary nonacademic institutions to join the exclusive club. Such institutions, which offered many teacher education programs, found themselves in difficult straits when pressure was put on them to improve. Their transformation into bonafide academic (degree granting) institutions has been slow and painful. The CHE was not fully aware of major social, political, and economic developments that were working against its exclusionary policy and undermining its "guild" orientation.

Around 1990 the system of higher education entered a stage of crisis for which there are visible and hidden reasons (Gotlieb and Chen, 1992). Funding for higher education decreased drastically from 1973 until the mid-1980s because of economic difficulties. The universities struggled by cutting faculty positions (especially those of younger and beginning academics), limiting expansion to a minimum, and restructuring. However, the ever-growing demand for higher education, which stems from the public school reform and a changing demand for educational opportunities in higher education, could not be satisfied in times of decreasing means. Other reasons for the crisis are the change of the professoriate in terms of academic ethos (from a European tradition to a North American standard) and the change in the age gap (a large body of old guard and a small group of young faculty). Finally, the student body also changed in terms of numbers, social strata, ethnic background, range of academic achievements, and instrumental views of studying in higher education.

In 1992, the Ministry of Education responded to the developing crisis by initiating a long-range plan to open ten new comprehensive colleges around the country by the end of the decade. These undergraduate, liberal arts colleges need to be accredited by the CHE and are expected to open within the next few years. This massive initiative is yet another example of the political power of the Ministry of Education and its central role in reshaping Israeli society. The decision to democratize higher education calls for a major transformation of postsecondary studies (Chen, Gotlieb, and Yakir, 1993). It is already influencing the curriculum in some of the teachers colleges which are among the ten sites selected for general undergraduate studies, and will probably affect the entire Israeli teacher education world, since potential candidates might choose the new alternative for a more generalized higher education over the current teacher education options.

THE TEACHER EDUCATION SYSTEM

The Structure of the System

At present, three types of institutions have teacher education programs:

1. *Departments of teacher education in universities* prepare teachers for junior and senior high schools. Students can either enroll in a postbaccalaureate one-year program or begin their training in the third year of studies toward an undergraduate degree and study for two years.

In both tracks, students enter the teacher education program after establishing a strong disciplinary basis, and their studies center around education and pedagogy. Upon graduation they are awarded a B.A./B.Sc. degree and a teaching diploma. One university offers a B.A. in teaching in a special three-year program. In 1990, 1500 student teachers received a baccalaureate and teaching diploma. Of those, 765 studied in the five universities that have teacher education programs. Since then, the universities are sustaining or losing the number of students enrolled in their teacher education programs while the number of graduates from the teachers colleges is increasing.

2. *"Academic" colleges for teacher education* (those authorized by the CHE to grant an undergraduate degree) prepare teachers for early childhood education, for elementary and junior high schools, and for special education. Students study four years and their program includes simultaneous study of subject matter and pedagogy. Graduates receive a B.Ed. degree and a teaching certification.

There are today eight fully accredited such programs and five more stand to be accredited in the immediate future. In 1991, there were 14,678 students in the 31 teacher training colleges in the country. Of these, 9,540 were enrolled in the eight "academic" colleges. These colleges reflect historical, ideological, religious, and career-choice differences. For example, two colleges are sponsored by the Kibbutz Movement. There is a college that prepares teachers for the public religious schools. Another college prepares teachers to teach physical education; and another prepares teachers to teach in vocational schools.

3. *Nonacademic colleges* prepare teachers in three-year programs for the same grades and populations as the academic colleges and in a similar intertwined curriculum. Graduates of these programs do not receive an undergraduate degree; upon graduation they are awarded only a teaching diploma. In 1991, the twenty-three nonacademic colleges prepared 35 percent of all prospective teachers enrolled in teachers colleges. These institutions differ from one another in ideological and religious orientations.

The ideological affiliation of some teachers colleges reflects the multidimensional nature of Israeli society. This phenomenon is unique to the colleges, primarily because of their historical development. (Ideological affiliation does not exist in the universities.) For example, the two colleges that prepare teachers according to the kibbutz ideology were established prior to the State in a period when Socialist-Zionist ideology was very dominant. They were affiliated with social and political streams rather than with the existing universities. There is still a significant impact today of the kibbutz ideology on the curriculum and philosophy of these teacher education colleges (Dror, 1992a).

Israeli Arabs study in most university and college programs, but they also have two institutions which prepare teachers specifically for teaching in Arab schools, primarily in the elementary grades and in early childhood programs. The two Arab teacher education colleges are now in the process of moving from certificate-granting to degree-granting institutions, as are some of the other colleges seeking to achieve the higher status termed here as "academic."

Teacher education is highly controlled by the Ministry of Education, especially in the academic and nonacademic colleges. Since the Ministry grants the teaching certificate, it dictates part of the teacher education curriculum and requires administrative accountability. The Ministry also developed the entrance examination for college candidates and decided on a cut-off point for that test. Based on supply and demand forecasts, the Ministry decides on annual quotas for each college and on the extension, elimination, or reduction of departments in the colleges. The Ministry subvents the budgets of the colleges while universities are budgeted through a central committee of the Council of Higher Education. This total control of teacher education by the government has been a major obstacle to long-term planning, administrative autonomy, and academic development in the colleges.

In a small country such as Israel it is surprising to find such a stratified and complex teacher education system. However, the introductory comments of this chapter shed some light on the situation, and the historical review that follows later explains much of this ambiguity.

Student Population

Students are admitted to most teacher education programs (except for Arab or religious programs) after military service. In the colleges the average age of freshmen is 21 to 22, and 89 percent are women. (In early childhood and elementary education 100 percent are women.) In 1991, 89 percent had a complete matriculation diploma from high school and 11 percent were admitted temporarily until they complete the missing exams (Kfir and Feigin, 1992). Students enrolled in the colleges for teacher education generally score lower on the entrance examination than those enrolled in university undergraduate studies (Kfir, Fresko, and Arnon, 1992). Examination of the universities' catalogues shows that this gap exists mainly between the teachers colleges and the prestigious university departments but is very small when compared with other undergraduate departments. It seems, therefore, that the teachers colleges have difficulties in attracting the highest level of the student population (Ariav, Kfir, and Feigin, 1993).

The students come from diverse ethnic and socioeconomic backgrounds and many of them apply to the academic colleges as a "second choice" when they realize that they would not be admitted to the more prestigious departments in the universities (Oshrat, 1991). About half of the graduates do not enter the teaching profession upon graduation or they leave teaching within five years (Oshrat, 1991).

Faculty

In the university, the teacher education faculty usually includes a small, regular tenure-track staff, who also teach in other university departments and engage in research, and instructors who are often veteran teachers and doctoral students. Since university programs are not responsible for teaching prospective teachers subject matter knowledge, the faculty teach only foundation and methods courses. The teaching load is eight semester courses per year and salaries are low (the median annual income of academics is about $21,400 [Chen, Gotlieb, and Yakir, 1993]). Tenure and promotion procedures emphasize research over teaching, and determine salary level and benefits. University faculty have an independent union to which teacher education instructors belong. Teacher education departments, as in other countries, are often weak in the university hierarchy as well as in their own schools of education.

Faculty in the colleges is composed of three types of instructors: subject matter teachers, educational foundation teachers, and general or subject-specific methods teachers. The first and second groups of instructors include professionals whose doctoral or master's degrees are not necessarily connected to education, but rather are awarded in a specific discipline such as sociology and psychology in educational foundations, and mathematics and geography in the disciplinary domain. Methods instructors usually have school experience and a master's degree. The faculty body is significantly larger than in universities because of the size of the college programs some institutions having over 600 instructors on the payroll. The teaching load in the colleges is double that in the universities and research funds are not easily available. College faculty members are employed by the Ministry of Education or by the colleges that function as corporations, and their union is the same as that of teachers in the school system. Tenure criteria focus on teaching quality and are bound to the union regulations; there are no promotion ranks, and salary is determined by level of education and years of teaching experience. Approximately 35 percent of the faculty in all teacher training colleges have doctorates, 60 percent have master's degrees, and the rest have professional equivalencies or are under standard (Kfir and Libman, in press).

DEVELOPMENT STAGES IN TEACHER EDUCATION IN ISRAEL

The major dilemma in the history of teacher education in Israel has been the tension between the "academization" and "humanization" orientations—between emphasizing the disciplinary content and scientific knowledge needed by novice and experienced teachers and emphasizing pedagogy and the personal development of the learner in the classroom as well as that of the student teacher (Dror, 1992b). Another persisting dilemma is how to prepare teachers to deal with the multicultural and conflict-laden society of Israel (Ben-Peretz and Dror, 1992). Policy decisions made in relation to these dilemmas have shaped teacher education conceptually and practically. The following historical summary of the development of teacher education illustrates these dilemmas and highlights major issues that confront teacher education in Israel. The development of teacher education in Israel can be divided into five stages.

Pre-1948. The prevailing conception underlying teacher education in the period preceding the establishment of the State was based on the Central European, and especially the German, tradition. This approach emphasized field experience and the integration of subject matter and pedagogic studies. It was carried out in a few high schools where teacher training and secondary education were combined. The opening of a pedagogic department in the Hebrew University in Jerusalem in 1936 was a turning point in the monolithic perception of teacher education in the country. The department was established in order to address the growing need for secondary school teachers as waves of Jewish refugees from Europe arrived in the country. It also reflected the budding social debate about the need to separate teacher training from high school studies and make it more professional. The department was created with a strong American/British orientation, which, contrary to the European view of teacher education, regarded teacher education as an academic field for professionals (Ben-Peretz and Dror, 1992). The European-American dichotomy and the high school-post-secondary distinction typified later thinking and policymaking (Gotlieb, 1991).

A distinctive feature of the pre-state period was the fact that despite the low level of teacher training, the profession itself was perceived as highly prestigious (Orbach, 1976). This was partly due to the particular conditions of the Jewish community at that time, and partly because of the potent Jewish ethos that places a high premium on learning and teaching.

1948-1962. The rapid growth of the Israeli population in the early years of the State brought about an acute shortage of professional teaching personnel. Unqualified people were hired to teach, quick courses were offered as alternatives to teacher training, and teacher dropout increased (Dror, 1992b). The most significant change in this period was the separation of teacher education from the high school and the transformation of the existing programs into two-year postsecondary institutions called "seminars." These programs, which resembled the normal schools, required that candidates complete high school and focus their study according to the age of students and the clusters of subject matter that they would eventually teach (for example, the upper elementary grades/math and science track).

The first Minister of Education, Professor Dinour, initiated in 1952 a symposium on teacher education in which he advocated the notion of "academizing" teacher education by affiliating the teacher seminars with the university. The idea fell victim to the philosophical disagreements between the seminars and the universities about the academic vs. humanistic-pedagogic nature of the programs. The seminars also feared losing their ideological orientation once they would be taken over by the university.

1962-1979. When mass immigration was tapering off and a process of stabilization was setting in, attention was again given to the nature and quality of teacher education. The Dushkin Committee Report, based on studies of teacher education in the United States, England, and other countries, recommended a revision of the training schemes. It suggested concentrating teacher education in a few large institutions, lengthening the preparation period to three years, tightening the curriculum, increasing admissions requirements, changing the selection of teacher educators and their teaching load, and establishing a standing council to examine and promote ways to "academize" the profession (Dekel, 1982).

While most of the recommendations were implemented by the mid-1960s under the supervision of the Ministry of Education, the recommendation relating to the promotion of "academization" was rejected by the Ministry, which refused to relinquish its responsibility to another authority. Whether consciously or inadvertently, these recommendations led to another interesting development (Ariav and Seidenberg, 1992). The elite of graduates from the seminars, who were admitted on a personal basis to undergraduate programs in the universities and completed their academic studies, did not stay in teaching in kindergarten through grade 8. Rather, they used their newly acquired knowledge to move "up" to teach in high schools. Hence, the hope that the reform would create a substantially better cadre of teachers for primary schools was not fulfilled.

A significant catalyst in the reform of teacher education in this stage was the restructuring of the school system and the creation of the junior high schools that would include grades 7 and 8 and the freshman year of high school. Teachers in these schools were expected to have a better grounding in subject matter and their preparation had to be more academically rigorous, similar to the training provided in the universities (Praver, 1965). The operational translation of the school reform to teacher education was devised by the Peled Commission in 1976, which called for changes both in the university and the seminar programs. Some seminars arranged an accreditation system with a university to grant a baccalaureate degree, but others introduced on their own a new course of study for the preparation of junior high school teachers.

1979-1991. Toward the end of the 1970s, discontent grew with the process of teacher education and with the decreasing social status of the teaching profession. The tension between the teacher education programs in the universities and the seminars became more acute. The Ministry of Education refused to allow the universities to open elementary school training programs because of their strong academic orientation. At the same time, recruiting highly qualified students for the seminar programs became difficult because the universities would not give credit for coursework completed in the seminars to those wishing to enroll for a B.A. degree program. Many bright students were dissuaded from studying in the teacher education seminars by the fact that it was not part of the process of accumulating "academic capital" (Gotlieb, 1991).

It was the 1979 Etzioni Commission, headed by a supreme court justice of that name, that resulted in a breakthrough in the previously held conception of teacher education. While earlier attempts sought to establish closer links between the universities and the seminars on the basis of unequal partnership, the Etzioni Commission suggested turning the seminars into academic institutions. In addition to reiterating earlier suggestions for change, such as raising admission requirements and the quality of the faculty, reducing the number of training seminars, and bringing the curriculum more in line with academic norms, the Commission further recommended the setting up of uniform standards of pedagogical training for *all* age groups (Etzioni, 1981). The academization of the profession was perceived as an important step in enhancing its status specifically and improving education in general.

This time, the Ministry of Education adopted the recommendations of the Etzioni Commission and asked the CHE to devise a model for implementation. Following the British reform of teacher education in the late 1960s (Mann, 1979; Evans, 1985), the CHE suggested guidelines for the academization process of the five largest seminars. These selected institutions were to become teachers colleges authorized to grant a B.Ed. degree to students completing a new four-year program, irrespective of the particular grade level of teaching certification earned (Chen and Gotlieb, 1989). The guidelines outlined the new curriculum structure and content, stated specific and higher admissions thresholds, and explicitly described the required faculty profile (CHE, 1981). The guidelines, however, failed to address issues of academic governance and decision making, finances and budgets, academic resources and facilities, as well as ways to implement effectively the guidelines and the

supervisory processes for performance evaluation (Ariav and Seidenberg, 1992).

The academization started with five (and then extended to eight)
large institutions in the early 1980s. Early in its deliberations the CHE
emphasized the limited scope of this process and directed the creation
of a small elite of the teaching force. The psychological reason behind
this move was the belief that the new degree could reach a high status if
it would become exclusive and match the university's B.A. The economic
reason for this decision was the fear that the cost of opening academic
programs for all prospective teachers would be very high. However,
these bureaucratic decisions could not withstand the social forces that
were pushing to transform the entire teaching force rather than creating
an elite cadre. The trade union movement and the society at large saw
the academic colleges as providing avenues for social mobility and new
alternatives for entering higher education. With an overwhelming number of students applying to the colleges, the concept of an elite became
the "norm." This unanticipated development helped to change the profession and to elicit increased financial support from the Ministry of
Education.

The "pioneer" colleges targeted for this new development were left
to interpret and apply the guidelines on their own, receiving their academic status piecemeal. Every college had to receive a separate accreditation for each department from the CHE—a long and tedious process
that took ten years. By 1991, the eight colleges were almost fully acade-
mized, and although they still offered the nonacademic three-year program, fewer and fewer students opted to take it. Since the early 1990s,
the majority of students in teacher education programs in Israel have
been enrolled in "academic" programs and graduate with a baccalaureate and a teaching diploma. Yet, while the academization process was in
full swing, graduates holding B.Ed. degrees encountered difficulties in
applying for graduate studies because their B.Ed. programs did not
include prerequisites for admission to the universities. It was then that
the colleges and their students realized that the B.Ed. degree in Israel is
a "step degree" of its prestigious sisters—the B.A. and B.Sc.

Parallel to the reform in preservice education, efforts are being
made to "academize" the teaching force. Practicing certified teachers in
preschool programs, elementary schools, and junior high schools, who
do not have an academic degree, are encouraged and receive incentives

to complete their studies toward a baccalaureate. They can do so in either the academic colleges or in the universities. The majority choose the colleges. The growing numbers of "returning teachers" flooded the academic colleges in the last few years (Mor, 1993), raising new problems ranging from curriculum and staffing to budgetary concerns. These numbers, though, are still a drop in the bucket considering the large percentage of teachers without either an academic degree or teaching certification in the Israeli school system. In 1992, only 21 percent of all elementary school teachers, 61 percent of all junior high school teachers, and 33 percent of all special education teachers had attained academic degrees, and in the last decade the percentage of noncertified teachers dropped from 16 to 8 percent (Israeli Government Bureau of Statistics, 1993).

1991-present. The 1991-92 academic year marked an end of the era of a major transformation in the development of teacher education in Israel. That year the eight academic colleges held a symposium to examine legal, financial, and political issues that have impeded their progress and academic freedom. They created a forum for the heads of the academic colleges that, together with officials from the Ministry of Education, searched for ways to discuss and solve lingering problems.

In 1991-92 the CHE established an evaluation committee to examine the accomplishments of the academic colleges. The committee reviewed the curricula of the colleges and concluded that generally they fulfilled the CHE's guidelines (Keidar, 1992). However, the committee criticized various curricular issues and recommended that the colleges collaborate in developing a core curriculum for the subject areas. Most important were the suggestions that the colleges need to become full-fledged and academically autonomous institutions through a change in the Law of the CHE, and that the college faculty need to have promotion levels similar to those of the university. The last recommendation suggested that evaluation performance for tenure and promotion should be based on excellence in teaching with some attention to applied research. The heads of the colleges have been working on these issues very seriously since the report was published and have managed thus far to have a representative in the CHE.

During the same year, the Ministry launched a large-scale study to assess the impact of the academization process on the colleges and on the actual work of teachers in the schools. This study, headed by a team of researchers from four of the academic colleges and the Hebrew University in Jerusalem, is now in its fourth year. The study first examined the changes that have occurred in the academic colleges in the process of academization with regard to the teacher education curriculum, student population, faculty, facilities, and structural and functional issues. It also looked at the perceptions of school teachers and administrators about the importance and meaning of the academization of the profession. Next, the focus will turn to exploring whether academic teachers teach any differently than those not holding academic degrees, since the rhetoric of the reform was built on the assumption that improved teacher education would result in better schooling. The findings thus far show that the colleges have indeed made significant progress in most of the studied areas, but these efforts by themselves are not sufficient for the breakthrough for which everyone has been hoping.

During this stage, all of the academic colleges have begun to engage in research in teacher education. Studies range the entire gamut of research that currently exists in North America, Europe, Australia and other countries. The entry of research as an important component on the agenda of the colleges is a very significant development because college instructors are still expected to carry a heavy teaching load, leaving research activity for the university faculty. Indeed, this change is continuously challenged by the universities and the CHE, which try to maintain the historic two-tier system that distinguishes between prestigious academic institutions and the practical and professional schools.

One of the results of this development was the establishment by the Ministry of Education of the MOFET Institute—a national center for research and staff development for the "academic" and "nonacademic" teacher education colleges. The Institute has a grants committee to support research efforts, sponsors workshops, courses, and professional seminars, issues publications and a journal, and has even sponsored in 1993 an international conference on teacher education. The sole target population of the MOFET Institute's activities is teacher educators.

The developmental stages of teacher education in Israel shed light on the ongoing struggle to improve the profession, and illuminate the dilemmas and issues that have preoccupied preservice training for over half a century. Examining a single institution will better illustrate some of the issues at stake. While it is difficult to generalize from a case study, the experience of Beit Berl College does provide a perspective and better understanding of the overall picture.

BEIT BERL COLLEGE:
AN ILLUSTRATIVE EXAMPLE

Located in a rural area in the central part of Israel, Beit Berl College is the largest teacher education institution in the country. There are currently about 5300 students enrolled and close to 600 faculty members (the equivalent of 350 full-time positions). Central to the college is the School of Education which is responsible for all preservice and in-service departments and programs. Four preservice departments (early childhood, elementary education, secondary education, and special education), two departments for nonschool educators (informal education and disadvantaged youth), and an in-service department work with thirteen disciplinary departments such as the departments of mathematics, geography, and English) to create a web of curriculum programs. The School of Education also operates a program for the training of novice principals, special programs for immigrant teachers, and a large institute for the preparation of teachers for Arab schools. A dozen centers operate under the auspices of the School of Education to provide educational services and "lab school" experiences to the students, faculty, nearby communities, and various public schools.

In addition to the School of Education, there is a large department for special programs such as programs for librarians, editors, and counselors, as well as programs for gifted children, grandparents, and "burnout" teachers. There is also on campus a special program for students who, although they have finished their military service, have not completed study for the high school matriculation examination.

The college, set among area kibbutzim and moshavim, has only a few buildings of more than one story. In recent years, major construction has been underway to increase space and renovate old structures. There are student dormitories, a guest facility built with a generous donation by the city of Wiesbaden, Germany, as well as all the other normal academic facilities, such as main and professional libraries and laboratories. Although the College is very close to some towns in the coastal area north of Tel-Aviv, the campus has an informal rural ambience.

Students in the College usually come from the central part of the country, which is the most populated, and they are from urban, suburban, kibbutz, and moshav communities. The student body is very diversified in terms of cultural, religious, and ethnic background. About a third of the students are experienced teachers completing work toward the B.Ed., seeking certification as principals, or taking in-service courses. In many cases they study together with the younger students who are in the pre-service programs.

The faculty is diversified not only in cultural and ethnic origins, but in academic and professional background as well. About 40 percent hold doctoral degrees, some from famous and well-known universities abroad, and about 50 percent have a master's degree, usually from Israeli universities. The provost is nominated by a board and oversees the financial, administrative, and academic functioning of the College. The budget is highly dependent on funding by the Ministry of Education.

A Brief History of the College

The campus was built in the early 1950s by the Labor party as a school for continuing education for workers of the newly born state. The idea and the selected location reflected the socialist ideology of the dominant culture of Israel at that time. During the 1960s, the Kibbutz Movement, which is strongly affiliated with the Labor party, established a small two-year school for teacher education for pre-Kindergarten through 8th grade at Beit Berl. In the late 1960s, the Labor party opened an undergraduate college on campus to allow students who did not meet the universities' admissions requirements to have an opportunity to receive higher education. The faculty was mostly from Tel Aviv University and work began on the accreditation of the new college as an academic institution. In the late 1970s, when the CHE rejected the idea of such a liberal arts college, and suggested instead opening a comprehensive academic college for education, the two rather different programs on site were merged. Interestingly enough, the failure to achieve academic recognition of the liberal arts college paved the way for the transformation of the existing programs into an academic college of education for preparing teachers for elementary and junior high schools.

The secondary and informal education departments were established soon after as four-year programs, drawing heavily on the faculty of the former programs which existed on campus. In 1980, on the verge of the most recent reform movement, they were accredited by the CHE as academic programs leading to teaching certification and a B.Ed. degree. With this precedent "at home" and the changing national climate toward teacher education, the departments on early childhood, elementary education, and special education and all the disciplinary departments began to reconstruct their programs according to the CHE guidelines and apply for accreditation.

At the present time, the "academization" of Beit Berl College is almost fully completed. Since the College was selected as one of the ten sites for the new liberal arts colleges around the country, programs are now being developed to open an undergraduate liberal arts college on campus in the 1995/96 academic year. It is quite ironic that the position of the CHE is coming around full circle to accredit as comprehensive the College that it refused to recognize only fifteen years ago. Clearly, circumstances have changed, and the College is capitalizing on the new opportunities.

Because of the original ideological affiliation with the Labor party, the College and the Party were financially intertwined. The realization that an academic institution could not be governed by a political party, coupled with a major financial crisis that began in 1989, led in 1990 to the relinquishment of this direct financial involvement. However, as noted earlier in this chapter, many colleges of education still maintain their affinity to social ideologies rooted in the pre-state era or the early years of the State of Israel. Beit Berl College today still advocates values and ideas promoted by the Labor party, such as Jewish-Arab coexistence, equal opportunities for all segments of the population, multicultural learning environments for students and faculty, social responsibility, and community involvement.

What has changed in the last wave of reform?

Between 1980 and the present, the College has undergone the following changes in order to meet the guidelines set by the CHE in 1981:

1. The curriculum structure and contents have changed as the academic program became an integrated four-year course of study (Ariav, Feigin, and Emanuel, 1991).

2. Admissions requirements include the high school matriculation diploma and a certain score on the college entrance examination (Kfir and Feigin, 1992). The latter requirement was recently raised and steps

are being taken to have candidates take the entrance examination required for university admission.

3. The faculty has changed in two ways: (a) new faculty members must have at least a master's degree and those holding doctorates receive preference, while veteran faculty members are strongly encouraged to continue their studies toward higher degrees; and (b) there is an increase in the number of full-time instructors and a decrease in the number of part-time instructors.

In addition to the expected changes as listed above, many important unanticipated changes have occurred in Beit Berl College during the time of the reform. Among the most interesting to observe are the following:

(1) The ethos of the college has changed drastically. The ethos of a teacher education program is defined by Katz and Rath (1990) "as a combination of the affective quality and content of the relationships among all participants. Together these attributes of a program constitute an ambience through which candidates' values, attitudes, norms, and dispositions may be affected" (p. 251). The ethos of a program seems to be the most significant parameter that makes a difference in a teacher education program (Kennedy, 1992). Faculty are now required to submit syllabi in advance for all courses, and many work in support teams to discuss, learn, and develop their courses. Internal staff development as well as instructional assistance is offered by colleagues and guests from other institutions in Israel and abroad. The process of tenure and promotion is dealt with more carefully and is not automatic. Students are expected to become more independent and responsible for their own learning as the curriculum has become more rigorous and demanding. Opportunities for making choices and being autonomous learners have made the old mentality of "in loco parentis" obsolete. Some of the changes described below are related to the changing ethos of the college.

(2) Restructuring the decision-making process to align it more closely with common procedures and norms of higher education represents a major change at the College. This was made possible partly because university faculty were involved in the establishment of the College of Education and its academic organs, and partly because the new

leadership of the College realized that following the CHE guidelines is a necessary but insufficient condition for becoming an academic institution. Therefore, Beit Berl College has served as an example for other colleges in governance issues. Specifically, the College moved away from a centralized and bureaucratic decision-making process to more democratic, broad-based processes. The College has a provost, a clear structure for the School of Education and the Department of Special Programs (deans, department heads, working committees), an academic council (senate), a curriculum committee, a promotion and tenure committee, a Dean of Student Affairs, and a variety of operational committees parallel to those existing in the universities. Department heads are usually elected by the faculty and their appointments are on a rotational basis. Budgetary management has also become less centralized and more autonomous in the various departments. All these changes have increased the number of faculty and students who take part in making decisions.

(3) Educational leadership has become a major component of the College's mission since the higher status it has been accorded allowed it to offer expert help previously assumed to be available only in the universities. Some examples are:

- Partnerships with schools where the College faculty is involved in curricular, instructional, and managerial changes.
- Provision of guidance and services to the community and schools through the numerous centers in the College (for example, The Center for Adolescents and Family, The Center for Language Development, and The Center for Children's Literature).
- Development of community-related programs such as the Second Chance Program for young people who do not have the matriculation diploma and the Program for Gifted Students of nearby school districts.
- Provision of school leadership through the in-service department, which has been officially designated as the staff development center for the school district, and the Beginning Teachers Project.

(4) Research has become an important segment of the College's life with increasing numbers of faculty involved in studying their own practice and inquiring into aspects of the College programs. A small research

team, started in 1989, is now a department involving faculty members interested in doing research. The research team was established initially to help conduct internal evaluation in the College as the reform era came to an end. The department today provides professional assistance to those who seek help, initiates studies, carries out studies sponsored by the College administration, and leads a national study on "The Academization of the Institutions in Teacher Education and the Teaching Profession: Achievements, Problems, and Developments." Numerous reports, journal articles, and papers presented at professional conferences in Israel and abroad are the overt products of this research activity at the College. There is a growing involvement and interest by faculty members in conducting research. However, lack of a research tradition in a teaching college and lack of promotional incentives contribute to the difficulty of attracting faculty to engage in research.

(5) Networking and international relations have become the most visible benchmarks of institutional maturity. Beit Berl College was the driving force behind the formal networking of all the academic teachers colleges in 1990 and the creation of a forum and lobby of the heads of these colleges. More interesting, however, are the devoted efforts of the College to reach out and connect internationally with educational institutions abroad. These efforts are carried out by two departments of international relations:

- Toward Europe and Asia. This department has been functioning for many years and works primarily with government agencies and municipalities, political groups, and universities, particularly in Germany and Austria. It is involved in fund raising, promotion of academic ties, and various educational initiatives.

- Toward English-speaking countries, especially those of North America. The department was established in 1991 to develop relationships with North American universities in the areas of joint research, group visits of students and faculty, individual faculty exchanges, jointly sponsored conferences, workshops, and colloquia, and arrangements for graduate studies for Beit Berl College students. The College annually hosts more than twenty-five individuals and groups from North American academic institutions and educational organizations, and has recently initiated with its partner institutions an international action research consortium on multicultural issues in teacher education. Through a biannual newsletter, a brochure, a videotape, and a descriptive kit, all in English, it is now possible for individuals and institutions outside Israel to learn about the College. Currently, Beit Berl College has formal relationships with more than ten universities in the United States and Canada.

The rapid growth and host of activities generated by the two departments gives testimony to the reciprocal needs and desires for international connections of both Beit Berl College and institutions of higher learning abroad. This development is a major breakthrough for a college that only a decade ago struggled for academic recognition and economic survival.

Future Change and Development

Beit Berl College, as well as the other academic teachers colleges, has attained impressive achievements. Nevertheless, the dynamics of change in times of social anxiety call for a heightened awareness of possible future developments, and require proactive measures to be taken in order to face them. Following are four areas which are on the agenda of the College at the moment, the first two being specific to the College, and the last two shared by many other colleges:

(1) *Improving the quality of pedagogic studies* is a primary concern for the College. The methods classes and student teachers' field experience (practicum) were not addressed by the CHE when the reform was initiated, because it was assumed that these areas were strongholds of teacher training institutions. Efforts over the last ten years to reconstruct courses in educational foundations and subject areas left the pedagogic studies behind. The pedagogic faculty and the faculties of the educational foundations and disciplinary areas grew apart, widening the gap between theory and practice. Work has just begun on the reconceptualization of the pedagogic studies, including emphasis on critical and reflective pedagogy, integrated courses of didactics and educational foundations, and collaborative work with cooperating teachers and professional development schools.

(2) *Planning for constructive interrelationships between the School of Education and the liberal arts college* to be opened shortly at Beit

Berl College is a difficult challenge. The history of higher education, both in Europe and North America, indicates that in such circumstances there is a tendency for the liberal arts college to overshadow the education school and gain supremacy. This is especially dangerous when the two programs offer different degrees, with the B.Ed. being perceived as less valuable than the B.A., and with different program lengths (four years for B.Ed. and teaching diploma vs. three years for B.A.). Work is now beginning on planning combined programs and tailoring the curriculum to fit newer and more flexible demands.

(3) *Initiating advanced clinical degrees for practitioners*, who find the graduate studies in the universities too research oriented, is an important step although not realistic in the near future. Work needs to be done in the colleges to open M.Ed. and Ed.D. programs for teachers, administrators, and other field-based educators who wish to continue their studies beyond the B.Ed. but are not interested in the more theoretical and research-oriented M.A. and Ph.D. It is possible that the changing nature of higher education in Israel would eventually transfer the responsibility for all teacher education as well as clinical graduate degrees to the colleges, allowing the universities to focus upon research-oriented graduate studies. Similar trends have occurred in recent years in several European countries (Bone and McCall, 1990).

(4) *Changing the working conditions of the faculty and establishing tenure and promotion criteria* seem to be crucial to improve instruction, enhance research, and acknowledge the academic status of teacher educators. Because faculty in the teachers colleges are members of the teachers' union and many are employed by the Ministry of Education it is impossible to introduce academic standards of teaching, research, tenure, and promotion. Efforts to change this situation are very slow and are hampered by the union and the Ministry of Education, which object to them on financial and political grounds. Recently, the CHE appointed a subcommittee to examine the issue and is slowly moving to change this situation.

SUMMARY

Continuous waves of reform in teacher education have contributed to the professionalization of teaching but have neither raised its social status nor influenced the quality of education. This is not surprising considering that, while "there are many stimulating ideas in the reform reports, there are also ill-defined questions, incomplete rationales, questionable solutions, and unexamined assumptions" (Tom, 1986, p. 37). In fact, findings of the TELT Study debunk some of the underlying beliefs of many reform proposals and portray them as common myths (Kennedy, 1992). Reforms are rarely systemic in nature and do not operate in a sociopolitical vacuum. In Israel, reforms have succeeded in turning teaching into an academic profession. However, from a more critical perspective, they played a role mainly as a barrier against further erosion in the public image and status of the teaching profession, and they served social needs as demand for higher education increased.

The above description, and in particular the "close-up" on Beit Berl College as a case study, demonstrates that reforms provide impetus for change, but the nature, quality, and velocity of the change are unpredictable and uncontrollable. Too many social, economic, and political forces participate and interact in a way that impact the context in which the reform takes place. Hence many issues have remained unresolved, new problems have emerged, and additional opportunities have arisen.

It is apparent today that revision of preservice education needs to go together with a radical change in the working conditions of teachers as well as in their job descriptions. Revision should go hand in hand with school reform and there should be sufficient resources for experimentation and implementation. Such changes also require the careful examination of the socioeconomic forces which work in the society to undermine potential achievements, as well as the forecasting of trends that might impact reform efforts.

The complexity of Israeli society and political changes being experienced at the present time make future planning for teacher education very complicated. Nevertheless, a few brave decisions by the Ministry of Education, such as drastically changing teachers' and teacher educators' working conditions and recognizing the full autonomy of the colleges as academic institutions, could provide a springboard for further growth. The role and attitude of the CHE could also contribute to a substantial change in the professionalization of teaching if and when teacher education is fully "accepted into the club" of Israeli higher education.

The authors wish to acknowledge the assistance of Fradle Freidenreich in the preparation of this chapter.

REFERENCES

Ariav, Tamar; Feigin, Naomi; and Emanuel, Dalia. [*The Curricula of the Academic Colleges for Teacher Education*], Report no. 1. Jerusalem: Department of Teacher Education, Ministry of Education and Culture, 1991.

Ariav, Tamar, and Seidenberg, Aaron. "Beit Berl College 1980-1990: A Case of the Professionalization of Teacher Education in Israel." Paper presented at the 39th World Assembly of the International Council on Education for Teaching, Paris, August, 1992.

Ariav, Tamar; Kfir, Drora; and Feigin, Naomi. "The 'Academization' of Teacher Education in Israel," *Teaching Education* 5, no. 2 (1993): 151-161.

Ben-Peretz, Miriam, and Dror, Yuval. "Israel." In *Issues and Problems in Teacher Education: An International Handbook*, pp. 139-154. Edited by H. B. Leavitt. New York: Greenwood, 1992.

Bone, Tom, and McCall, James, eds. *Teacher Education in Europe: The Challenge Ahead*. Proceedings of a Conference. Glasgow: Jordanhill College, 1990.

Chen, Michael, and Gotlieb, Esther. ["Towards a New Era in Teacher Training in Israel"]. In [*Planning Educational Policy: Position Papers and Decisions of the Standing Committee of the Pedagogic Secretariat*]. Edited by D. Pur. Jerusalem: Ministry of Education and Culture, 1989.

Chen, Michael; Gotlieb, Esther; and Yakir, Ruth. *The Academic Profession in Israel: Continuity and Transformation*. Princeton, N.J. Carnegie Foundation for the Advancement of Teaching, 1993.

Council for Higher Education. [*Committee for Academizing Teacher Education in Teacher Training Institutions—Provisional Model of the Curriculum for the "Boger Hora'a" (B. Ed.)*]. Jerusalem: Council for Higher Education, 1981.

Dan, Yossef. ["The Process of Becoming a Teacher Education College"], *Mahalachim: The Levinsky Teachers College Annual* 1 (1983): 22-32.

Dekel, Yehoshua. "Trends in Jewish Teacher Education in the Land of Israel: 1904-1962." Master's thesis, Bar-Ilan University, Ramat-Gan, Israel.

Dror, Yuval. ["Between 'Academization' and 'Humanization' in Teacher Education in Israel from the Turn of the Century until the Late 1980s: History of an Educational Dilemma as Supportive of Policy Planning in Education"], *Drachim Be'Hora'a* 1 (1992a): 11-37.

Dror, Yuval. "Teacher Education for Ideological Societies: Taking Oranium, the School of Education of the Kibbutz Movement, as an Example," *Westminster Studies in Education* 15 (1992b): 45-52.

Eddy, Audry. [*Changes in the Status of Teachers during the Past Ten Years*]. Report no. 10. Tel Aviv: Institute for Social Research, Tel Aviv University, 1992.

Etzioni, Amitai. ["Report of the National Committee Which Examined the Status of the Teacher and the Teaching Profession"], *Hed Ha'chinuch* 53, no. 18 (1981): 7-17.

Evans, Keith. *The Development and Structure of the English School System*. London: Hodder and Soughton, 1985.

Gotlieb, Esther E. "Global Rhetoric, Local Policy: A Case Study of Israeli Education and Teacher Training." In *Understanding Reform in Global Context: Economy, Ideology, and the State*, edited by M. B. Ginsburg. New York: Garland, 1991.

Gotlieb, Esther E., and Chen, Michael. "The Visible and Invisible Crisis in Israeli Higher Education Circa 1990." Paper presented at the World Congress of Comparative Education, Prague, 1992.

Holt, Maurice. "The High School Curriculum in the United States and in the United Kingdom," *Journal of Curriculum and Supervision* 8 (1993): 157-173.

Israeli Government Bureau of Statistics. [*Report on the State of Education in Israel.*] Jerusalem: Ministry of Education and Culture, 1993.

Katz, Lilian G., and Rath, James D. "A Framework for Research on Teacher Education Programs." In *Research in Teacher Education: International Perspectives*, edited by R. P. Tisher and M. F. Wideen. New York: Falmer, 1990.

Keidar, Binyamin. [*Report of the Examination Committee of the Academization Process of the Colleges for Teacher Education.*] Jerusalem: Council for Higher Education, 1992.

Kennedy, Mary M. *Findings on Learning to Teach.* East Lansing: National Center for Research on Teacher Learning, Michigan State University, 1992.

Kfir, Drora, and Libman, Zipora. [*Faculty of the Institutions for Teacher Education and the Academization of Preservice Education.*] Report no. 8. Jerusalem: Department of Teacher Education, Ministry of Education, in press.

Kfir, Drora, and Feigin, Naomi. [*Have Students' Characteristics in the Academic Teacher Colleges Changed in the Process of Academization?*] Report no. 4. Jerusalem: Department of Education, Ministry of Education and Culture, 1992.

Kfir, Drora; Fresko, B.; and Arnon, R. *Occupational Entry and Professional Advancement of Beit Berl College Graduates: A Survey of Ten Cohorts* (1979-1988). Report no. 1. Beit Berl, Israel: Beit Berl College, 1992.

Mann, John. *Education.* London: Pitman, 1979.

Mor, Doron. ["Continued Studies toward a B. Ed. Degree in Academic Colleges for Teacher Education"], *Dapim* 16 (1993): 83-99.

Orbach, Ephrayim. ["On the Development of a Theory on 'Transfers in Education'."] Doctoral dissertation, Hebrew University, Jerusalem, 1976.

Oshrat, Zipora. ["A Comparative Study of Education Students in Teacher Training Colleges and the University."] Paper presented at the 9th Conference of the Israel Educational Research Association, Bar-Ilan University, 1991.

Praver, Yehuda. [*Instructions for the Implementation of the (Junior High School) Reform in the Teacher Education Institutions.*] Jerusalem: Ministry of Education and Culture, 1965.

Tom, Alan R. *How Should Teachers Be Educated? An Assessment of Three Reports.* Bloomington, Ind.: Phi Delta Kappa Educational Foundation, 1986.

Chapter 8

TEACHER PREPARATION IN CHINA

Jingbin Zhang

The world is changing, and society is changing with it. Education in all its aspects is also changing. Above all, science and technology are developing very rapidly. As a consequence the goals of education are developing in two directions. On the one hand, the most advanced levels of science and technology require education to provide specialists—an elite. At the same time, the masses must be trained to supply support levels for the entire scientific-technological sector, already vast and growing rapidly. This is the main task of elementary education. Changes in curriculum methods, equipment, and other aspects of schooling necessitate changes in teacher training.

BASIC ISSUES IN THE REFORM OF TEACHER EDUCATION

The following basic issues relating to teacher education have been addressed in China:

Teacher qualifications. Educational policy on teacher preparation in China places high priority on subject specialization, including knowledge, skills, and abilities. A second priority is on methodology. Teachers should recognize and consider these questions: How do teachers teach and students learn? What is taught and learned? How should teaching and learning be evaluated? Third, teachers should have general and scientific qualifications such as command of natural and social sciences relevant to the teacher's field of specialization; and general knowledge of language and literature, foreign languages, philosophy, and the arts. Finally, teachers should have the ability to study on their own and do research work.

Psychological qualifications. Teachers should be career oriented, devoted to their students and confident in their career choice. They must recognize that their work can be highly satisfying despite its limited material rewards. They must be resolute and courageous in order to overcome the difficulties associated with their profession. They should be creative and eager to make progress. They should be able to deal with people in a variety of situations.

Moral qualifications. Teachers help to form a child's character. They must strive to be worthy of the title, teacher. They must teach wisdom as well as science.

Defining the Teacher's Role

As disseminators and constructors of civilization, teachers are a link between the past and the future. They hand down the ancient Chinese culture to their students while preparing them for the new world. Since it is the role of education to contribute to a nation's economic productivity, teachers are also responsible for transforming general laborers into technicians, scientists, and knowledge workers. Increasingly, China's leaders recognize that the effectiveness of educational policy depends greatly on the quality of their classroom teachers. Deng Xiao-ping (1983) has declared, "Teachers hold the key to a school's success in training qualified individuals of socialist construction and training workers who develop morally, intellectually, and physically, and with both specialist consciousness and culture." [P. 105]

It is the teacher's role to design and guide classroom instruction. That is, China's educational policy holds the teacher responsible for planning the content of classes in accord with designated goals, the syllabus, and students' level of preparation and ability. The teacher selects and combines the best teaching methods for the situation.

Teachers must also teach by personal example. Historically, teachers have had high prestige in China, especially among primary and secondary school students. They must use their prestige to help motivate students, paying close attention to students' learning activities.

Teachers should be theorists as well as practitioners of education. They should constantly reflect on their experience and then research, develop, and enrich educational theory. Educational theory in China has been criticized as being divorced from practice; teachers are in a position to address this problem.

The high status of education in China helps people to recognize that educational reform is needed. One of the most important prerequisites for reform is to produce better qualified teachers fully trained in modern methodologies. Teacher training is thus an urgent task.

Primary and Middle School Teachers in China

According to the statistics of the Planning and Construction Department of the State Education Commission (1990), in 1990 there were 5,582,000 primary school teachers, 2,470,355 junior high school teachers, and 562,266 senior high school teachers in China. (Student enrollments at these levels were 122,414,000 in primary schools, 38,685,500 in junior high schools, and 7,173,100 in senior high schools.) Among senior high school teachers less than half (45.5 percent) had a college degree or better. Among junior high school teachers less than 7 percent had a college degree. The vast majority of primary school teachers are graduates of a middle teachers' school or a senior high school (Education Development Study Center, 1991).

The Cultural Revolution (1966-1976) left a gap in China's teaching corps. During that decade, few teachers were trained and many left teaching never to return because of the abuse and humiliation that were heaped upon them. Making up the consequent teacher shortage is a hard task faced by the Chinese system for training teachers.

PROBLEMS IN THE HIGHER NORMAL SCHOOL CURRICULUM

Teacher education programs have long been the foundation of China's educational system. Until the mid-1960s, these programs, like the Chinese educational system itself, have been the products of a highly centralized, government-controlled economic plan. As a consequence, the Chinese government, not professional educators, controlled the entire teacher preparation process, from matriculation to graduation.

Within the last decade, however, the Chinese government has initiated a number of political and social reforms that have benefitted teacher education programs by granting them a greater degree of autonomy. Because of the lasting effects of the former system, change is understandably slow. Much more remains to be done to improve the program content and the governance of teacher education programs to China.

Since 1978, "reform" and "opening" have been the main policies of the new Chinese government. Under the aegis of "reform" the government has taken steps to change virtually every social, economic, and political structure, including the school system and teacher preparation programs. "Opening," especially within the last few years, has come to mean that the Chinese people seek to exchange information with other countries in nearly every conceivable area: education, economics, science, technology, art, and culture. These major policy changes have begun to have a positive influence on China's teacher education programs.

Curriculum presents a more striking problem. I will use the mathematics curriculum of higher normal schools as an example. Under the current plan the four-year undergraduate course calls for 128 to 134 weeks of classroom instruction; eight to twelve weeks of examinations; six to eight weeks of practice teaching and probationary teaching; two to six weeks of science research; two to four weeks of social practice; two to four weeks of military training; four to six weeks in reserve; enrollment and graduation, one to three weeks; winter and summer vacation, 36 to 44 weeks. In social practice, students spend some time going to factories, the countryside, or other places to keep abreast of developments in production and to discover the change in people's lives in order to understand the progress of society and the advantages of socialism. In general, 50 to 55 percent of total class hours are dedicated to required courses in one's specialty, 30 to 35 percent in required core courses, and 8 to 15 percent in electives.

These requirements present several problems. Mathematics, for example, has a higher proportion of required courses than many other disciplines. Also, course content does not accurately reflect teacher training needs. Because fewer electives can be taken, the relation between a student's mathematical specialization and his or her future teaching career is not very clear. Students easily conclude that learning higher mathematics is of no use. In fact, the teaching of higher mathematics ought to improve students' mathematical thinking skills, especially their ability to inquire into elementary mathematical theory, to solve problems, and thus to teach from a perspective of deeper understanding. At the same time, the lower proportion of electives means students cannot acquire a range of knowledge or give full play to their interests and strengths.

Practical training must be greatly strengthened. Many teacher training programs provide only six weeks for practice teaching in middle schools. Some normal universities also arrange an additional two weeks for students to teach on a probationary basis. This is very little practice indeed. More time must be given to developing students' teaching skills and course content related to the vocation of teaching must be increased.

Course content is generally outmoded. Education and psychology curricula need to be enriched. Scientific and mathematical and educational methodologies are especially weak. The content of mathematics education has to be updated, especially with respect to the use of computers and calculators in teaching. To prepare qualified teachers for a changing world, course content must be changed constantly, and new knowledge absorbed into the curriculum. While I have emphasized problems in the discipline of mathematics, comparable problems exist in other specializations offered in higher normal schools.

REFORM AND DEVELOPMENT OF CHINESE TEACHER EDUCATION

In general, preservice training for primary teachers is completed in middle normal school and in higher normal schools for junior and senior high school teachers. In-service training is offered in higher normal schools, colleges of education, and advanced teacher training schools. The goal of preservice training is clearly to provide basic qualifications for teaching. In-service education promotes continuing development in teachers' command of their specialization.

Chinese teacher education now faces both challenge and opportunity. In accord with the policies of reform and opening, some comprehensive universities have undertaken training of middle school teachers. More and more middle schools prefer to employ graduates of these programs, so higher normal schools are facing keen competition in the talent market. In any case, China's economic, scientific, technological, and cultural development have created the demand for both greater numbers of graduates and higher standards of preparation in the higher normal schools. But this situation also provides a new opportunity for development in those schools. In recent years, teacher education has seen some changes.

Changes in Preservice Training

Pedagogy. One such change has been a greater emphasis on pedagogy. According to the *Undergraduate Special Catalogue of General Higher Normal School* of the State Education Commission of China, most higher normal schools now add the word "education" after the names of former areas of specialization. For instance, "Department of Mathematics" is now called "Department of Mathematics Education." This means the training emphasis and professional scope of the department must give first priority to preparation of middle school teachers and promote the combination of the various disciplines with pedagogy as well. Teacher training is making an effort to strengthen curricula in education, psychology, and middle school subject matter.

For example, Capital Normal University in Beijing first addressed the basic teaching skills of its students with special attention to language skills and mastery of standard Chinese characters. All students are required to pass an examination in these areas before they graduate. Some departments—biology, mathematics, Chinese, English, education and others—have added teacher training courses in their disciplines in recent years. They have had good initial results with microteaching in this program, which has been funded jointly by the university and Beijing. Microteaching is a process involving videotaping a student teacher in a simulated classroom. Following the teaching exercise, usually accomplished in fifteen-minute segments, the student and a master teacher analyze the filmed exercise searching for ways to improve teaching techniques.

Curriculum. Higher normal universities are modifying their curricula to strengthen students' basic education, foster individual abilities, and widen their range of knowledge. These schools are developing a curriculum based on core courses and working out realistic ways to apply such parameters as "specialized" and "general," "required" and "elective."

Many higher normal schools are offering more elective courses to increase students' adaptability as well as broaden their general education. Secondary specializations now available include computers, English, music, art, and others. These afford a constructive outlet for students who do well in their studies and have time for extra work. Some specialists could be rewarded with special course diplomas recognized by the State.

Competition. Some higher normal schools or their experimental departments offer a standard test in core courses at the end of the sophomore year. Those who pass have wider freedom to select courses, according to their level of knowledge and interest, from among three categories: teacher education, research, and applied studies. Those who do not pass are classified in the lower rank of higher special course students. At the same time, the school reclassifies 3 to 5 percent of the best special course students in the higher rank. In this way, outstanding students are recognized and lower-achieving students eliminated.

The admission and assignment system. The government of China has taken some measures to give the higher normal schools special advantages in the admission system. Like the higher-ranked universities, they can enroll new students from the first batch. (In China, colleges and universities are classified in several levels, entering students are classified into batches according to ability, and schools admit students from the batch which corresponds to their level.) They are also allowed to enroll a certain number of recommended students—outstanding seniors recommended by their high schools for admission to higher normal schools. Recommended students need only an interview or a comprehensive exam given by the higher normal school, and are not required to take the standard entrance exam.

The monopoly of teacher training by normal schools, schools of education, and teachers' advanced studies schools is being broken. Comprehensive universities, and TV universities or colleges now offer training for teachers in primary and middle schools. As more alternatives for teacher education are developed, it becomes necessary to transform the single teacher training model into a comprehensive one. The new model allows for some teachers to become qualified in two or even three subject areas according to the needs of middle schools. This has been welcomed by both schools and students. The proliferation of possibilities has increased competitiveness among the various programs for preparation of teachers.

Teacher training can now be undertaken on a full-time, part-time, or occasional basis. Most occasional training is done through evening or correspondence courses at universities and colleges. More teachers thus have more opportunities for training.

In-service Teacher Training

As science and technology develop, the need for lifelong education becomes more urgent. In the Chinese educational system, the need for in-service training for teachers has come to be universally appreciated.

Although educational background is not the sole determinant of one's teaching level, it is a condition for promotion and a standard for the general quality of teachers. Newly assigned middle school teachers now have had a higher special course, or an undergraduate or graduate degree, especially in big and middle-sized cities and some "opened" areas of China. But even here there are still some teachers with no required education background. Universally, schools encourage them to take further courses and try hard to get a diploma. In remote areas and most of the countryside, both teacher quality, especially in primary grades, and conditions for running a school are less advanced. So it is a difficult task to raise teacher quality, improve school conditions, and regularize elementary education across the board in the countryside and remote areas of China. Colleges of education and teachers' advanced study schools offer some regular courses which correspond to the courses of normal schools. Middle-aged and young teachers are required to take the regular in-service courses whether they have a diploma or not. They can be promoted after passing examinations in these courses. This policy benefits teacher quality in general and helps to fulfill the need for constant educational development.

The reform of teacher education in China continues, though it still has some distance to go to catch up with the global demand for educational change. It seems certain that the distance will be reduced through the recent efforts of Chinese educators and policymakers. China's education experts and persons with breadth of vision have offered many suggestions for educational development. Some think that China ought to lengthen the course of study for a teaching diploma. Four years of higher normal school education is not enough, for students need not only to learn their subject but also to be trained in the skills of teaching. Others think course content should be adjusted constantly to suit the needs of present and future teachers. Some suggest that pretraining and in-service training should be organically related. Teachers should be required to take advanced courses at regular intervals. Some propose a strict examination system for teachers that would eliminate the unqualified (Zhang, 1992). As in any vocation, the status of teachers is raised when there is a real possibility of dismissal. Such a vocation is respected by the people.

To prepare qualified teachers for the changing world, the pace of reform in Chinese teacher education must continue to accelerate.

REFERENCES

Department of Planning and Construction of the State Education Commission. *The Achievement of Education on China*. Beijing: State Education Commission, 1990.

Education Development Study Center of the State Education Commission. *The Perplexity and Challenge that is Faced by Future Education*. Beijing: People's Education Publishing House, 1991.

Xaio-ping, Deng. *Selected Works of Deng Xiao-ping*. Beijing: People's Publishing House, 1983.

Zhang, Jingbin. "A Reform in the Course of Teaching Material and Method is Imperative." *Studies in Higher Education*, nos. 3 and 4. Beijing: Capital Normal University Publishing House, 1992.

Chapter 9

THE "TAKE-OFF" OF INTERNATIONAL COMPARATIVE STUDIES IN EDUCATION

Torsten Husén

By its very nature education tends to be provincial and ethnocentric. Each region or nation has by its history a system of formal or informal education closely tied to its culture and traditions. There has been a marked difference between the school and the university in this respect. In Europe the use of Latin as the *lingua franca* alleviated the ethnocentrism several hundred years ago. In the nineteenth century, when research began to become a major task at many universities, an inherent trend of universalism worked against provincialism.

The comparative study of educational institutions as a scholarly endeavor did not really take off until well into the 1950s. Such studies were promoted by a set of conditions in the field of international politics after World War II whose common denominator was the setting up of intergovernmental agencies and cooperative international programs. Let me identify some conditions that were conducive to making studies of education on a comparative basis a discipline with pragmatic implications.

DETERMINANTS OF COMPARATIVE STUDIES

Right from the outset UNESCO made promotion of education a top priority. In cooperation with the World Bank and the Ford Foundation it took the initiative in setting up an International Institute for Educational

Planning (IIEP) located in Paris and attached to the UNESCO head-quarters. Other intergovernmental agencies followed suit, even though their activities were confined to Western and/or industrialized countries.

The Council of Europe launched an educational program in the mid-1950s. I chaired a European seminar on school reforms held in 1958 (Husén and Henrysson, 1959). About 1960, the Organization for Economic Cooperation and Development (OECD), the club of highly industrialized countries inside and outside Europe, started an educational program closely related to its program on scientific and technological personnel. After all, OECD had as its overriding objective the promotion of economic growth of its member countries. A major component of the program was to make proper use of academic talent wherever it was to be found. Particularly in Europe, where postprimary education in a grammar school, *lycée*, or *Gymnasium* preparing students for the university traditionally had been the privilege mainly of the upper or middle classes, "democratization" (that is, the equalization of postcompulsory education) was seen by an increasing number of policymakers as benefitting both the individual and the society at large. In 1961, the OECD office of Scientific and Technical Personnel in collaboration with the Swedish government organized an international seminar on "Ability and Educational Opportunity" (Halsey, 1961). The participants, many of whom were leading social scientists, were strongly committed to the idea of expanding educational opportunities for able young people from disadvantaged social strata who so far had been strikingly underrepresented in institutions of higher learning.

The research endeavors that materialized in the establishment of IEA (International Association for the Evaluation of Educational Achievement) made it possible to conduct international comparisons with *empirical* methods. Prior to 1960, there were no international standards that could be used in making cross-national comparisons simply because there were no internationally valid instruments by means of which accurate comparisons could be made. Therefore in the ongoing debate in the wake of Sputnik, subjective comparisons were conducted on the basis of analyses of curricula, syllabi, examination papers, and, not in the least, on-site visits, which were often referred to as "educational tourism."

After the war many countries in the industrialized world were involved in reforming their school systems and needed to evaluate the outcomes of these reforms. In developing countries that were entering a postcolonial era, efforts were made to build a coherent system almost from scratch. In my home country, Sweden, where a major school reform was prepared by commissions during the 1940s, a pilot program in a number of municipalities in the 1950s preceded the introduction of a common comprehensive nine-year basic school all over the country. The pilot schools were compared with the traditional schools, particularly with regard to how well students performed in the lower secondary grades where the reform envisaged an integration of the various school types running parallel to each other.

IEA can take credit for having been able to develop internationally valid standards for comparing student achievement. This empirical approach was able to build on the advancements made in educational psychology, survey research, and sampling statistics. These three together constituted the IEA methodology applied for the first time cross-nationally. From the outset the advancements in psychometric methods had been made mainly for educational purposes. I only need to mention Alfred Binet and Edward Lee Thorndike. Large-scale achievement testing became common almost a half century ago in countries such as England, the United States, and Sweden. Survey research by means of questionnaires and interviews administered to individuals, sampled randomly from a large population, was introduced later. It was pioneered and used extensively in the United States after World War II. The Gallup polls, marketing studies, and studies of work satisfaction are well-known examples of this work. The idea of taking out a representative sample which was investigated, with a specified margin of error, by questionnaires or interviews instead of including the entire population was, indeed, a revolutionary idea in the social sciences. I am old enough to remember how in the mid-1940s a request came to the Bureau of Conscription, where I worked, for information about how many conscripts had a driver's license. I suggested that we should sample every tenth or twentieth individual among the 600,000. I was met by a strong skepticism and the entire card file (this was before Hollerith cards) was searched. The figure arrived at was, of course, without any error of estimate!

The IEA survey approach to comparative studies, as it shaped up some thirty years ago, represented a "paradigm shift," to use a term that lately has become fashionable. But IEA has also lately come under attack for being "positivistic" and one-sidedly quantitatively oriented.

This, however, has been the very strength of the original IEA approach. After all, it was advanced in order to make accurate cross-national comparisons possible and to get away from the subjective, sweeping, and impressionistic assessments that earlier dominated the scene.

As I have repeatedly pointed out, survey methodology has clear limitations that need to be supplemented by qualitative and ethnographic methods. The fact that, say, thirteen-year-olds in one country are performing better than students of the same age in another country is in itself an interesting and important fact. The next step is to identify by means of questionnaires certain measurable factors that help to explain these differences. But in order to dig more deeply into the pedagogical reality we need to visit a reasonable sample of schools and apply paradigms of a more qualitative and interpretative character. I have also pointed out that comparative studies need both a quantitative and a qualitative approach. They, indeed, supplement each other. (See Husén, 1989.)

In a paper I presented at a Williamsburg conference in 1967, to which I shall refer later, I reported studies of the "reserve of ability" on a comparative basis (Husén, 1969). Data from the IEA twelve-country study of achievement in mathematics showed that the earlier the selection for academic tracks and programs takes place, the more of a social bias against children from lower classes went into the selection process. One policy conclusion was that the comprehensive type of public education served the democratization objective by keeping the young students under the same roof and by and large in the same program even though ability grouping was a common practice.

In the early 1960s, education began to be seen as a major instrument in international military and trade competition. This was the time when the concept of "human capital" was making its way into the debate among both economists and educational policymakers. I remember having lunch in 1959 with Professor Theodore Schultz at the Faculty Club of the University of Chicago where I was visiting professor at the Center for Comparative Education. He tried out his ideas on me.

The Soviet expansion in Eastern Europe and the famous speech by Winston Churchill on the iron curtain in the late 1940s, as well as the establishment of the North Atlantic Treaty Organization (NATO), marked the emergence of two super powers each of which tried to expand its realm of influence. The Soviet Union established a belt of satellite countries with monolithic and unitary political and educational systems. On the other side were NATO and the Marshall economic assistance program out of which grew OECD with the aim of promoting recovery and growth of the Western European countries.

In 1957, Sputnik became, at least in the United States, a turning point in conceiving the role of education. When the Soviets placed a satellite into orbit a bit earlier than the United States, that event was regarded by many Americans as evidence that the U.S.S.R. was ahead of the rest of the world with regard to this particular type of technology and was also superior in the teaching of relevant school subjects, in this case mathematics and science. Those interested in educational policy no doubt remember the consequences. Within a year of the launching of Sputnik the U.S. Congress passed the National Defense Education Act, legislation that would previously have been unthinkable but after Sputnik was hastily and unanimously accepted by the policymakers. What before 1957 would have been regarded as bordering on high treason now became highest virtue. Delegations of American educators, including such people as Henry Chauncey and George Bereday, hastened to Moscow to learn why the Soviets were so successful in educating scientists and technologists. Reports on Soviet and American education were published and brought leading comparative educators into the limelight (Bereday et al., 1960).

Europe had also its share of the attention that the new technological achievements brought to comparative education. In the late 1950s educational researchers from a dozen Western countries got together at the UNESCO Institute for Education in Hamburg and began to contemplate empirical comparative studies of students' achievement in mathematics and how cross-national differences could be explained in terms of resources, school structure, and methods of instruction. The International Association for the Evaluation of Educational Achievement, known under the acronym IEA, was born (Husén, 1967). At the same time Hamburg was also the meeting place for European educators who in the early 1960s decided to form the Comparative Education Society for Europe. Its first international congress was held in Amsterdam in 1962.

In the United States an International Education Act was passed in 1966, but alas, it was not funded by Congress. It carried a direct relationship to what I shall dwell on now.

Student exchange, including a massive influx of students from developing countries to universities in the United States and Europe, mounted in the 1960s and could be counted in six digit numbers. This raised questions of the equivalence of examinations and diplomas in various countries—another task for comparative education.

Last but by no means least, we should not forget the agencies involved multilaterally or bilaterally in foreign aid. The experts involved in their activities were forced to think in comparative categories. Again, agencies like UNESCO and the World Bank were sponsoring the establishment of the International Institute for Educational Planning in Paris.

THE WILLIAMSBURG CONFERENCES

It is against the background I have painted here in very broad strokes that two Williamsburg meetings in 1967 have to be viewed. They were outcomes of the heightened interest in international education reflected in the International Education Act of 1966. There were also some Americans who had been instrumental in promoting various activities that could be subsumed under the heading "international education." Several of them were actively engaged in "internationalizing" education, including the two conference architects, James A. Perkins and Philip H. Coombs. In February, 1967, some twenty-five people attended a planning conference where the issues to be dealt with at the full conference in October were put on the table. Some 150 people from 52 countries participated in the October meeting.

The Williamsburg meeting, beginning with a background paper on "World Crisis in Education," (Coombs, 1968) was organized under favorable auspices. Comparative education had experienced a breakthrough in the early 1960s on both sides of the Atlantic. The Vietnam war, however, was casting its financial shadow over the federal budget and prevented the funding of the International Education Act, which had been submitted by the Johnson administration. But even considering that drawback, international cooperation, foreign aid, and comparative studies accompanying these endeavors were strongly supported and, indeed, en vogue. Even though a few representatives from Eastern countries participated (but none from the Soviet Union) the "world" at that time was by sheer necessity conceived of as Western plus the Third World countries (except China). I remember a colleague from one Eastern country making a snide remark about "American imperialism." At that time, as was the case until recently, no one could conceive of a breakdown of the Eastern European bloc which appeared to be firmly cemented forever.

The Williamsburg meetings in 1967 were seminal in the process of building up an international network, particularly in higher education, and gave birth to comparative studies in this field. Williamsburg was a breakthrough for global perspectives in education, including the cross-national comparative perspective.

The list of participants at Williamsburg cuts across all categories of experts in education. There were scholars, policymakers, planners and university presidents, all with the common denominator of being leaders in their respective roles not only in their home countries but in many cases on the international scene as well. Among the 150 participants were former, present, or prospective ministers of education, such as Hans Leussinck and Gabriel Betancour, and rectors, vice-chancellors, or presidents of leading universities, such as Clark Kerr, Eric Ashby, and James Perkins. There were planners of reforms in education, such as Friedrich Edding and Philip Coombs, and leading intellectuals who had orchestrated cross-national debates, such as Raymond Aron who along with Jean Paul Sartre and René Maheu graduated as top students from École Normale Supérieure. There were pioneers in educational research like Ralph Tyler, and in adult education like Bertrand Schwartz.

One should realize that this was a unique opportunity for constructive dialogue across territorial and disciplinary as well as other boundaries, which under normal circumstances prevented concerned efforts to tackle problems in a way that Philip Coombs in his background document referred to as systems analysis. The overriding problem that cut across the issues dealt with in the group sessions was how to reconcile the hopes of the individuals and the needs of society on the one hand and the capabilities of the economies on the other.

Most of the Williamsburg conference participants had in one way or another been involved in international activities in education beyond their own national borders. Thus, the scene was now set for conducting comparisons and for an exchange of experiences and scholarly information, in short an opportunity to widen the perspective beyond the provincial one. Global interdependence in education became evident in a more tangible way than the intergovernmental organizations had been able to make us recognize. The choice of participants and the themes selected for the conference contributed to making this interdependence more concrete. It was suggested that the UN General Assembly should designate 1970 as the "international education year." This occurred and was, indeed, auspicious for the founding of the International Council for Educational Development (ICED) that year. Its first president, James A. Perkins, was the main architect of the Williamsburg meeting.

The Williamsburg conference took place less than a year before the 1968 crisis at universities in many countries, to which the French referred as "les événéments." As already pointed out, the participants felt that the overriding problem was the imbalance between demand and supply in education. This was the major crisis problem so aptly spelled out with so much convincing evidence by Philip Coombs in his background paper and a year later in his book (Coombs, 1968). The other source of crisis was the widening gap in educational provisions between the rich and the poor countries. The summary report from the conference also pointed out the need for improving educational structures, programs, and management in an innovative way. Traditional inflexibility had to be replaced by "fresh approaches and new ventures." Increased international cooperation was needed in order to achieve such goals.

How much foresight did we have? To be sure, the imbalance between demand and supply has been haunting us all the time since the mid-1960s, particularly in the developing countries, exacerbated by the oil crisis, inflation, and ensuing austerity measures. Whereas the expenditures per student per year have been rising in real terms in the rich countries, they have been falling in the poor countries. The need for innovative strategies is still as urgent as it was then and has been abundantly evidenced by ongoing but not always successful efforts to revise national systems of education.

There were emerging problems, though, which we did not foresee or to which we did not pay enough attention. The enrollment explosion at many universities and the undersupply of teaching and guidance provided by faculty had begun to stir up unrest among students who began to feel neglected. The writing on the wall began to be visible, but not visible enough to be regarded as a major issue. In 1981 I wrote an essay on futurological studies for the UNESCO journal *Prospects* (Husén, 1982). I pointed out the student unrest on both sides of the Atlantic as something we did not foresee in the mid-1960s, along with the slowdown in economic growth in the 1970s after the oil crisis and the downtrend in birthrates in the rich countries during the two decades after Williamsburg. (My colleague at Columbia University, George Bereday, to whom I had dispatched a reprint of my UNESCO paper, sent me a letter along with some newspaper clippings from 1967, some of them from the *New York Times*. In the letter he said that he "stood up in the plenary session and protested that student unrest was not discussed." I cannot remember this, perhaps due to opportunistic forgetfulness!)

Comparative studies in education existed before what I have here described as the takeoff period of comparative education in the 1960s. They once grew out of very pragmatic concerns. In Britain they were offshoots of the problems encountered in administering education in its colonial empire. In Germany they were referred to as *Auslandpädagogik*.

Early pioneers in the academic world were Isaac Kandel and Robert Ulich in the United States and Nicholas Hans in Britain, all scholars transplanted to countries that were not their native lands. In the 1960s the first systematic handbooks in comparative education were published, such as that by Bereday (1964) and another by Harold Noah and Max Eckstein (1969). A *Comparative Education Review* began publication under the auspices of the Comparative and International Education Society founded in 1956. The journal, which is still flourishing, came out with a special issue on the state of the art in comparative education in 1977.

Since societies for comparative studies had been formed in various regions and countries, it was felt that an international coordinating body should be set up, not least for organizing world congresses. This led to the establishment of the World Council for Societies of Comparative Education, which organized the first international congress in Ottawa in 1970. The latest congress of the Council took place in Prague in July, 1993.

The pioneers and the first generation of comparativists came from the humanities, typically with a background in history and philosophy. The establishment of the Comparative Education Center at the University of Chicago by C. Arnold Anderson, brought in sociology and economics as contributing disciplines. The 1960s also saw cross-national studies of achievement in mathematics and science by educational psychologists and statisticians under the auspices of IEA. Thus the empirical methods of the social sciences made their way into comparative education. Another noticeable development during the period I am sketchily reviewing is the entry of comparative policy studies pioneered by political scientists.

SPIN-OFFS AND "RINGS ON THE WATER"

The International Council for Economic Development (ICED) made a point of holding its annual Board meetings in various parts of the world. It has been quite natural for the host country to seize upon the opportunity to draw upon the experts present and to get their views and comparative perspectives on its domestic problems in education and on ongoing reforms.

In some instances ICED has been called upon to conduct more systematic policy reviews similar to those carried out under the OECD auspices. Thus, in 1987 some ICED Trustees participated in one review requested by the Spanish Ministry of Education. The system of higher education in Spain was then in a state of crisis with students occupying university premises. Quite recently a similar review took place in Mexico. Both reviews were coordinated by Philip Coombs. Needless to emphasize, exercises like those just mentioned, which last only a few weeks, cannot be regarded as scholarly studies in depth with all the documentation that goes with such endeavors. But they possess an indisputable quality of highest value for policymakers and practitioners. They have been conducted by people who possess what one may call connoisseurship, people who have spent a long career in higher education as teachers, administrators, and researchers and who can view problems with a similar perspective but with different eyes than those who are daily faced with them.

Creative endeavors in central human affairs, such as in education, often demonstrate their value by their often unexpected spin-off effects. In looking back on Williamsburg and its aftermath a good descriptive metaphor would be "rings on the water." The conference was a major "splash" simply by bringing together high level people to an exchange of views and experiences. This started a process of "rings on the water." Ideas were exchanged and diffused all over the world. Common problems were identified and viable solutions contemplated. Provincialism yielded to more global approaches. People realized that their own system was not necessarily better than all other systems. This awareness implied that nations cannot borrow wholesale from each other, but by looking at the other systems one can get a perspective that provides insights into how one could go about improving one's own system.

I think that those of us who came from highly industrialized and rich countries with established and expensive systems of education have, by the exchange of experiences hinted at above, gradually become aware of the extent to which our own system is determined by our own history and traditions and how easy it is to be ethnocentric. Many have taken it for granted that the Western system of formal education as embodied in primary, secondary and tertiary institutions, such as the *Volksschule*, the *lycée*, or the *Gymnasium*, could serve as self-evident models to be emulated by Third World countries. I still remember how shocked René Maheu became when, at a meeting in Bellagio, Italy, in early 1972 I ventured to suggest a reassessment of the adequacy of the Western model of formal schooling for Third World countries.

CONCLUDING OBSERVATIONS

Many of the major problems identified in the late 1960s are still with us. For example, those of us who are from Europe note a problem in education that has become increasingly pressing: the rising immigration of foreign labor and the concomitant problem of providing multicultural education. In the United States provisions for bilingual education were part of the Elementary and Secondary Education Act of the mid-1960s. But in Europe the so-called guest workers (*Gastarbeiter*) then constituted a peripheral problem in education. But by now it has moved up on the priority scale. In Sweden, until the early 1960s an ethnically very homogeneous country, now some 10 to 15 percent of the school children come from homes where Swedish is not the mother tongue.

The European Common Market (EC) and the Maästricht Treaty on the European Union (EU) have given actuality to an integration of the European educational systems. The fact that an increasing number of university students are spending at least one academic year in another country within Europe have spurred debates on equivalence of degrees and diplomas. This has had an effect on curricula in secondary education, at least in schools which are directly preparing for the university. But the increasing number of students from Third World countries in European and American universities contribute to reinforce the tendencies hinted at. With ample justification we can talk about a globalization of education. Thus, comparativists in education can foresee a busy time in the coming years.

REFERENCES

Bereday, George Z. *Comparative Method in Education*. New York: Holt, Rinehart and Winston, 1964.

Bereday, George Z.; Brickman, William W.; and Read, Gerald H., eds. *The Changing Soviet School: The Comparative Education Society Field Study in the USSR*. Cambridge, Mass.: Riverside Press, 1960.

Coombs, Philip H. *The World Educational Crisis: A System Analysis*. New York: Oxford University Press, 1968.

Comparative Education Review. Special issue on "The State of the Art: Twenty Years of Comparative Education." *Comparative Education Review* 21, no. 2 (1977): entire issue.

Halsey, A. H., ed. *Ability and Educational Opportunity*. Paris: Organization for Economic Cooperation and Development (OECD), 1961.

Husén, Torsten. "Educational Research at the Crossroads? An Exercise in Self-criticism," *Prospects* 19, no. 3 (1989): 351-360.

Husén, Torsten, ed. *International Study of Achievement in Mathematics: Comparisons between Twelve Countries*, Vols. 1-11. New York: Wiley, 1967.

Husén, Torsten. "Present Trends in Education," *Prospects* 12, no. 1 (1982): 45-56.

Husén, Torsten. "School Structures and the Utilization of Talent." In *Essays on World Education*, edited by George Z. Bereday. New York: Oxford University Press, 1969.

Husén, Torsten, and Henrysson, Sten, eds. *Differentiation and Guidance in the Comprehensive School*. Report on the 1958 seminar conducted under the auspices of the Council of Europe. Stockholm: Almqvist and Wiksell, 1959.

Noah, Harold J., and Eckstein, Max A. *Toward a Science of Comparative Education*. New York: Macmillan, 1969.

Chapter 10

THE CASE FOR
INTERNATIONAL
COMPARISONS

John P. Keeves

The remarkable expansion worldwide of the provision of education at all levels—elementary, secondary, college, and adult recurrent programs—during the twentieth century is widely recognized. Of particular interest is the rapid growth toward universal secondary education in many countries in the fifty years since the termination of hostilities in World War II. These developments have occurred with British, French, German, and the United States school systems as models, and with school systems in developing countries drawing commonly from one, and in some cases during different periods, from more than one of these four countries. With so much in common between educational systems across the world, it is not surprising that an interest in international comparisons has emerged. Moreover, without these common origins of national educational systems, international comparisons would not be meaningful.

The interest in international comparisons has been strongly supported by politicians and policymakers in the field of education, who increasingly realize that national development is sustained by an educational system of high quality which provides not only a well-trained work force but also a well-educated citizenry. These politicians and policymakers wish to know how their national educational systems perform in comparison with those of other similar countries. Furthermore, with the increasing costs of provision as their educational system expands, they also wish to know whether value is being obtained for the money spent.

However, there is commonly less support from educational administrators who view cross-national comparisons as a threat to their autonomy and authority.

The growth of interest in international comparisons has not been limited to the study of educational systems. It has been extended to economic and social indicators of national well-being and prowess in a wide range of sporting activities. Nevertheless, it is in education that a field of scholarly work has emerged during the twentieth century that has acquired the name of *comparative education*. While this field is able to trace its roots back into antiquity, the seminal work in 1817 of Marc-Antoine Jullien, who emphasized objective observation, the collection of documents, and thorough and systematic analysis, laid the foundations for later developments. The provision of an educational system of the highest possible quality is of such importance to each and every country that the field of comparative education has had a very important function in the expansion in education that has taken place during the twentieth century. Furthermore, the publication by UNESCO of the report *Learning to Be* (Faure, 1972), which is concerned with the development of education in the years ahead, has introduced concepts of a worldwide learning society and lifelong educational programs. These concepts shape the new frontiers of education across the world. In the future, comparative studies will inevitably continue to have an important place.

While scholarly work in the field of comparative education has been rich in detail and description, it has commonly been poor in the quality of analysis carried out, and weak in the accounts provided of why certain developments have taken place in certain settings at certain times that are mirrored by similar developments elsewhere. The failure of comparative education to provide an explanation of the most important phenomenon of the present century, namely the growth of education worldwide at all levels, has arisen from the lack of firm evidence on which to base an explanation. This lack of information was first acknowledged in early 1957 by a group of scholars who had assembled at the UNESCO Institute for Education in Hamburg in the then Federal Republic of Germany. The group recognized that there was little empirical evidence to support the sweeping assertions that were being made at that time about the relative strengths and weaknesses of different national systems of education. The expansion of secondary education in the United States over the previous decades had left the schools exposed to strong criticism for a decline in standards and a lack of intellectual rigor. Similar concerns were emerging in other countries, where secondary education was in the process of rapid expansion. The launching of Sputnik by the former Soviet Union in mid-1957 no doubt contributed to concern in the United States, but it is important to note that the issues were already being considered in Europe at a center that brought East and West together.

The scholars meeting in Hamburg were concerned with the problems of evaluation in education. Many of them were educational psychologists and psychometricians. They argued that it was inadequate to consider merely the inputs to education and the conditions under which schooling was conducted. For effective evaluation it was also necessary to examine the outcomes of education in terms of achievement, attitude, and participation. They advanced the bold idea in 1958 of conducting a study of the educational achievements of students belonging to different national systems of education and they gained the endorsement of the Governing Board of the UNESCO Institute for Education for an "international study of intellectual functioning" (Foshay et al. 1961, p. 8). The idea of cross-national surveys was further discussed in 1959 and a group of educational research workers from twelve countries agreed to launch a feasibility study. They sought to find out whether appropriate instruments could be developed that were meaningful cross-nationally and whether a methodologically and administratively sound study could be conducted that would yield evidence from a wide range of school systems. Such a study would support the making of valid general statements that held across countries.

It is important to note that from the outset this group of scholars was not interested in conducting a cognitive olympiad, or in generating a set of performance indicators that would merely establish the well-being or otherwise of a school system. They rejected the strong data-free assertions that circulated in the United States and Europe in 1957, and they sought evidence of the factors that influenced educational outcomes cross-nationally. They also recognized that commonly there is insufficient variation within a particular school system to ascertain factors that had an influence on educational outcomes. Only by extending their investigations across systems would there be sufficient variation to enable such factors to be identified. They saw the educational world as an international laboratory, in which different school systems experimented in different ways in order to obtain optimal results in the education of their youth. The recency of development of national educational systems had already ensured that the schools of different countries largely had common goals. Moreover, the success of the German university system in the latter decades of the nineteenth century and the early decades of the twentieth century had ensured that throughout Europe and the United States the school and university systems of each country were moving in a common direction with respect to scholarly knowledge. However, different countries employed different methods to achieve common ends. If research could obtain evidence from across a wide range of systems, then there was likely to be sufficient variability to permit the detection of previously concealed factors that have meaningful and consistent influences on educational outcomes.

The efforts of this group of scholars were supported by the ease of air travel that was quite suddenly available in the late 1950s, and by the emergence in the early 1960s of powerful computers and accurate optical mark reading instruments that permitted the relatively rapid processing of large amounts of data. Developments in the statistical analysis of quantified and categorized data have continued to strengthen their work. Moreover, it is important to acknowledge the generosity of foundations and governmental agencies in the United States and various institutions in Sweden (both affluent countries with international perspectives) that have sustained this work over the intervening decades.

After the initial steps in 1959, this group of scholars gradually consolidated their efforts with the establishment of a cross-national research organization, the International Association for the Evaluation of Educational Achievement (IEA) that has had its offices first in Hamburg from 1959 to 1969, then in Stockholm from 1970 to 1989, and more recently from 1990 in The Hague. The membership of the organization has grown from an initial twelve countries to a current list of fifty-three systems, with many more countries having participated in one or more of its studies. Today, IEA is an organization with a strong following of member systems and a vigorous program of research and evaluation studies.

TEN KEY FINDINGS FROM IEA RESEARCH

The case for international comparisons cannot be argued without evidence. It is necessary to show first what IEA has achieved from thirty-five years of research activity. The discussion that follows is limited to ten key findings. Some results are now well-known, but not associated with IEA by name. At the time they were first presented they were novel and had started as a hunch or hypothesis in the thoughts of an IEA research worker. Their presentation emphasizes that IEA is not concerned with crude comparisons and the conduct of an educational "horse race" with countries listed in order at the finishing post. Measurement of a country's level of educational achievement is merely a first and necessary step on the path toward finding out why countries differ in their levels of achievement. The fact that newspaper headlines are captured by reporting the rank order of a country, particularly in a situation where a specific country has performed poorly, cannot be ignored. While IEA research workers have steadfastly tried to avoid such publicity, they have been well aware that it can sometimes be used to generate further funding. Their primary aim is, nevertheless, to develop an understanding and explanation of educational processes. The ten key findings listed below are presented in more detail in a recently published monograph titled *The World of School Learning: Selected Key Findings from 35 Years of IEA Research* (Keeves, 1994). Full information to support these findings is to be found well scattered in the very large number of publications that present the results of IEA studies. For each finding a statement is first presented, a brief comment is provided, and the implications of the finding for policy and practice are given.

1. Effects of Retention and Participation

The average level of achievement within a country at the terminal secondary school stage is inversely related to the proportion of the age group enrolled at school or participating in the study of the subject under survey.

This finding establishes that in those countries where a higher proportion of the age group remain at school the average level of achievement of those students at the terminal year of secondary schooling is lower. Likewise, in a particular country, where an increase in retention rate occurs it must, by implication, be expected that the average level of achievement of the students will drop proportionately. This finding has been shown to hold in the areas of mathematics and science, and must be expected to hold in other subject areas.

Implication for educational planning. In school systems where changes in retention rates occur over time there is need in educational planning to make allowance and to provide for changes in the average levels of student achievement.

2. The Best Do Not Suffer

At the terminal secondary school stage, when equal proportions are compared there are no differences in levels of achievement, irrespective of the proportions of the age group retained at school. The best students do not suffer with increased retention rates.

Countries differ greatly in the proportions that they hold at school at the terminal secondary school stage. As a consequence, while the average level of achievement of the group is lower the higher the proportion retained at school, there are small and inconsistent differences across countries in the levels of achievement of the best 5 percent and the best 10 percent of the total age group. Thus there is no evidence of drawing on a larger pool of more able students nor of deterioration in standards of the better students.

Implication for educational planning. The shift from a highly selective school system to universal secondary education does not necessarily lead to a deterioration in the standards achieved by the better performing students.

3. Effects of Curricular Time

Students' achievement in mathematics, French as a foreign language, and science is positively related to the time given to the study of the subject at school, both in comparisons across countries and between students within countries.

It must be pointed out that the effects of time are also found to be cumulative across the years of schooling. However, sometimes where this relationship between time and achievement does not show up within a country, there is insufficient variation between students in the time they are given for studying the subject. Subsequent work, in other studies has indicated that time assigned in the curriculum can be broken down into "nonengaged" time and "engaged" time or "time on task" and it is the latter that relates most strongly to achievement.

Implication for educational planning. The design of the school curriculum requires decisions on the levels of achievement sought, and the relative emphasis to be given to each subject area, and as a consequence the relative amounts of instructional time to be assigned to each subject at each grade of schooling.

4. Time Spent on Homework

The achievement of students is related to the time spent on homework after other factors influencing achievement have been taken into account.

It should be noted that while a consistent relationship is found between time spent on all homework and achievement in mathematics and science at the lower and middle secondary school levels, there is no consistent relationship between achievement and time spent on homework in the subject area under survey. This suggests that time spent on homework must be considered to be an index of motivation to succeed at school as well as an extension of instructional time by the undertaking of additional work in the subject area at home.

Implication for educational planning. Careful consideration should be given to the amount of time which should be assigned to homework in each subject area and across all subject areas in order to augment instructional time but without prejudicing motivation.

5. Opportunity to Learn

The average level of student achievement across countries is positively related to the opportunity that the students have to learn the content of the items tested.

Opportunity to learn has been measured in IEA studies by asking teachers, either individually or in a school group, to judge what proportion of the students tested in their school had had the opportunity to learn the content of the items included in a test. Where there is variability across schools within a country, the existence of a relationship is also detected between opportunity to learn and achievement.

Some reviewers of the IEA program of research have contended that the relationships recorded between opportunity to learn and achievement in mathematics and science indicate that the tests employed favored those school systems and schools where students had the advantage of learning the content tested. In this way they have implied that the tests were biased in favor of particular groups. However, the tests were developed to provide a very broad and representative coverage of the curricula that were offered across all countries involved in the testing program.

Implication for educational planning. Students need to be provided with opportunities to learn specific subject matter content, and sufficient time needs to be allowed for its presentation if that content is considered important for them to learn.

6. The Textbook and Its Effects

In less developed countries the use of a textbook has an effect on student learning. However, the same effects have not been reported from studies in more developed countries.

In the more developed countries a very high proportion of students commonly possess or have access to a text book. As a consequence, the effects of availability and use of a textbook can only be estimated in less developed countries where sufficient variability exists. There is some evidence, however, that schools in which the students performed better in reading possessed more reading materials in the school, had a student newspaper, and had more library books per student than had the lower performing schools.

Implication for educational planning. It is necessary for each student to possess a textbook for each school subject being studied. In addition, schools need an ample supply of reading material in a school library if the effective development of students' reading skills is to occur.

7. Reading Resources of the Home

The level of reading resources of the home is positively related to student achievement, as are other indicators of language usage in the home, such as the use of a dictionary in the home and whether or not the language of the home is the language of instruction.

The questions that are used in surveys to measure the level of reading resources in the home must necessarily be relatively simple and consider only the number of books in the home and the use of a mother tongue language dictionary in the home. Nevertheless, such simple measures provide moderately strong and consistent relationships with educational achievement not only in reading comprehension, but also in other subject areas such as mathematics and science.

Implication for educational planning. In circumstances where students lack an adequate supply of reading resources in the home, schools need to develop ways of augmenting the supply of appropriate reading materials that are made available to students.

8. The Status of the Home

Measures of the socioeconomic status of the home are positively related to student achievement in all countries, at all age levels, and for all subject areas.

Information that has been used in order to obtain measures of socioeconomic status include: father's occupation, level of father's and mother's education, and in more recent studies, mother's occupation, although special scaling procedures have to be adopted to scale information where the mother undertakes home duties. The occupational and educational scales employed are of necessity very simple, because information is obtained in IEA studies from 10-year-old and 14-year-old students. Nevertheless, the relationships recorded are moderately strong and highly consistent. Slightly stronger relationships were recorded in the mid-1980s than in the early 1970s, suggesting that there was increased polarization in the societies under survey in the effects of the circumstances of the home.

Implication for educational planning. In comparing the levels of achievement of students in different schools, allowance must be made in appropriate ways for the differences in the status of the homes from which the schools draw their students.

9. Learning Conditions Make a Difference

Although the effects of home background variables are similar across subject areas, the effects of the learning conditions in the schools differ among subject areas, and in some subject areas are equivalent in the size of their influence to the effects of the home.

The Equality of Educational Opportunity Survey in the United States (Coleman et al. 1966), through assessing student performance with scores on a verbal ability test, contributed to a questionable belief that schools made little contribution to student learning. The evidence collected in IEA studies over an extended period of time, even though the studies have sometimes produced evidence that is now known to be an underestimate of the contribution of the effectiveness of schools to student learning, has shown that the influence of the learning conditions in the schools is clearly related to the nature of the subject area under survey.

Implication for educational planning. Considerations of efficiency and equity require that the learning conditions in the schools should be both raised and equalized in order to increase student learning at all levels of schooling, in all subject areas, and for all students.

10. Sex Differences in Educational Achievement

Differences in achievement found between the sexes vary in size and direction across countries, across school subjects, and over time.

Boys tend to show superior performance in science and mathematics and girls in narrative reading skills and response to literature. In those countries where strong programs have been set up to improve the performance of girls in science, gains were recorded between 1970-71 and 1983-84 not only at the lower secondary school stage but also at the terminal stage of schooling. It was only in the English-speaking countries that girls showed superior performance on the reading and listening tests of French as a foreign language. In the cognitive tests in civic education, boys generally performed better than girls.

Implication for educational planning. Programs are effective in reducing the gender gap in science, and need to be maintained where they exist, and introduced where they do not exist in specific subject areas.

These ten key research findings have been drawn from the results presented by the fifteen major studies that IEA has conducted during the thirty-five years it has been active in the area of international comparative research. While much of the publicity given to IEA research has been directed toward the findings presented from studies in the areas of mathematics and science, it is necessary to recognize that IEA has deliberately sought to undertake investigations across all areas of the curriculum where it is meaningful to examine achievement, attitude, and participation outcomes.

THE RANGE OF IEA STUDIES

The studies carried out by IEA are now considered in terms of four domains, and a cycle of investigations is planned for the long-term future in each of the four domains: mathematics-science cycle, language cycle, civics-arts cycle, and the special studies cycle. The grouping of studies into four domains does not deny the importance of undertaking, as was done in the IEA Six-Subject Study in 1970-71, investigations in different subject areas simultaneously so that the interrelations between subject areas can be examined.

In table 1 information is given on the fifteen studies from which results have been published, although for two of these studies additional data collection is still in progress, namely the Preprimary Study and the Computers in Education Study. Moreover, planning is under way for three further studies. In the first, achievement in mathematics and science will be investigated simultaneously. In the second, achievement in several foreign language areas will be investigated at the same time. The third study will examine civic education and, as in the earlier study conducted in 1970-71, will be particularly concerned with the development of civic attitudes and values.

For each study listed in table 1, details are provided of the date of testing, the age or grade groups investigated and the number of countries that participated in the study. In general, the studies have been cross-sectional surveys. However, in the Second Mathematics Study and the Classroom Environment Study, attempts were made to test the same students on two occasions, and thus to introduce into the investigation a longitudinal component with respect to student performance. It has become clear from these two attempts that such longitudinal studies do not necessarily yield the information needed to estimate accurately the effects of schools and teaching behaviors. The problem would appear to be that measurement at only two points in time does not yield difference scores of sufficient reliability for the teasing out of effects. It is clear that performance needs to be measured at least at three or four time points.

Table 1

List of IEA Studies and Populations Tested

Name of study	Date of Testing	Student populations tested	No. of systems
Science-Mathematics Cycle			
First Mathematics Study	1964	13-year-old	12
		pre-university	
First Science Study	1970-71	10-year-old	19
		14-year-old	
		terminal secondary	
Second Mathematics Study	1980-82	10-year-old	20
		13-year-old	
		terminal secondary	
Second Science Study	1983-84	10-year-old	24
		14-year-old	
		terminal secondary	
Language Cycle			
Reading Comprehension	1970-7	10-year-old	14
		14-year-old	
		terminal secondary	
French as a Foreign Language	1971	14-year-old	8
		terminal secondary	
English as a Foreign Language	1971	14-year-old	9
		terminal secondary	
Written Composition	1985	end of primary schooling	21
		end of compulsory schooling	
		pre-university	
Reading Literacy	1990-91	9-year-old	31
		14-year-old	
Civic-Arts Cycle			
Literature	1970-71	14-year-old	10
		terminal secondary	
Civic Education	1971	10-year-old	10
		14-year-old	
		terminal secondary	
Special Cycle			
Pilot Twelve-Country	1960	13-year-old	12
Classroom Environment	1982-83	Grades 5 to 8	11
Computers in Education	1989	10-year-old	21
	1992	13-year-old	
		terminal secondary	
Preprimary	1987-91	4-year-old	17
	1992		
Future Studies			
Third Mathematics and Science	1995	10-year-old	
		13-year-old	
		terminal secondary	
Foreign Languages	1996-97		
Civic Education	1997-98		

This would seem to pose major problems for the conduct of a large cross-national investigation, because of the difficulties encountered in maintaining contact with the students in the samples.

Only in the Second Science Study undertaken in 1983-84 were deliberate attempts made to maintain close links with the First Science Study, which was conducted as part of the Six-Subject Study in 1970-71. This strategy of carrying out a repeated study over an interval of fourteen years provided important information on change in standards of achievement in science in different countries, which in general were found to have risen, and on changes in the magnitude of differences in performance between boys and girls, which in general, as has been mentioned above, were found to have fallen. Of particular interest in this study was the examination of changes in the science curriculum, as well as changes in the proportions of students participating in the study of science.

The magnitude of the IEA program of research, the coverage of subject areas, the range of age groups investigated, and the number of countries involved are very substantial. The IEA studies represent a huge research effort that has been sustained over a third of a century. The number of students involved in each testing program (for example, in the Second IEA Science Study over 250,000 students were tested), together with the large number of teachers and schools in so many countries involves not only sound organization but also very considerable good will from school systems, administrators, teachers, students, and their parents. IEA has been deeply indebted to them for their support.

Not only are the findings from the IEA studies of considerable importance to policymakers and planners, as has been implied in the discussion of the ten research findings recorded above, but each of the reports of the fifteen studies which have to date published their results also contains findings of importance for classroom teachers and school principals who have given generously of their time to enable the program of research to be fulfilled.

Other organizations have also sought to conduct cross-national studies that on the surface are similar to those undertaken by IEA. Their efforts have generally been shortlived for a variety of reasons. In order to understand why IEA has been able to maintain its program of research over a period of thirty-five years, and to have grown from a mere handful of countries to a large, although changing, group of fifty or more, it is necessary to identify and examine the key characteristics of IEA research.

With a knowledge of these characteristics it should be possible to understand why IEA has continued, has gained strength over time, and has been able to overcome the many problems encountered in the type of research endeavor it has chosen to pursue.

KEY CHARACTERISTICS OF IEA RESEARCH

It is clearly necessary to identify the key characteristics of IEA research studies in order to understand how the nature of the IEA work differs from that of other organizations that have sought to undertake what on the surface would appear to be similar types of studies. Such studies differ substantially from those conducted by IEA in both design and purpose.

The first important characteristic is that IEA research is *collaborative* and is carried out by educational research agencies. Membership of IEA is primarily considered in terms of countries. However, where there is more than one education system within a country, it is possible for each system to be represented, with the limit of no more than two systems from each country. A system is customarily represented by a research institution or governmental research agency within a country, and that institution or agency nominates a person to serve on its behalf as a member of IEA. There is also a small number of individual and honorary members of the organization, whose election is based on their contributions in the past to the work of IEA. Decisions on the activities of IEA are undertaken by the members within an assembly. Although such decisions are inevitably affected by the availability of funding, no one country or member has influence other than that exercised in informed debate. In a similar way, within each specific study carried out by IEA decisions on the conduct of the study are made as a result of informal and scholarly debate. While for each study a Steering Committee guides the planning of the study and an International Coordinator undertakes the task of administration of the study, all decisions are made on the basis of consensus achieved in a democratic way. In the processes of the design, the operation, the analysis of data, and reporting of a study, it is commonly not possible for a particular country or a particular individual to carry weight in decision making except on the basis of quality of argument. As a consequence of this collaboration, the instruments and the design employed reflect consensus across countries to undertake an agreed-upon program of research in which each participating country has had equal say at the time decisions were made.

The second important characteristic of IEA research is that it involves *comparisons* across countries and systems of education. The emphasis is on the differences and similarities across systems. Generally, relationships are examined that apply across systems. However, it is also common to identify a relationship that is common to several systems, and sometimes a relationship that is unique to a particular system. Nevertheless, frequently relationships are hypothesized to exist although there is no evidence from a study to support their existence. This is still very useful information to have obtained because it demands a critical reexamination of the processes thought to be operating.

A third characteristic of much IEA research is that it is *confirmatory* in nature. IEA researchers generally approach a research situation with clear ideas of what they believe to be the important forces that are operating in that situation. Their ideas are derived from theory or are based on an agreed upon understanding of how things work. IEA researchers are rarely satisfied merely to describe. They commonly seek to explain in terms of cause and effect relationships that they have hypothesized to exist. In more recent years they have developed detailed causal models for examination. Such models are best viewed as collections of hypotheses. These models and hypotheses must be tested in ways that confirm their existence. Thus the work is essentially confirmatory in so far as specified models and hypotheses are tested. Where an explicit or latent hypothesis is not confirmed, it is by implication rejected. This shift to a confirmatory approach has occurred gradually in recent years. It derives from a clearer understanding of how educational processes operate.

This leads to a fourth characteristic of IEA research, in so far as it involves a concern for *process as well as product*. While there is an identifiable concern for the outcomes of education, assessed in terms of achievement, attitude, and participation, the interest of IEA researchers is in the development of an understanding of how things work. This has led to the construction of models of the teaching and learning processes that operate in schools, as well as models of curricular processes. However, the exercise in the analysis of data is not merely to construct the model, but to test the model against observed data and to confirm or reject the structure of the model, in whole or in part, according to whether or not it is compatible with the evidence obtained from the real world. The examination of processes in this way provides an explanation of the forces at work. Moreover, the opportunity to test models by replication across many countries permits the models of educational processes to be generalized across different school systems.

A fifth important feature of IEA studies is the concern to measure *performance* where possible by what have come to be known as performance measures, rather than to rely solely on multiple-choice test items as has been common in the United States. As a consequence of this concern for performance, approximately 20 percent of the items in the tests employed in the First IEA Mathematics Study in 1964 were constructed response items and had to be laboriously scored by hand. Likewise in the Six Subject Study, a practical science testing program was developed and used in a limited number of countries at the 14-year-old and terminal secondary school levels. The IEA Study of Literature in 1970-71 involved the writing of extended answers of an essay type that had to be scored carefully. Similarly the studies of French and English as foreign languages used tests of writing, speaking, and listening with very precise and detailed marking schemes in order to measure student performance accurately and consistently. The more recent IEA Study of Written Composition employed essay-type questions but has reported a lack of consistency in students' responses to writing tasks of different kinds. The introduction of performance tests into a study places a heavy and costly burden on that study. However, the gain in the meaningfulness of the outcomes measured outweighs the costs and the time taken for administration and scoring.

A sixth characteristic of IEA research is the concern for the findings from the studies to provide information for *planning, policymaking, and practice*. In the examples given above, care has been taken to try to present the results obtained from the studies in a manner that illustrates this concern. Some of the earlier reports of IEA studies were written in a way that would gain recognition from the academic and scholarly world. This was necessary because IEA research had to maintain credibility, even though some of the authors of the reports were among the foremost educational and psychological research workers in Europe and the United States. In more recent studies attempts have been made to write for different audiences such as policymakers, teachers, administrators, as well as other research workers. Underlying these efforts is an awareness of the importance of making the findings of the studies available in such a form as to influence planning, policymaking, and practice.

The seventh important characteristic is that the research undertaken is *multidisciplinary* in nature. Although many of the original group of IEA researchers were psychometricians, there is no exclusive commitment in IEA research to psychometric methods. Researchers are free to draw from any appropriate discipline and to employ any appropriate method to answer the questions and to examine the problems they have chosen to consider. While IEA studies draw on ideas from psychology, they also use ideas derived from sociology, demography, economics, history, and anthropology, as well as from classroom observation. What is important is that the chosen research problems are addressed in the most effective way and in the most appropriate theoretical context.

An eighth important characteristic is that the research is necessarily *multivariate*. Educational research situations are complex. Many factors operate, and it is rarely possible to conduct an experimental study where schools and students are randomly assigned to treatment and control groups. As a consequence, it is necessary to obtain information on many factors and to use procedures of statistical analysis to exercise control so that the effects of particular factors can be estimated accurately. Unfortunately this leads to a weakness that is present in some IEA studies, namely, that of collecting information on too many factors and too many variables. However, this is the price to be paid for the multivariate nature of educational processes, as well as collaboration in which the interests of many people must be satisfied.

A ninth key characteristic, which only in the past few years has it become possible to examine in an effective way, is that educational data and processes are *multilevel* in nature. In studying the performance of students within a school system it is commonly necessary to sample school districts at a first stage, and then to sample schools within districts, and subsequently to sample students or classrooms from within schools. Sometimes it is possible to test the same students on several occasions. The procedures employed for the analysis of data must take into consideration these different levels, in part because they are built into the design of the samples, and in part because they also reflect the manner in which educational processes are at work. Unless appropriate consideration is taken of these different levels of operation in the analysis of data, the estimates made of the effects of different factors are likely to be seriously biased. While not all analyses that have been carried out in previous IEA research studies must be argued to be unsound, in the examination of school and classroom effects, where the results have sometimes been disappointing in the past, it is now possible to undertake analyses in a more appropriate way and so obtain better estimates of effects.

The tenth key characteristic of IEA research studies is that they, in the main, employ *large sample survey procedures*. In order to obtain data that is truly representative of a country or system it is necessary to draw a large complex sample. Furthermore, the sample must be drawn in such a manner that accurate estimates of error are obtained. The multilevel structure of the large complex IEA samples means that quite large errors are found for variables measured at the school and classroom level, while much smaller errors are recorded at the student level. It is only possible to obtain significant school and teacher effects if a sizeable number of schools and classrooms are sampled. The consequences of these requirements are that large numbers of students must be tested and the tests must include multiple-choice items so that some scoring can be carried out by an optical mark reader and the analyses undertaken using a powerful computer. It would be highly desirable to employ other research methodologies such as ethnographic and anthropological procedures, and the IEA Classroom Environment Study employed detailed observations in the study of student and teacher behavior in the classroom. While other research methods have been used in preliminary investigations and follow up studies, IEA has generally had to return to large sample survey procedures in the undertaking of its research studies.

It is important to emphasize that IEA research studies have never been without their problems. The work planned is always ambitious in the extreme, not only in size and complexity across different countries working in different languages, but the theoretical issues addressed are complex, and frequently there are only tentative suggestions as to how the data might be appropriately analyzed. IEA has been fortunate to enlist the services of some of the outstanding educational researchers of the twentieth century across the world to participate in its program of research. The names of Benjamin S. Bloom, John B. Carroll, Torsten Husén, A. N. Oppenheim, G. F. Peaker, T. Neville Postlethwaite, Robert L. Thorndike, and Douglas A. Walker quickly come to mind as authors of reports of studies. Moreover, IEA has also been able to call upon the services of J. W. Tukey, K. G. Jöreskog, H. Wold, and James S. Coleman to give advice and assistance on statistical analysis when help was needed.

The problems encountered in IEA studies have often been associated with the complexities of organization of the studies across a large number of countries, with the accompanying problems of coordination and time delays and with the desperate shortage of funding for a costly enterprise. It has only been through the dedicated efforts of so many that so much has been accomplished.

THE INVESTIGATION OF EDUCATION IN A CHANGING WORLD

The large data banks held by IEA are only now after thirty and more years of research opening up the possibilities of investigating in a systematic way the manner in which schooling is conducted in a changing world. A sufficient number of countries have maintained their involvement in IEA studies and have supplied sufficient details in their national case studies for it to be possible to examine the changes that have occurred over time not only within countries but also across countries. In the field of science, ten countries participated in the IEA science studies in both 1970-71 and 1983-84 and a report (Keeves, 1992) was prepared that examined as far as was possible the changes that had occurred over the fourteen-year period. Likewise, in the field of reading comprehension, there were eight countries that took part in the reading studies in both 1970-71 and 1990-91. While the amount of information that is common to the two studies is limited, there is sufficient for an examination of the changes that have taken place in the teaching of reading and in reading performance over a twenty-year period.

The important finding from the longitudinal study of the ten school systems in the field of science education was that over the fourteen-year period there was increased emphasis on the teaching and learning of science from the time of beginning school right through to the terminal secondary school stage. Students in elementary schools were, in general, beginning to learn science at an earlier age, were more frequently given access to a text book, and were more involved in undertaking experiments in their science classes. At the lower and middle secondary school level the evidence indicated that the study of science was mandatory in nearly all countries in 1983-84, where fourteen years earlier some students had been able to opt out of learning science at this level. At the terminal secondary school level with increased retention rates over time, a substantially larger proportion of the age group were studying some science, although in some countries the proportion of those at school who were studying science had declined. In Sweden and the United States the proportions of the *age-group* studying science at the Year 12 level had also declined. The consequence of this increased emphasis on teaching and learning science was that there were striking gains in levels of science achievement at the 10- and 14-year-old levels in most countries over time. Where a particular country diverged from this highly consistent pattern of results in so many respects there must be great cause for concern.

The change in performance of the students in an educational system over time, both relative to that in other systems as well as in absolute terms, is of considerable interest to politicians and policymakers in the field of education. Such concern for standards of achievement is of particular importance in many developing countries, where both the educational system and the population are growing rapidly and considerable cost is involved in supporting education. However, the maintenance of educational standards is also of consequence in the more highly developed countries where provision for education is a substantial component of the national budget. Furthermore, both politicians and policymakers seek information that would provide directions for change in the school system, as well as policies and practices that are known to be beneficial. The cross-national comparative studies conducted by IEA have, as indicated above, provided in the past such information on many occasions and to many countries.

International comparative studies have the capacity to yield a wealth of important information in the study of education in a changing world, if the potential for them to do so is widely recognized. IEA studies should seek not only to map change but also to investigate the factors associated with change in educational performance.

REFERENCES

Coleman, James S., et al. *Equality of Educational Opportunity*. Washington, D.C.: U.S. Department of Health, Education, and Welfare, 1966.

Faure, Edgar. *Learning to Be: The World of Education Today and Tomorrow*. Paris: UNESCO, 1972, and London: Harap, 1972.

Foshay, Arthur W.; Thorndike, Robert L.; Hotyat, F.; Pidgeon, Douglas A.; and Walker, David A. *Educational Achievement of Thirteen-Year-Olds in Twelve Countries*. Hamburg: UNESCO Institute for Education, 1962.

Keeves, John P. *The World of School Learning: Selected Key Findings from 35 Years of IEA Research.* The Hague: International Association for the Evaluation of Educational Achievement (IEA), 1994.

Keeves, John P. (ed.). *The IEA Study of Science III: Changes in Science Education and Achievement: 1970 to 1984.* Oxford: Pergamon, 1992.

Chapter 11

THE DIM SHININGS
OF INTERNATIONAL
COMPARISONS

Gerald W. Bracey

In "Why Can't They Be Like We Were?", now referred to as the "First Bracey Report on the Condition of Public Education," I wrote that "international comparisons have generated considerable heat, but very little light" (Bracey, 1991). The nearly four years since those words were written have done little to change that assessment, although I now think that at their worst such comparisons even generate confusion. As examples of the kinds of beaconless heat I have in mind, I offer these quotations:

American students are performing at much lower levels than students in other industrialized nations (Shanker, 1993a).

International examinations designed to compare students from all over the world usually show American students at or near the bottom (Shanker, 1993b).

Yet even America's best high school students, as international comparisons reveal, rank far behind students in countries challenging us in the multinational marketplace (Gray and Kemp, 1993).

In mathematics and science, American high schoolers finish last or next to last in virtually every international measure (Gerstner et al., 1994).

If there were substance behind these claims, then there might be a glimmer behind the heat, but as we shall see, all these statements are false.

I should early attend to the fact that skeptical readers might observe that I have used international comparative data in all four of my reports to date and then ask why I continue to report data which I claim have little utility (Bracey, 1992, 1993, 1994). The answer might be cast as "research report judo" in which the reports are turned on themselves to defeat them. Where international comparisons have not been used to show that American schools have actually failed, they have been used to show that the schools are in dire trouble and that American students do not stack up well against those in Europe and especially those in Asia. I use the reports' own data to conclude that, whatever else they reveal, they do not show any of these things.

I must confess right off, however, to skepticism about these reports that comes, in large part, from my examination of them but also from having lived in Europe, Asia, and Africa. Many countries have neither the tradition of testing nor the tradition of social science research that are so much parts of the American social fabric. It is naive to think that the absence of these two traditions can be overcome by sophisticated sampling techniques generated in this country. Others who have lived abroad have the same intuitions as I have.

There are, in addition, a host of cultural factors that may well affect outcomes in significant ways that are difficult to quantify. Let us consider one of the lesser but well-known series of studies, that of Harold Stevenson and colleagues at the University of Michigan, and, especially, James Stigler now at the University of California at Los Angeles (Stevenson and Stigler, 1992). These are flawed studies which would not have passed peer review save for the fact that they accord with the general impression of school failure and thus, unfortunately, take on a patina of credibility simply for the commonness of their conclusions.

At the most obvious, the results of these studies have been overgeneralized. The cover of the Stevenson and Stigler book, *The Learning Gap*, reads, in its entirety, "Why American Schools Are Failing and What We Can Learn from Japanese and Chinese Education." One would expect, then, to see inside an examination of "American Schools." But what one finds instead are data almost entirely from mathematics assessments and almost entirely from grades 1 and 5 (there are some data from kindergarten). Data from secondary schools are nowhere to be seen.

And, of course, no data from colleges. Japanese students work exceptionally hard in high school because the key factor to success in their lives is getting *into* the right college, of which there are only a few.

Once in college, they party, carouse, skip class, and cheat openly. American students work less hard in high school and shift into another gear for college, recent reports of binge drinking notwithstanding.

Beyond this problem of failing to examine the whole system, there are methodological problems both obvious and subtle. Stevenson has never reported much information about his Minneapolis sample, but his descriptions of his Chicago and Beijing samples are revealing (Stevenson et al., 1990). The Chicago sample was 29 percent black and Hispanic, thus containing almost 50 percent more of these minority groups than the K-12 population as a whole. As we shall see later, other results show black and Hispanic students scoring below the lowest country (Jordan) and the lowest state (Mississippi) in mathematics. Twenty percent of the Chicago students did not speak English at home. Family income was weighted toward the lower end of the economic spectrum.

By contrast, the Beijing sample was, for China, an educated elite. (Incomes, of course, are not comparable in any meaningful way.) It is naive to believe that the government of China would open its low-achieving schools to an American researcher. The two samples are thus not representative of their nations nor are they comparable to each other and they should never have been compared.

Beyond these obvious problems are some factors that surely affect achievement but which cannot be fit into a regression equation or other quantitative indicators. In Chicago, the typical child lived in a home with two siblings. In China, because of the population control policies, most students were from families with an only child. China, a nation long accustomed to having more than ten children per family in order that a few might survive to take care of their parents in their old age, has recently had to adapt to a state of having one child per household. Stories abound about the attention lavished on these children.

In addition, about 10 percent of the Chicago homes contained at least one grandparent, which was the case in 50 percent of the Beijing homes. The Chinese children are thus in a much more adult intensive environment, something known to affect achievement. But how does one quantify what we might call the "granny factor?"

There are other such cultural factors that might affect performance. Japan has an old saying: "The nail that stands out gets hammered down." Apparently, so do the Scandinavian nations. What does such an attitude do to achievement? Raise the floor? Lower the ceiling? Some of the data from the Second International Mathematics Study (SIMS) show variability for Japan to be smaller than for the United States and to decrease over time, suggesting pressures on both ends of the achievement curve. The same SIMS data show the American variance increasing, an outcome so common that it has a name, the educational "Matthew Effect": In American classrooms the cognitively rich get richer, the poor get poorer.

Beyond these problems, there is the telling fact that Stevenson's results do not accord with those of other studies, something with which Stevenson has consistently refused to come to terms. From Stevenson's results has come the common statement that only 1 percent of American students perform as well in mathematics as 50 percent of Japanese students. As we shall see later, other studies do not find anything of the kind.

We might note in passing that if these 1 and 50 percent figures were true, it would contrast starkly with another statistic from domestic tests: the proportion of students scoring about 650 on the SAT mathematics test is at an all-time high (Bracey, 1994). Two hypotheses might be advanced to account for this growth other than general increases in mathematics achievement: (a) it results from growing numbers of high-scoring Asian students, and (b) it results from the SAT becoming more popular in states where it has typically not been taken by a large proportion of seniors. If this latter were true, it would be possible to add high-scoring students without digging deeply into the talent pool.

Neither of these hypotheses holds up under scrutiny. Asian students do in fact score higher than those of any other ethnic group but they constitute only 8 percent of all testtakers, up from 4.5 percent a decade ago and far too few to account for the numbers seen. Examination of state results over the past few years reveals that the growth in the number of SAT takers has been in states like Pennsylvania, Connecticut, New York, and other states where well over half of the senior class were already taking the SAT.

Finally, in the consideration of the Stevenson studies, we must deal with the ability-effort dimension. Many people have taken Stevenson's work to indicate that Americans believe in ability while Asians believe in effort. To take only one representative comment, Katherine Merseth of Harvard University had this to say:

A predominant view in America is that one either "has it" or one doesn't. Effort receives little credit for contributing to successful learning in mathematics—or, for that matter, in any subject. For example, American, Japanese, and Chinese mothers were asked what factors among ability, effort, task difficulty, and luck made their children successful in school. American mothers ranked *ability* the highest, while Asian mothers gave high marks to *effort*. This led the researchers to conclude that "the willingness of Japanese and Chinese children to work so hard in school may be due, in part, to the stronger belief on the part of their mothers in the value of hard work (Merseth, 1993, p. 549).

The researchers who reached this conclusion are Stevenson and his colleagues. But an examination of the data reveals that this is one place where Stevenson and company have misinterpreted their own results, as has Merseth. Luck and task difficulty count for little among mothers of any country. American mothers do rate ability as more important than Chinese and Japanese mothers rate it, but they rate *effort as more important than ability*. The differences between American and Asian mothers' ratings of effort is not large, a maximum of one point on a ten-point scale. American children show precisely the same pattern: they think ability is more important than Asian children do, but rank effort as more important than ability and almost equal in importance as Asian children think it to be (Stevenson and Stigler, 1992). Both mothers and children rate ability and effort as almost equally important, with effort winning out by a little. To me this is an instance of international comparisons not only generating heat rather than light but of leading people to the wrong conclusions.

The Stevenson studies show the most problematic aspect of all international comparisons: the numbers look pristine and precise on the page but they are, in fact, beclouded by numerous methodological and cultural factors that obscure their meaning.

I now turn to other international studies of achievement. I will largely ignore the early studies because they were badly affected by sampling problems, test construction itself, and, at the upper grades, selection biases. Even the most recent studies have reported information from countries that did not sample representatively, but at least these nonrepresentative samples are identified as such. Test construction remains a problem as it is now known that even mathematics problems do not travel well. In reading, the problem has been recently addressed through "back translation" in which one person translates a passage and a second translates it back to the original language. The fidelity of the original to the back translation is then compared.

The selection problem, one of the worst in early studies, has been eliminated by not testing upper grades where tracking and dropout rates can have profound impact. The First International Mathematics Study did not take into account that at the time only about 20 percent, the top 20 percent, of European students attended upper secondary school compared with more than 80 percent of U.S. students (Rotberg, 1990).

The Second International Mathematics Study (SIMS) attempted to cure this problem by testing only students who were in academic tracks and were taking advanced science and mathematics in upper high school. This unfortunately introduced another selection bias: countries differ in the proportions of students in such tracks. In the eighth grade, Japan ranked first, Hungary was near the top, and Hong Kong was in the middle of the pack. At twelfth grade, Hong Kong ranked first, Japan second, and Hungary near the bottom. It is conceivable that Hong Kong has first-rate secondary schools and that Hungary's are awful. More likely, however, these results come from the proportion of students still taking mathematics in grade 12: 2 percent in Hong Kong, 12 percent in Japan, and 50 percent in Hungary. Hungary has a long tradition of emphasizing mathematics, something that is important in another study, the Second International Assessment of Educational Progress. The decision in recent studies to eliminate high school from the assessments, of course, means that a much smaller part of the system is being looked at.

SIMS was afflicted also by the lack of a match between curriculum and test that worked to the detriment of U.S. scores. For instance, it administered an algebra test in the eighth grade. Only about 20 percent of U.S. students take algebra as a formal course in eighth grade. Even so, American students finished 12th out of 21 countries, hardly a stellar performance but much better than the "last or next to last" characterization often given of U.S. scores. (In fact, at the eighth grade the U.S. finished 11th in arithmetic, 17th in geometry, and 19th in measurement. At the twelfth grade, U.S. students finished 14th of 15 countries in advanced algebra and 12th of 15 in calculus.)

Ian Westbury at the University of Illinois thought it would be interesting to see how American students who actually take algebra compare to their Japanese counterparts. The latter had finished with the highest average scores of any nation. He found that the American students actually did somewhat better. This should be considered unfair and biased toward America since it takes 20 percent of an American grade, presumably the academically most able 20 percent, and compares them to an entire Japanese cohort. When Westbury compared this group to the top quintile of Japanese students, however, they still scored slightly higher although the proper conclusion would be "no difference" because the scores are so close (Westbury, 1992).

In another analysis, Westbury found that the arithmetic scores of the top 50 percent of American classes were identical to those of the top 50 percent of Japanese classes—66 percent of the items correct. However, the bottom 50 percent of the Japanese classes had a score of 55 percent, not far behind their upper peers. The American lower 50 percent, however, compared poorly to either the upper 50 percent of U.S. classes or the lower 50 percent of Japanese classes, averaging only 37 percent correct (Westbury, 1993). This theme of the upper half of American students being "world class" in mathematics and the lower half only "third world" will be repeated in other data shown below. Along with the Americans' high finishes in reading, it is perhaps the most consistent finding of international comparisons.

Whether all American students should take algebra in the eighth grade (as it seems that most European and Asian students do) is a question raised by SIMS. According to mathematics educator Thomas Romberg, we already ask children to do things in the eighth grade that are more difficult than algebra so it is not an issue of talent or prior skills (Romberg, 1992). I am given to understand, though, that most reformers would prefer to see algebra woven throughout the elementary and middle school curriculum.

Lawrence Stedman argued that international comparisons in general and SIMS in particular are relevant to curriculum problems and recently pointed to a set of recommended educational reforms that emanated from an intensive study of the SIMS results: "U.S. mathematics programs [in the eighth grade] are characterized by an inordinate amount of review of old material, a low-intensity approach to content that skims many areas, and a repeated delay of challenging material." Stedman lists a few other characteristics of the middle school mathematics curriculum and recommendations made on the basis of SIMS data and then concludes:

So there it is—a guide to reforming junior high mathematics programs that comes directly from an international assessment—reorganize the spiral curriculum, reduce review and remediation, lessen teacher workloads, and eliminate ability grouping. I think that most educators would consider that useful (Stedman, 1994, p. 144).

However, most of the proposed SIMS-based reforms have been argued for some time, and most seem obvious simply from an examination of the current middle school mathematics curriculum and other research conducted in this country. Justifying international comparisons on the basis that they lead to recommendations already made on the basis of domestic studies seems to be tortuous, indirect, expensive, and redundant.

The Second International Assessment of Educational Progress in mathematics and science (IAEP-2), conducted by the Educational Testing Service (ETS), was released in 1992 and met with a collective groan in the United States. Although ETS listed the countries alphabetically in its press release and warned against rankings due to sampling differences in some countries, the media quickly rearranged the scores to produce a rank order. American students ranked 13th of 15 and 14th of 15 in mathematics at grades four and eight. While American 9-year-olds finished third in science, American 14-year-olds finished 13th (LaPointe et al., 1992a, 1992b). "An 'F' in World Competition" wailed *Newsweek*, which attempted to explain away the high finish of American 9-year-olds (*Newsweek*, 1992).

We are a nation obsessed with ranks, something that provides little information about what to do next. Little noticed among the rankings were the *actual scores* of American children. These were quite close to the international average, as had been, for that matter, eighth graders' scores in SIMS (in twelfth grade, students were tested on functions and calculus, topics most often taken in college, and scores were below average). For mathematics, the average scores were 63 and 58 for 9- and 13-year-olds respectively. For U.S. students they were 58 and 55, respectively. In science, the international average was 62 and 67 for 9- and 13-year-olds respectively, while the U.S. science averages were 65 and 67.

A look at the 95th percentiles on IAEP-2 also reveals most countries tightly bunched and, indeed, the U.S. 9th percentiles are higher than several countries which have higher averages. (There is some indication of ceiling effects for the 13-year-old mathematics 95th percentile of Taiwan and Korea). Again, this study, much larger and more sophisticated than those of Stevenson and colleagues, does not corroborate their claim of vast differences in achievement between students in the United States and those in Asian nations.

IAEP-2 also brings into focus a new problem not dealt with in other studies and dealt with only anecdotally in this one. Archie LaPointe, Executive Director of the Study, reported that as the names of those children chosen for the Korean sample were called, the children stood and exited to thunderous applause from their peers. Apparently in Korea at least, IAEP-2 really was an educational Olympics and it was a tremendous honor to be chosen.

I cannot imagine American students responding in this way. They are the most tested in the world, "bubbling" in 100 million answer sheets a year according to the National Center for Fair and Open Testing (FairTest). It takes something to get them up for yet another test. Something like IAEP-2 is a "yawner." It enters and disappears from their lives in one day and has no impact on anyone or anything. When a school district I worked for participated in the first National Assessment of Educational Progress (NAEP) state-by-state mathematics tryout, about half of the teachers participating reported to me that they had difficulty keeping their students on task, and this in a district that sends about 85 percent of its students to college.

The impact of motivation should not be underestimated. When I was Director of Testing for the Commonwealth of Virginia, cheating was common enough that we developed a computer program to detect unusual changes in test scores. One year the program produced the name of a small, rural district where the scores had shot up. In our role as policemen, we visited the district. We found that the new superintendent had decided that his students, not being headed to college or careers where academic skills weighed heavily, simply did not take the tests seriously.

The superintendent had hit on the notion of taking the test out of the realm of academics and placing it in the realm of athletics: just as in sports, the goal was to outscore the archrival neighboring country. During the week of testing teachers had dressed as cheerleaders and held pep rallies in the auditorium where the grades affected were cheered on by their peers in other grades. Scores rose 15 to 30 percentile ranks depending on age and test. No international comparison has tried to obtain any indication of motivation, leaving all results suspect.

The international comparisons in mathematics and science have been the most publicized. It is not mere conjecture to claim that is because they played into the hands of the Reagan and Bush administrations, both of which had a goal of privatizing schools through vouchers and choice. As part of this agenda came a constant barrage of bad news in the hope of creating enough desperation on the part of the public that it would permit the transfer of public funds to private schools. "A public school is one that performs a public service," said then-Secretary of Education Lamar Alexander in a marvelous verbal sleight of hand.

This attitude could be seen in the reaction to a study conducted by the International Association for the Evaluation of Educational Achievement (IEA), *How in the World Do Students Read?* (Elley, 1992). More accurately, it could be seen in the nonreaction to this study. LAEP-2 was released in February, 1992. The Educational Testing Service and the U.S. Department of Education orchestrated a press conference and coverage was widespread. When the IEA reading results came out, no one knew it. They were released in July, 1992 but did not appear in the United States until late September. They appeared then only because a friend in Germany had sent *Education Week* reporter, Robert Rothman, a copy when the report appeared in Europe. *Education Week* ran the story on page 1 of its issue for September 30, 1992 (Rothman, 1992). *USA Today* also carried the story on page 1 of its issue for September 29, 1992 (Manning, 1992). (Although the *USA Today* report appears to predate that in *Education Week*, the latter publication appears two days earlier than its publication date.) The *USA Today* story carried a quote from Francie Alexander, then a Deputy Assistant Secretary of Education, who dismissed the study as irrelevant. "This is OK for the '80s," said Alexander. "But for the 90s and beyond, kids are going to have to do better."

By November, 1992, the story had filtered into educational monthly periodicals and the headline of one reveals how ready people are to see schools as performing poorly. In its November, 1992 issue, the *American School Board Journal* (*ASBJ*) carried the headline: "Good News: Our 9-Year-Olds Read Well; Bad News: Our 14-Year-Olds Don't."

The good news, according to *ASBJ*, was that American 9-year-olds finished second in the world in reading among students from thirty-one nations. They finished second only to Finland, a small, homogeneous, educationally concerned nation that does not spend much time worrying about how to teach Finnish as a second language. The "bad news" was that 14-year-old Americans tied for eighth place. "How can it be," I wondered in a letter to the editors of *ASBJ*, "that in a study of thirty-one nations, where a 16th place finish would be average, an eighth place finish is 'bad news'?"

More to the point, like other American publications, *ASBJ* had got caught up in ranks and was ignoring scores. The study was reported on a 600-point scale identical to that of the SAT. The second place 9-year-olds were 22 points out of first place. The 8th place 14-year-olds were 25 points out, only three points further away. As with many studies, developed nations bunched together such that small differences in scores made large differences in ranks. For example, the distance from second place France to eighth place America was only 14 points.

The IEA reading study remains largely unknown even within educational circles. When I lecture around the country I ask audiences, mostly school administrators, how many have heard of it. Often no one has, and in a room of 200 the number seldom reaches five.

A recent report from the National Center for Education Statistics (1993), *Education in States and Nations*, provides some data that throw light on how the United States fares in international comparisons and, paradoxically, presents other data suggesting that such comparisons may mean nothing at all. The report contains eighth grade mathematics data from IAEP-2 transformed into NAEP scales and then combined with the eighth grade state-by-state results from the 1992 NAEP mathematics assessment. If we add to these data other reporting categories from NAEP, we find the following situation at the top:

Student Population	Average Scores in NAEP Scale Points
Asian students in U.S. schools	287
Korea	285
Taiwan	283
Advantaged urban students in U.S. schools	283
White students in U.S. schools	277
Hungary	277

The number one ranking of Asian students in American schools is curious given that many of them attend schools with characteristics not generally associated with high achievement and certainly raises a question about the sources of their high scores. When only white students in the United States are compared with students in other countries, they tie with Hungary for third place. Together, whites and Asians make up 70 percent of the K-12 student body in the United States and they score among the best in the world.

As noted earlier, the overall average for U.S. students was close to the international average. But if a large proportion of Americans score at or near the top, then another proportion must be scoring low. And it is. Looking at the bottom of the scale we find this:

Student Population	Average Scores in NAEP Scale Points
Jordan	246
Mississippi	246
Hispanic students in U.S. schools	245
Disadvantaged urban students in U.S. schools	239
African-American students in U.S. schools	236

Juxtaposing the top and the bottom ends of this scale suggests that an education reform agenda aimed at the typical school or at all schools is misguided.

It also suggests that criticisms of works such as *Perspectives on Education in America*, better known simply as "The Sandia Report," are also misguided (Carson, Huelscamp, and Woodall, 1993). Stedman put such a critique this way:

The most significant weakness of the Sandia report, however, was its focus on trends and its failure to assess the quality of student performance in absolute terms. This left the report greatly imbalanced. The basic point is this: Although U.S. students' performance generally has been stable, it remains at low levels. Few students achieve proficiency in the major academic areas; most have major gaps in their knowledge and skills. These are poor results for twelve years of schooling. Democratic society and the many workplaces expected in the 21st century require better than what the schools are producing (Stedman, 1994, p. 145).

For the most part, the low levels of achievement to which Stedman refers come from NAEP data and Stedman is engaging in the kind of criterion-referenced interpretation of NAEP that Forsyth (1991) has shown is not valid. Moreover, these low levels, if they be such, exist all over the world. The reports of achievement, particularly the achievement of such Asian nations as Japan, Korea, and Taiwan, often carry the implication that these countries have monolithically good systems with high national standards which all or almost all students attain. This is not true and an examination of the data relating to this point calls into question the utility of comparing nations at all on the basis of average scores.

Education in States and Nations contains not only scores of countries and states, but indications of the range within each country and state. The range is enormous. As one moves from the average scores in mathematics of 13-year-olds for Mississippi and for Jordan at the bottom to that of Taiwan at the top, one traverses a range from 246 to 285—39 NAEP scale points. As one goes from the 5th percentile in Taiwan to the 95th, one traverses a range from 222 to 345 or 123 NAEP scale points. If the chart went from the 1st to the 99th percentile, perhaps another 20 or 30 points would be added. The *intra*-nation variability swamps the *between*-nation variability. How, then, can one speak of "American schools" or "Taiwanese schools" or the schools of any nation or state? In view of the enormous within nation and within state variability, it does not seem meaningful.

As an aside, we might also note that the huge variability of scores has an implication for projects in which national standards are being developed in various subjects. Where can we place a standard that people will consider credibly high without failing large numbers of students? And what do we do when that happens? No one has yet answered this question satisfactorily.

In this chapter I have dealt largely with the results of international comparisons in terms of their focus—test scores. I have not dealt with other important factors such as curriculum and teaching strategies which introduce variability. For example, Mayer and colleagues administered a computation test and a problem-solving test to American and Japanese students. They then divided the computation test scores into six levels of achievement. The Japanese students outscored American students on the computation test, but at all six levels the American children outscored the Japanese on the problem-solving task (Mayer, Tajika, and Stanley, 1991). Such an outcome is consonant with anecdotal reports that Japanese schools focus on rote aspects of mathematics.

Nor have I dealt here with a very important factor, Opportunity to Learn (OTL). This omission is occasioned because it has never been systematically factored into any of the studies, although OTL shows much variation from country to country.

The most that international comparisons have shown is that U.S. students perform much better in mathematics than has been alleged and that they are near the top in reading. Aside from that, the studies give little or no guidance about how to improve any nation's educational system, unless, of course, a nation adopts the test as its curriculum, something that seems to have happened on occasion (LaPointe, 1994). But, given the tremendous variability of scores within countries and the large number of factors other than quality of instruction that can and do introduce variability among countries, I see no reason to change my 1991 conclusion: international comparisons generate much heat, little light.

REFERENCES

Bracey, Gerald W. "Why Can't They Be Like We Were?," *Phi Delta Kappan* 73 (October, 1991): 104-117.

Bracey, Gerald W. "The Second Bracey Report on the Condition of Public Education," *Phi Delta Kappan* 74 (October, 1992): 104-117.

Bracey, Gerald W. "The Third Bracey Report on the Condition of Public Education," *Phi Delta Kappan* 75 (October, 1993): pp. 104-117.

Bracey, Gerald W. "The Fourth Bracey Report on the Condition of Public Education," *Phi Delta Kappan* 76 (October, 1994): 114-127.

Carson, C. C.; Huelskamp, C. M.; and Woodall, T. D. "Perspectives on Education in America," *Journal of Educational Research* 86 (May-June, 1993): 260-310.

Elley, Warwick B. *How in the World Do Students Read?* Hamburg: International Association for the Evaluation of Educational Achievement, July, 1992.

Forsyth, Robert A. "Do NAEP Scales Yield Valid Criterion-Referenced Interpretations?" *Educational Measurement: Issues and Practices* 10 (Fall, 1991): 3-9.

Gerstner, Louis V., et al. *Reinventing Education*. New York: Dutton, 1994.

Gray, C. Boyden, and Kemp, Evan J., Jr. "Flunking Testing: Is Too Much Fairness Unfair to School Kids?" *Washington Post*, 19 September 1993, p. E1.

LaPointe, Archie E. Personal communication, June, 1994.

LaPointe, Archie E.; Mead, Nancy A.; and Askew, Janice M. *Learning Mathematics*. Report No. 22-CAEP-01. Princeton, N.J. Educational Testing Service, February 1992.

LaPointe, Archie E.; Askew, Janice M.; and Mead, Nancy A. *Learning Science*. Report No. 22-CAEP-02. Princeton, N.J.: Educational Testing Service, 1992.

Manning, Anita. "U.S. Kids Near Top of Class in Reading," *USA Today*, 23 September 1992, p. 1.

Mayer, Richard E.; Tajika, H.; and Stanley, C. "Mathematical Problem Solving in Japan and the United States: A Controlled Comparison," *Journal of Educational Psychology* 83 (1991): 69-72.

Merseth, Katherine. "How Old Is the Captain?" *Phi Delta Kappan* 74 (March, 1993): 549-553.

National Center for Education Statistics. *Education in States and Nations*. Report No. NCES 93-237. Washington, D.C.: National Center for Education Statistics, 1993.

Newsweek. "An 'F' in World Competition," 17 February 1992, p. 57.

Romberg, Thomas. Personal communication, June, 1994.

Rotberg, Iris. "I Never Promised You First Place," *Phi Delta Kappan* 72 (December, 1990): 296-303.

Rothman, Robert. "U.S. Ranks High in International Study of Reading," *Education Week*, 30 September 1992, p. 1.

Shanker, Albert. "World Class Standards," *New York Times*, 4 July 1993, Sect. 4, p. 7.

Shanker, Albert. "The Wrong Message," *New York Times*, 11 July 1993, Sect. 4, p. 7.

Stedman, Lawrence. "The Sandia Report and U.S. Achievement: An Assessment," *Journal of Educational Research* 87 (January, 1994): 133-147.

Stevenson, Harold W., and Stigler, James. *The Learning Gap*. New York: Summit Books, 1992.

Stevenson, Harold W.; Lee, Shen-ying; Chen, Chuansheng; and Lummis, Ma. "Mathematics Achievement of Children in China and the United States," *Child Development* 61 (1990): 1053-1066.

Westbury, Ian. "Comparing American and Japanese Achievement: Is the United States Really an Underachiever?" *Educational Researcher* 21 (June/July, 1992): 18-24.

Westbury, Ian. "American and Japanese Achievement . . . Again," *Educational Researcher* 22 (April, 1993): 21-25.